Joachim M Werdin

INEDIA

NON-EATING

FASTING

SECOND EDITION
2016 December

INEDIA, NON-EATING, FASTING
second edition, significantly changed

In your life, your mind is a horse that is pulling a cart (which is your body). The cart is inertly following the horse, it does not make decisions on its own. The cart moves ahead when the horse is walking, it stops when the horse is standing and it rolls back when the horse is not in control.

INEDIA, NON-EATING, FASTING
second edition, significantly changed

Joachim M Werdin

Edition II, December 2016, with corrections and extended material.
ISBN 978-83-940498-6-7

Original title in Polish "Inedia, Niejedzenie, Post."
(ISBN 978-83-940498-2-9).
Translated by the author from Polish to English.

To contact the author:
e-mail: jmw [at] niejedzenie [dot] info
http://inedia.info
http://breatharian.info
WeChat: joachimwerdin
Skype: joachimwerdin
Youtube: www.youtube.com/user/joachimwerdin/

This book has no copy rights, it is entirely free and belongs to no one. You can use it in any way. You can translate, copy and distribute it in any form. In fact, I would like you to share it with other people.
Use it for the good of yourself and others.
About the price of this book, read the last page.

Knowledge that I have built for myself and from which I have drawn information to place here is timeless. Everybody can read it and write it down. I have done it for those who still prefer to use material sources like books.

When I am teaching in my seminars, I explain much more then is written in this book. If all would be written here, this book would be several times bigger. Therefore, I encourage you to participate in my seminar.

I have written this book, share this basic information from my knowledge because I Love people.

IAM is the Consciousness – everything else is IAM's creation.
IAM is the creator of Life.
I am the Master Creator of my life.
I allow my Inner Joy to emanate freely so that I feel Love and see Light.

WHY THIS BOOK?

Nine years passed between publishing the first edition of this book and "Life Style Without Food". During that time, when giving seminars or meeting with friends, I was talking and writing to many people about topics described in LSWF that is inedia, fasting, proper nourishment, self-development, Consciousness and Life. Two years later, I updated this book with new materials, so now we have the second edition of this book.

In summer, 2014 when in China, I was talking with people about topics mentioned above, I understood how important it is to publish new materials forthwith. I saw and felt how seriously local people are interested in those topics and how sincerely they are looking for information that I know.

Many people that I have met were asking me similar questions. That gradually made me finally decide to write more details, to better explain and to add more materials.

I have written this book in order to give you more information, if you are interested in inedia, fasting, proper nourishment, self-development, Consciousness, Life, etc.

During those past years I noticed how big is the lack of knowledge, how many beliefs about those topics prevailed among people. Beliefs are limitations. When enslaving man they constitute barriers against manifestation of the Inner Power. Getting rid of beliefs is a process to freedom of the man. A free man does not have beliefs.

I hope that information included in this book will help you in getting rid of beliefs. Such a process will be happening if you use that information for benefiting yourself and others.

It is worth knowing that for yourself, you are the most important being in the universe, therefore, take care of yourself, that means giving yourself the highest regard, seeing yourself as an admirable man and do Love yourself.

At the same time do not compare yourself to other people, so that you do not suffer and do not feel superior to them. Every man is a different universe, therefore comparing yourself to others is useless.
You are not better, you are not worse, you are just different and you are experiencing Life in a different way that is called 'your life'.
Words like 'better', 'worse', 'good' or 'bad' are nothing more than just expres-

sions of human beliefs. These beliefs narrow your view, understanding of people, ability to learn and experience Life.

Get rid of fears and awes and allow your Inner Joy to manifest itself through your body, because this is how you are creating Life and that is how Love can freely emanate from you.

From then on, you do not need or seek any help. That is how you are becoming a happy man who naturally shares joy and Love with others. The more you share, the more you receive. Others will be following such a life style, people will become free, thus the world becomes paradise.

It is difficult to beguile or stultify free people in order to enslave them, therefore free people do not have rulers, lords or guides. They know and utilize their natural Inner Power, they consciously create their own life.

I am dreaming about such man and mankind. I see in future, mankind is like that. This is why I am sharing my knowledge in form of information contained in this book. It is my goal to make man return to living in 'natural state' on Earth.

The content of this book is the sum of two books: "Life Style Without Food" published in 2005 and "Life Style Without Food – Addendum" published in 2014. Except for removed errors and redundant sentences, and adding some sentences, the contents of this book does not differ much from the sum of the contents of the two books.

THIS IS ONLY INFORMATION

Information is any data coming to your senses, for example, sentences that you read in a book or a lecture that you listen to.
This book contains just information. All information can be (partially or completely) true or false regardless of where it is found. 'Great spiritual master', 'enlightened guru', a book, Internet, TV and others are sources of information. None of these and no other source of information can give you knowledge.

Knowledge is something you build up by experience, using the information you receive. The information itself is not knowledge. To build up your own knowledge, you can use information from different sources. Having checked the information out and having experienced it, you can say:
'I know'. Until then you were believing, you did not know.

Belief has an unbreakable connection with doubt. Actually, belief is the same thing but seen from the other side. What you believe as true, you also doubt it. When you doubt something, at the same time you also believe it. Also when you believe, you may be questioning and searching until you gain knowledge. When you know, you do not ask, you just know, period.

Therefore do not blindly believe what is written in this book or other; it is better to find it out by yourself. You can take advantage of all information here in any way. For example, you can test it on yourself in order to build up your own knowledge. If you are going to blindly believe what is written here, you may suffer as a consequence.

When you believe any information you receive to be your knowledge, you become a slave to the information source. A group of people believing in a so-called authority (guru, master, teacher, expert) can be easily manipulated. This was how religions, -isms, parties, cults and other organizations, which are controlling people and their life style, have been established and continue to prosper.

In other words, I suggest that you think for yourself. Use information and treat all 'spiritual masters', 'recognized authorities', mass media etc. as sources of information only. Then work with the information yourself, not allowing others to manipulate you. Test it yourself; experience it yourself, because if you do not, you will never know, you can only believe.

Let me say it again – this book is only information and nothing more.

> All information is:
> ↑ entirely true
> or
> ↓ entirely false
> or
> ↑↓ partly true and partly false.

Every bit of information is exactly that, regardless of its origin. Whether it comes from me or from a president or from an alcoholic or from the highest authority or from a hopeless villain or from a king or from a henchman or from evil or from angel or from extraterrestrial entity – it is still only information and it has one of the three above mentioned characteristics. Always be aware of that. For when you are aware, it is much more difficult to mislead you.

When they tell you something, especially when they want to convince you to believe something, just ask them this question:
"Is that your knowledge, your belief or just information that you have?"

Information is not your knowledge. Knowledge cannot be put across intellectually. By listening, reading or watching you can receive information only, nothing more.
You are building your knowledge through experience. You can also remember/recall it (withdraw it from your instinct) or receive it from intuition.
Information can be easily passed to others. Knowledge is built by you for yourself.

Therefore this book is just information for you, it is not your knowledge. What is written here can be true or false. You may want to check it out for yourself.

In addition, truth and falsehood are relative, because they depend on circumstances. For example, 2+2 may equal 4, or 2+2 may equal 30, or different result is possible depending on the number system. What is true in one system may be false in another. Truth and falsehood are relative.

That is why I repeat, do not believe what is written in this book. Also, be wary of believing other sources. Listen, read and watch with the awareness that what comes to you is just information which can be true and false at the same time. What that is for you, you will find out for yourself by experiencing it.

Based on information, you can build your knowledge. When you harness information to serve you, then you experience and acquire – this is how you build your knowledge. However, that will be your knowledge. For other people, your knowledge will be just information because you will not be able to transfer your knowledge to them intellectually.
Knowledge is a structure built in your memory or data that you draw from your intuition. Intuition is the source of knowledge.

Do you understand the difference between these statements?
1. I know.
2. I doubt.
3. I believe.
4. I have information.

Believe ≈ Doubt.	=	Lack of knowledge.
I believe.	=	I do not know but I suppose yes.
I doubt.	=	I do not know but I suppose no.
You should believe.	=	You should not know.

By the way, let me ask you, do you know or believe in God? Why?

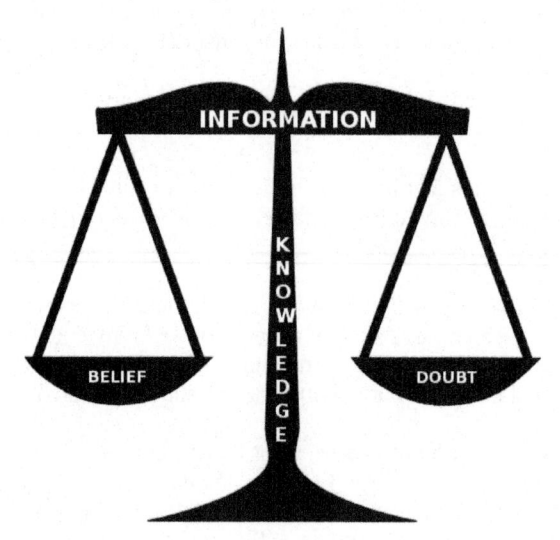

DEFINITIONS

Proper comprehension of what someone is saying or writing to you is the base of understandable communication. People may use identical words but intend different meanings. The word "god" is an example that evokes the largest number of images in respect to meaning. If you ask a hundred people to define the meaning of the word "god", you will receive dozens of definitions, among them many will be very different. Imagine how much misunderstanding can arise when those people talk about god. Therefore, it is possible that in a group of a few dozen people everyone will be speaking about different things.
I do not use the word "god" unless I have first made the meaning clear to my interlocutor or the definition is not important for the sense of a given sentence.
Please note the meanings of the words that I have defined below and have used in my writings.

The following are my definitions:

master – highly qualified specialist with sufficient practice and knowledge in a specific field or subject, e.g. shoe master, plumbing master, *qì-gōng* master, spiritual master, master in science.

teacher – man giving information about specific subject, information giver.

emotion – a perceptible rise of energy activity in the body caused by imagination or by external stimuli. Emotion is a program in the instinct and as such, can be built in, modified or removed. Emotions are adopted from the society in which man lives, as a result of automatic programming which begins from the moment of conception.

feeling – a perceptible attitude towards a subject (for example, man towards an animal) that can cause emotions.
Someone can be indifferent for you or you can feel something towards them, for example, you can Love them. Because of that feeling, you can evoke emotions in yourself, which can manifest, e.g. as laughter.

Love – (written with a capital **L**) is giving unconditionally, emanating Light and Warmth, sustaining Life, purely spiritual, peaceful, stable.
It is neither emotion nor affection. This Love is something that appears when Life is created. When man is under the influence of Love, man can trigger ecstatic emotions within and trigger feelings like love and joy.

In other words, when you are creating Life, you and those around you feel Love, something that is unexplainable and incomprehensible on an intellectual level.

☼

The yellow sun is the symbol of Love.

Realize this – the sun does not care about you, does not know what you do and does not bother whether you blaspheme it or pray to it. The sun does not even know that you exist. Nevertheless the sun gives you warmth, light, food, energy – everything necessary for your life. Without the sun there would be no life on Earth and your body would not exist.
In exchange for all of that, the sun wants nothing from you. The sun Loves unconditionally everything around regardless of how any being behaves. The same happens when you Love – you are creating Life. It can be felt that you emanate Love – this is how you are becoming the sun.

love – (written with a small **l**) is a conditional, emotional attraction, attachment and affection; it draws energy and aims for a deep physical experience; it is changing.
This love is a program (automatic mechanism) built into the instinct. Most people are familiar with love because they have loved and they were loved.

♥

A red heart is the symbol of love.

When you use symbols on social media on the Internet, be aware of what you intend to communicate. Is it Love or love? Choose the proper symbol.

You can Love someone without loving them. This is precisely what is happening in the case of the sun. It Loves you although you are not attractive to the sun. Sun does not yearn for you, it has no emotions associated with you.

being – life form consisting of mind and body.

man – a being who consists of an humanoid physical body, a spirit and a mind. I am using 'man' in this book, instead of 'person'. A person is not man.
"Traditionally the word man has been used to refer not only to adult males but also to human beings in general, regardless of sex. There is a historical explanation for this: in Old English the principal sense of man was 'a human being'"
– from oxforddictionaries.com.

spirit – 1. a being consisting of an immaterial body and a mind;
2. the invisible and insensible part of the body.

person – legal fiction, a description created in imagination and existing only on a media, for example, stone, wood, paper, plastic, disc, memory card. Examples include a description on an identity card or characteristics written in a passport. A person is not a living being, neither a body.

inedia
Inedia is the state of the mind, which manifests through the body. In the state of inedia the body naturally does not need food or drink to function properly. Inedia is normal for 'man in natural state', which is now rare on Earth. A man in the state of inedia is called an inediate.

inediate
An inediate is a man who does not need food or drink for their body to function properly. Inediate's mind and body function perfectly.
This word originates from the old Christian scripts describing saints who lived for years without eating and drinking. Presently the word inedia relates not only to Christian saints but describes any man living without eating and drinking regardless of their religion or beliefs.

non-eating
Non-eating is the state of the mind, which manifests through the body. In the state of non-eating the body naturally does not need food to function properly but it may need water. A man in the state of non-eating is called a non-eater.

non-eater
A non-eater is a man who does not need food for their body to function properly but they may need water. Non-eater's mind and body function perfectly.

liquidarian
A liquidarian is a man who consumes only drinks, which constitutes food for the body, like juices, herbal tea or milk. Liquidarianism is a liquid diet.

fast / fasting
To fast or fasting means to refrain from eating or from eating and drinking (dry fasting) for a period of time, due to a religious or traditional requirement or for healing the body. Fasting is one of the most efficient methods on Earth for removing illness and disease. Fasting is a medical procedure known on Earth since ever.

diet
A diet is a specific selection of foods. People follow a diet due to a belief system or a desire to keep the body in good shape.
There are thousands of diets, none of which are perfect. Every diet helps some people while harming others.

breatharianism
Breatharianism is a concept in which man lives only by breathing air. The air is enough to sustain the body properly. Thus, air is the only food that a 'breath-arian' needs.
This term was popularized by Hilton Hotema in the 1950's or 60's and later by Wiley Brooks to emphasize the substance that builds and sustains man's body.

breatharian
Every man who needs to breath to live is a breatharian. Air is food for humans.
Humans are breatharians. Whether they eat or not, has nothing to do with being a breatharian. Even if you eat tons of food every day, you are still a breatharian. If you do not believe me, stop breathing for 20 minutes and tell me the result.
Inediates and non-eaters are also breatharians because they still need to breath.
Hilton Hotema insisted that man is a breatharian by nature – that is to say, man's body is sustained only by air. Therefore man does not need so-called food which is considered poisonous and a drug.
Presently the term breatharian is often misused and misunderstood because people wrongly say 'breatharian' when they really mean 'inediate' or possibly 'non-eater'.

living on Light
Living on Light (or light) is a concept, introduced by some spiritually oriented non-eaters, about the ability of a being to live without food, and be sustained only by Light. This Light is not visible but is some kind of energy-like substance. Light and prana are often understood as being the same. Thus, it can be said that 'living on prana' and 'living on light' are the same.

You may be confused with these terms – non-eating, breatharianism, inedia. What are the differences among these terms? All three describe the state of man who does not eat. Allow me to explain the essence of these terms.

Non-eating emphasises exactly on what the two words mean, the state in which there is **no eating**. It is not related to drinking or breathing.

Inedia emphasises on **no eating** and **no drinking**.
It is not related to breathing.

Breatharianism emphasises on **breathing** as the source of body life.
It is not related to eating or drinking.

BEFORE WE START WITH THE TOPIC

VOGUE

In the beginning of 2001 I noticed a vogue (which later faded) for breatharianism, non-eating, "pranic feeding", going for "living on Light" in Poland. I am sure that in large part the vogue was created by the mass media. I can imagine that similar vogues happen in different places on Earth from time to time, so my observations in Poland may also be valid for other places.

Everything would be fine had it not looked like the so-called "blind run of flock of sheep". The "blind run" brought some people to a dead end and did more harm than good to them. It all resulted mostly from misunderstanding of the matter and insufficient knowledge.

Despite what some people and the mass media are promoting, inedia is mainly one of the by-products on the way to expanding the sphere of the Consciousness in which man lives, in other words, on the way to perfection, on the path of conscious self-development. Making non-eating the main goal and attempting to adapt the body to living without food, without the necessary spiritual considerations, can cause suffering to you.

One of the reasons why I have written this book is to deliver proper and practical information about: what the matter is about, which way of doing it is more beneficial, what should not be omitted, what should be considered etc. In doing so I focus your attention on the fact that non-eating can be a jump into the unknown. This can be dangerous because this can cause you to lose your material body.

It is worth remembering that inedia is related to conscious self-development, although a completely unaware man who is not interested in this matter, also can acquire the ability to live without inserting anything into their mouth.

From data that has come to me I conclude that the vogue of becoming an inediate and the race for living without food, appear in some places on Earth while disappearing in others. However, one trait is common – many people, like sheep, follow what others do and say, due to herd instinct. They do not know the subject deeply enough, they just read or hear something from someone and then they jump into the abyss. That method can be good for a worrier but it can cause physical injury and suffering.

From my observations, I have come to the conclusion that people cause the most damage to themselves by so-called "21 day process". They believe that this process is an efficient method for becoming an inediate. I have never met any man nor heard of anyone who became an inediate as the result of following "the 21 day process".
On the other hand, many people who have attempted to become a non-eater through that process, came to me asking for advice because they endured physical pain and mental suffering.

Other activities bringing adverse effects to people, that I have observed, are group gatherings lasting from a few days to a few weeks, organised by some people who were promoted on the Internet as non-eaters.
I see that their main purpose to organize such activities is to make money. Knowledge of those leaders is insufficient for efficiently helping those who were aspiring to non-eating.
The people seeking help, turned to those leaders with hope, gave them a lot of money, but after the meetings those people still had unresolved problems and hopes unfulfilled.
I felt that it was dishonest for these leaders to prey on the hopes of others.

WARNING

The main purpose of my activity regarding the subject of 'living without food' is to pass on to interested people information about methods for adapting the body for proper functioning without the need of eating and some material covering the ability of the body to live without the need of eating.

I have written this book in order to realize part of the purpose. However, please, do not look upon this information as an instructional manual leading through adapting your body for living without eating. The task I have decided to work out by writing this book is to deliver information only.

Adapting yourself to living completely without eating is a complex process, which most often requires you to live in a larger sphere of the Consciousness. You would be better off seeking advice from more experienced people. You might also consider looking for guidance from more experienced people. However, be aware of the fact that they cannot give you any guaranty or make you an inediate.

Furthermore, be aware that each and every man goes differently through this process; which is the reason why every man needs a customized method, personally worked out. It is worth remembering that there are as many methods of adapting the body for inedia as there are people who have gone through the process.

COMMON SENSE – please, pay close attention to this title. If you follow common sense, you will not experience the danger of degrading the health of your body.
In case of people living on Earth, inedia should not to be achieved by force. Inedia usually appears as a by-product of expanding sphere of the Consciousness in which man lives.
When you discover that something bad is happening to your body, go back to 'normal' eating. It is time to learn more, not to continue in the field that may hold unknown dangers for you. I guess, you see inedia across the field, but, let me ask you – so what? Even thou you see it from far distance, you may not reach that place. Even if you are a natural warrior, still, you can perish. Therefore, let common sense guide you.

BE A CO-AUTHOR OF THIS BOOK

For me, writing a book about a topic such as non-eating is a process that never ends. Whenever I think about the content already written, more things come to my mind. There is always something that I could add to make the subject more comprehensive.
My goal is to have the most comprehensive work up of this topic in one book. I know a lot in this matter myself and I am finding new things, but still it is not everything. The knowledge you possess about this topic is a valuable source. Therefore I invite you to together enlarge the collection of useful information contained in this book.

If you are living without food or doing long fasts, please describe your experiments, experiences and observations. Write about yourself, how you prepared your body for living without food, how you went through fasting and why you did it. Also, please write about the obstacles you encountered and what solutions you used to overcome them.

If you are not a non-eater, please also write to me. Every comment or suggestion from you may be valuable for me. What is missing in this book, what should be changed, what do you not like, etc.?

INTRODUCTION

'Man in natural state' is a being of unlimited abilities. Man can be limited by their own beliefs. Beliefs constitute barriers that cannot be overcome. The way to freedom of man, the being of unlimited abilities, requires removing these barriers.

Those who rule others know that man in natural state is unlimited. If someone wants to rule people, that is to enslave them, he can achieve that by convincing people to follow beliefs. Man is ready to do a lot in order to protect and realize their beliefs, even fight to death for them. There are many examples showing how people on Earth are blinded with their beliefs. Can you mention some of them?

Beliefs are programs built in the man's instinct. Intellectual explanation may create doubts, but rarely removes beliefs. Man often can explain to themselves why a given behaviour is senseless, but they still find it difficult to free themselves of such a conduct.

Explanation aiming to deeply intellectually understand why man in natural state can make so-called miracles, requires complete understanding of what man is and how individual constituents interact.

Since man is not an isolated object, you need to know the basics of what constitutes man. In order to have a complete picture, let us start from the beginning, that is from the Consciousness.

THE CONSCIOUSNESS

The Consciousness (written with capital **C**).

Imagine something that does not have any space, time or any other limitations. Actually, it is impossible for the intellect to imagine the Consciousness, because any such attempt already creates a limitation. But just for the sake of a visual representation here, imagine something that does not have any time, space, feeling, knowledge, abilities and anything that you can imagine, and even more.

> The Consciousness does not have,
> but It can create any:
> cause,
> light,
> dimension,
> space,
> time,
> power,
> energy,
> life,
> knowledge,
> limit,
> feeling,
> ability,
> origin,
> movement,
> thing that you can or cannot imagine.

Another word that intellectually can describe the Consciousness is 'Nothingness', because there is nothing in the Consciousness.

The Consciousness is almighty, all-knowing, all-existing, and all the other all- (s). The Consciousness is the cause of all causes. All matter, all spirit, all thinking processes and all life in its origin – all these, and even more things, have the Consciousness in their origin of existence. The Consciousness is everything that you are able and unable to imagine, and even more.

Other words used (in the same or similar context) for the Consciousness are, for example: God, The Dao, The Void, The Absolute, The Providence, The Universal Mind, The Cause, The Principle, The Universal Consciousness. Depending on the understanding and explanation of man, who uses these words, they may have another definition, which may or may not be the same as the above one. If you are unsure what someone is talking about, ask them about the definition.

If I was to describe the Consciousness graphically, I would draw a dot, point **0** (zero, the Nothingness). From the dot there would be lines spreading in all three dimensions, until the minus and plus infinity. Of course it is only a graphical representation of something, which is impossible to draw. Let us make a premise that this diagram represents infinity, something that has no limits. Such a representation of the Consciousness makes my explanation easier to understand. So the diagram below represents, for the intellect, the Consciousness.

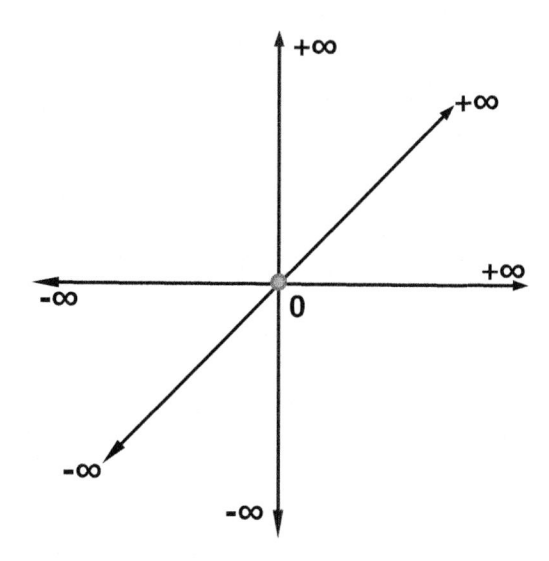

I have already written that it is impossible to comprehend the Consciousness intellectually. Let's do a comparison. A machine wants to comprehend the engineer who built it. This machine does not even have a tool (mind) which is necessary for thinking.
The intellect is the machine and the engineer is the Consciousness. The intellect does not have a tool capable to comprehend what the Consciousness is.

Nevertheless, it is possible and worthwhile to bring the intellect closer to comprehending the Consciousness. As a result, the intellect has a deeper grasp.

Then, what is the Consciousness?
It can be depicted in various ways. Every description of the Consciousness is untrue, it is only a depiction of an image in our imagination. When you leave the intellect and enter the intuition or even beyond, you can 'perceive' the Consciousness. However, upon returning, you will know that you are not able to grasp and describe the Consciousness.

Imagine that you are moving at the speed of light through the dark space of the perfectly empty cosmos without the smallest particle of light. You have been travelling for 15 billion years and still you see nothing. You have been moving endlessly and still there is only perfect darkness and nothingness. You cannot define space or time. If you were asked about space and time in the cosmos, you would answer that they do not exist or that they are limitless.

Now be aware, that limitless space and limitless nothingness is only a picture, just an image in the Consciousness. How much space and time does a picture in the imagination occupy? None. Completely nil. A picture in the imagination has nothing to do with time or space, because it is just a picture, which is an illusion.

Therefore, the cosmos which is limitless in space and time, is just an image or an illusion created by the Consciousness. It exists exclusively in the imagination, so it occupies zero space and zero time.
Interesting, isn't it? On the one hand, it is huge and infinite; on the other, it is ... nothing. This is why 'the Nothingness' is another name for the Consciousness.

This is, in big approximation, how the Consciousness can be described intellectually. It is limitless and does not occupy any space. It is everything and nothing simultaneously.

The Consciousness can be described as simultaneously both:
- all boundless universes with all matter, light, energy, Life and time, and every thing else;
    and
- nothingness.

Thinking about the Consciousness for the purpose of understanding It, is untrue and therefore creates falsehood. The Consciousness transcends thoughts because It contains everything. Truly, if something exists, it must be only the Consciousness, because everything else is just Its image.

If I was talking to you about the Consciousness, describing It intellectually and conveying by the intuition, I would have no way to make you comprehend what the Consciousness is. My explanations and I are just an infinitely small piece of what the Consciousness imagines. How can an image or micro thought describe its creator?

Let us continue. Imagine that you are still moving in that limitless cosmos. Now you notice flashes of lights, that is, you see result of Life creation. The Consciousness creates Life and entire galaxies made up of billions of stars which are suns. Whenever a star is created, you see light – that is the manifestation of Life creation. This is how the Consciousness creates beings in Its imagination.

Each of these beings, that is every star / sun, is a part of the Consciousness in Its imagination. Every of these parts lives and creates cosmic matter, like planets, moons, comets, star dust, water and elements. All of existence and Life are only images of the Consciousness.

It can be simply said that a galaxy, sun, black hole, and planet are pieces of the Consciousness; or to put is even more simply – they also are the Consciousness. Whatever exists is only the Consciousness.

In comparison, it is a somewhat similar to state that every hydrogen atom in the universe can say that it is hydrogen, and every droplet of water in the ocean can say that it is ocean water. Each of these atoms and droplets has qualities of the whole, if you forget about the illusion of space and size.

At this point, can you guess why I wrote: "IAM is the Consciousness – everything else is IAM's creation." as the motto of this book? Now it is obvious that man is also a piece of the Consciousness, similar to those suns and atoms. Man is also the Consciousness because there is only the Consciousness.

Do you understand? No?
Good, for that is normal. I also do not understand.
This is called philosophy – things can be considered and imagined endlessly when they are not comprehended intellectually.

SPHERES OF THE CONSCIOUSNESS

The Consciousness has no limits, so there is no place where it ends. The Consciousness is like the Nothingness, so we can say that it is point 0. Now, imagine that a sphere begins to emerge from the point 0. This sphere can expand from point 0 to infinity ∞.
In another way, you can imagine that a border of some kind was inserted into the Consciousness so that a limited part of the Consciousness was enveloped to form a sphere. Explaining this in visual terms it can be said that a spherical border was inserted or was created inside of the Consciousness. I call such a space a 'sphere of the Consciousness'. This is what I mean when I say that a being (for example a man) lives in a sphere of the Consciousness.

Unlimited number of spheres of the Consciousness can be created. There are five spheres of the Consciousness existing on Earth: the existence, the growth, the instinct, the intellect and the intuition. Visually these spheres of the Consciousness can be shown as in this picture.

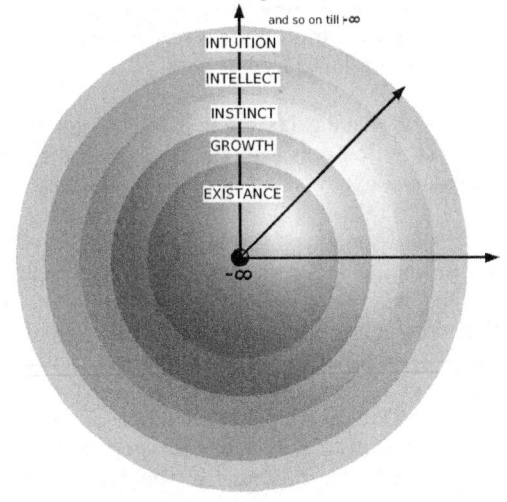

You see, the spheres are expanding from point 0 to plus infinity. I will not talk here about the expansion to minus infinity. I talk here only about the expansion from point 0 to the direction of Life, energy and mind, that is the creation of life forms by the Consciousness.

Remember, when the Consciousness expands from point 0, from the Nothingness, It creates Life. When you watch this expansion of the Consciousness, the creation of life, what you see is Light and what you feel is Love.

Limiting the Consciousness to a sphere makes the being, who lives in this sphere, limited (imperfect). A being from a larger sphere of the Consciousness has more abilities then a being from a smaller sphere.
A mineral (representative of the 'existence' sphere) has less abilities than a plant (representative of the 'growth' sphere). Comparing in the same way, an animal (representative of the 'instinct' sphere) can do more and knows more than a plant, but it has less abilities than man (the intellect sphere). So one can imagine that the beings living in the 'intuition' are more powerful than people.

At the same time, the above picture shows the process known as evolution (growth). The evolution of a being consists in expansion of the sphere of the Consciousness in which the being lives. A plant is more developed (farther in the evolution) than, for example, a rock or crystal. An animal is more developed (living in larger sphere of the Consciousness) than a plant. Man is even farther in the evolution.

In this process a being develops (evolves) themselves during the whole life because the sphere of the Consciousness in which the being lives is expanding. The more the sphere of the Consciousness (in which a being lives) expands, the more it is able to do, to imagine, to comprehend, and so on.

The intellectual development of a man, partially estimated as the intelligence quotient (IQ), can be used here as an example. Looking at man's history, one can draw a conclusion that man's abilities of comprehension, explanation, imagining, creating, finding solutions etc., were improving with time. So we can say, that the intellect (the sphere of the Consciousness) of an ordinary inhabitant of Earth has been expanding.

On the other hand, at the same time, the ordinary inhabitant of Earth has been active mainly in the intellect, therefore they have not been capable of doing things which are not possible in this sphere.

Every sphere is a limitation. If man remains in the intellect and they do not evolve more (that is they do not go beyond, to the intuition), man is not able to understand things which exist beyond the boundary of the intellect.

In a specific sphere of the Consciousness, a being creates and then uses a suitable body and specific conditions for living. Some examples. Man has more sensible and more sophisticated construction of the body compared to an animal. Also, human body contains less minerals and more water. Its energetic structure is more developed. An animal has more sophisticated body which contains less minerals compared to the body of a plant. A stone has the hardest body of the three, because it consists of almost exclusively mineral(s).

The beings living in the sphere of intuition own much more subtle bodies than people. In present time this body is invisible for most people, so it is considered immaterial.

Apparently, there is no such a thing as a sharp border between the spheres of the Consciousness. There is also no limit in the number of possible spheres which means that the evolution has no leaps. The evolution (expansion of the Consciousness sphere) of a being happens smoothly. In case of man the evolution means the process of expanding of their Consciousness sphere toward the intuition.

The evolution is just like that. There is no such thing as something better or something worse in the evolution, but there are spheres of the Consciousness and different innumerable possibilities to experience Life in them. Every being has the Consciousness in its essence (source or root). Every being is an experience of imperfection in a particular sphere of the Consciousness. It is the Consciousness itself which is experiencing. So it can be said that the evolution is a game played by the Consciousness.

The Consciousness is not limited in any way; however, the Consciousness, being omnipotent, can limit Itself in any way. In this case, the limited Consciousness is a sphere of the Consciousness.

Every sphere of the Consciousness represents a limitation. Every being is limited to a given sphere of the Consciousness. Man, while using instinct, intellect and intuition, is also limited, usually to the sphere of intuition. Potentially, man can grow in development much more.
This so-called 'spiritual development' consists in expanding the sphere of the Consciousness. The more a being expands the sphere of the Consciousness in which it lives, the more "spiritually developed" the being becomes.

When I explained the diagram "Spheres of the Consciousness", I wrote, "At the same time the above picture shows the process known as evolution (growth)." What I meant by 'evolution' was the development in creating Life. Life is associated with the development of forms, movement, energy and the expansion of space and time. In other words, the large the sphere of the Consciousness is, the more intensive movement occurs in it, the higher the vibrations are, the bigger the radiated energy is and the brighter it becomes.

Here are some examples:
Plants, which are bodies of higher vibration than minerals, have more movement.
Animals are clearly more busy, more alive than plants.
People have more energy and are higher vibrating than animals. As a result they usually live longer. If man does not degrade their body, man can live as long as the planet that man was born on.
Many invisible beings, called also 'spirits', are beings of higher vibrations than people. The spirits' vibrations are so high that their bodies usually are non-material and invisible to most people. They have more energy and can move more quickly.
Therefore the progression: minerals > plants > animals > people > invisible beings > and so on, shows beings of increasingly higher vibrations that are more and more 'developed'.

Here I explain the direction of the expansion of the sphere of the Consciousness described by the term "development of Life", which is the mechanism of the evolution of beings. This direction can also be called enlargement or expansion. It creates matter, beginning with ether and elementary particles, continuing to atoms, planets, galaxies and universes. The Big Bang hypothesis is thus supported and it aligns with reality.

The other direction of expansion of the sphere of the Consciousness is the opposite of the first one; it can be described by the term 'shrinking'. In this case the spheres of the Consciousness are expanding in the direction of the full, unlimited Consciousness that is understood as dimensionless, infinitely small, non-existing, and perfect nothingness.
In this process, the evolution regresses, galaxies lapse into black holes, vibrations decelerate to a full stop, energy decreases to absolute zero, darkness falls and everything disappears, lapsing into nothingness.

Initially, it is difficult to understand that both processes of returning to the Consciousness (also called explosion and implosion) are expanding the sphere of the Consciousness which is heading toward the disappearance of the limits. But when you realize that the Consciousness can be visually imagined as infinity and nothingness simultaneously, you will understand more easily that both expanding or shrinking the sphere of the Consciousness leads to the fullness of the Consciousness without spheres and limits.

These two opposite directions can be seen in activities of man. On the one hand, man studies and develops technology, creating new fields of life, and even travelling into the cosmos. On the other hand, man sits in silence and darkness in order to enter meditation and return to IAM, the Consciousness.

IAM

IAM (one word written in capitals), which cannot be comprehended with the intellect, is an illusory (imaginary) piece of the Consciousness.

IAM is an imagined, individualized part of the Consciousness,
like a drop of water is a part of the ocean.

the Consciousness

IAM is one with the Consciousness and exists in IT, like a drop of water is one with the whole ocean. IAM and the Consciousness are the same thing, but they are seen differently, considered differently and perceived differently by the intellect.

Thus the attributes of IAM are those of the Consciousness. IAM is in the Consciousness, at the same time being an imaginary piece of the Consciousness. IAM would not exist without the Consciousness and the Consciousness would not exist without IAM. In the same manner you can imagine that a drop of water would not exist without the ocean and the ocean would not exist without drops of water which constitute it.

IAM is the source, the essence, the primary cause and the creator of every being. Every being exists in IAM, because it has been created in IAM.
A being may feel that IAM is in him/her/it or the being may feel he/she/it is in IAM – it does not matter, because IAM is not limited by dimensions.

IAM is a particle of the Consciousness that has the same traits as the Consciousness, except that IAM 'thinks' that it is not the Consciousness, that it is something different, individualized and separated.
This is where all the fun, called Life, begins. IAM can be considered 'something real', something which emerges from the Consciousness and becomes separated from the Consciousness. The Consciousness which is 'nothingness' can be considered something unreal.

IAM is written in capitals "I", "A" and "M" in order to differentiate between "IAM" and "I am" which consists of the personal pronoun "I" and the verb "am". Therefore "IAM" is not the same as "I am".

To make this explanation even simpler, one can imagine that IAM is related to the Consciousness just like a hydrogen atom is related to the entire gas hydrogen found in the universe, or like a droplet is related to the water in the ocean, or like a grain of sand is related to the entire matter of the Earth. Every hydrogen atom in the universe can say that it is hydrogen of the universe, and every water droplet can say that it is water of the ocean.

Now you may think that there is a difference in size between IAM, which is a particle of the Consciousness, and a molecule or a droplet. After all, an atom occupies much less space than the entire hydrogen of the universe. Similarly, a droplet is many, many times smaller than the ocean.
Recall what I wrote about the Consciousness above, that It is not limited by dimensions, space, size or time. This means that the Consciousness can at the same time be as boundlessly huge as all the universes and as infinitely small as a point or nothingness, point **0**.

IAM is the same as and has the same traits as the Consciousness, thus both IAM and the Consciousness are the same matter. In order to imagine and later understand / explain this more easily, I have defined IAM as a particle of the Consciousness having the same traits as the Consciousness Itself.
In simpler terms, you can imagine that IAM is like a water droplet from an ocean, or a molecule of air from the atmosphere, or a grain of sand from the Earth.

You may wonder why I insist on the understanding of IAM. It is because

IAM is the essence of every being. IAM is the creator of everything that comprises a being.
IAM creates the mind, and the mind creates the rest that is Life, energy, matter (universes) and beings. Man is also a being that is created by IAM.

CONTEMPLATION OF IAM

Sit or lie down in a relaxed position. Stop thinking and move your attention away from the stimuli coming from your senses. If a thought appears, do not follow it, detach yourself from the thought and leave it alone.

Focus on IAM – that is what you are in the essence of you. Direct your attention away from your thoughts, mind, body or anything else. Only focus on IAM – whatever you imagine that is. Do not think about IAM, because IAM is beyond the creating power of mind, and also beyond any place and time. On the contrary, the mind is in IAM, therefore IAM cannot be created by thinking.

However, the mind, and the body through it, can feel the presence of IAM. Focus on this feeling. Tune yourself in for the appearance of IAM. Remain sitting or lying down in a fully relaxed state, but stay focused on IAM.

When IAM begins to manifest, you will feel that in form of indescribable joy and Love. At this point you will feel that your Inner Power originates from IAM.

That is the feeling of Inner Joy. Inner Joy is natural, you cannot create it. Inner Joy is what your body feels when IAM, which is the source of life of your mind and body, manifests itself through your mind into your body.

"I woke up contemplating my 'selves' (ego, personality, mind, thoughts, witness) when spontaneously they were seen for what they are – constructs, or vehicles for the IAM to function/experience on this level of existence ... It was so clear! Suddenly, all shattered and collapsed into the IAM that IAM and then stillness ... nothing ... for a moment/eternity ... So I KNOW ... all is created and sustained by and IS Life/IAM. And deeper still, everything/IAM unfolds from nothing."

Amara

THE MOST POWERFUL SAYING

The most powerful saying, so-called mantra, is this one:
"I am the Master Creator of my life."

For you own big benefit, when you wake up, before you open your eyes, repeat this sentence in your thoughts, many times. Then, when you get up, say that mantra aloud, even better, sing it with the full strength of your voice. You can also sing it in other situations, for example, when taking a shower, when jogging, when strolling in a park or on the beach.

I am the Master Creator of my life.

When you say that sentence, you state the truth about yourself. In the true reality, in your essence, you are the most highly experienced specialist, that is a master, in creating Life. Therefore, have the courage to acknowledge the truth by stating it with words.

By repeating this simple mantra, you can change your life tremendously for the benefit of you and the others. You will become much, much more aware of how your create your life and how much inner power you have to lead your life the way you wish to explore.

This simple mantra has changed people from being unconscious slaves and sheep of the society to self-sufficient free wolfs acting consciously.

THE MIND

The mind is created by IAM. The purpose of the mind is to create the game called Life. IAM creates mind, so that IAM does not have to do anything. IAM just sits back and enjoys watching the game.

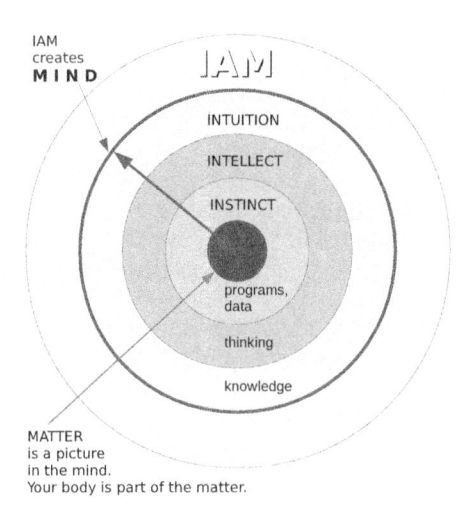

IAM creates MIND

IAM

INTUITION
INTELLECT
INSTINCT
programs, data
thinking
knowledge

MATTER
is a picture
in the mind.
Your body is part of the matter.

It is worth to be aware of the fact that everything is created by the mind, all the universes, all of the matter, your body and emotions, all of that is just an image, kind of a film, created in your mind.
All of these is unreal, that is why it is called Illusion, because it is imagined by the mind. When the mind is switched off, Life, including all of these things, disappears.
Your mind created your illusion, your game called 'your life'. Your universe and your body are parts of this game. You are not your mind, you are not your body, you are not your life.
The mind consists of three parts: intuition, intellect and instinct.

THE INSTINCT

It is one parts of the mind. It consists of data and programs. A program is a self-functioning mechanism which is working exactly the way it was created (written). The program does not think, it has no emotions and does not

31

do things which it was not destined (programmed) to do.

The instinct is a big collection of programs and data. The instinct does not think, does not deliberate, does not analyse, does not judge and does not create. The instinct runs programs and collects data thoughtlessly.

The data are:
- everything collected by the senses (knowingly or not) and conserved in the memory (most of it is forgotten);
- all circumstances, for example:
  - situations (e.g. behaviour of other beings);
  - factors (e.g. temperature, colour, sound level, space);
  - a result produced by a program.

There is a huge number of programs in the instinct. The working of the human body would be impossible without these programs. Actually, there would be no body without the programs, because the body is a direct result of the programs work.
In other words, the material world of your life, including your body, is created by your instinct, it is an image or a film in your instinct.

Here are just a few examples of the programs work:
- human can perceive with the senses and interpret it, so they can feel hunger, thirst or repletion;
- the heart beat frequency, the size of the pupil, amount of the sweat and many others are automatically controlled;
- responses caused by the reflex.

Emotional reactions of humans are programs responses to data. For example, when you hear or see something, you may start to feel happiness, sadness, sorrow, liking or anxiety – these are results of an impact by an external factor (that is data) on a program serving a particular field of man.

Another example: You are alone at home in a neutral mood. Unexpectedly someone knocks on the door. Having opened the door you see your beloved man, who kisses you and talks sweetly to you. What emotions arise in you?

Now something else: In a neutral mood you enter a room, where someone immediately shouts at you and throws insults at you. What emotions are arising in you now?

In the first scenario different emotions arise than in the second scenario unless man sufficiently controls them. To put it simply: in such a case specific data produces specific response by working program(s).

To be able to control your own emotions, in a way that allows you to experience them according to your will, may be one of the stages (or attainments) on your path of the spiritual growth.

When you control your emotions, you can decide, at any time, to feel happiness. Then you can remain in this state until you decide to elicit something else, for example, sadness.

If you cannot do it yet, different factors (e.g. behaviour of other people towards you) may be hurling you on the ocean of emotions like the wind hurls a leaf.

I suggest that you become well aware of what instinct is. The most important thing is to remember that instinct is a collection of programs and data. It contains all the emotions and feelings.
Instinct can be compared to the software of the computer. Turn on the computer and it begins to function precisely according to the instructions given by the software. The hardware, which is the machine called the computer, does not function without the software. You can compare this to a human. The body is the machine or hardware, the instinct is the software. The human body cannot function without instinct.

The software of a computer does not think; it merely gives instructions, precisely following the programs and data. When the software gives harmful instructions, it causes improper functioning of the computer and can even hang it up. A program that harms the functioning of the computer is called a virus.

Man's instinct works in exactly the same way. It follows the built-in instructions (programs + data), even thou this harms the body or leads to death. The harmful function is called an illness. The harmful set of instructions is called a virus.

Regardless of whether the activity of instinct is harmful or not, it functions just as in a computer, even if this activity leads to destruction of the machine, which is the body.

A SECRET

You may wonder why I wrote so much about the instinct instead of focusing on inedia, non-eating, etc. Let me reveal a secret. If you fully comprehend this, it will suffice for you to become an inediate or non-eater. Knowing this secret, you can create 'miracles' with your body.

The instinct holds the programs and data responsible for processes of eating, digestion and excretion. Normally, according to these programs, the human body must receive the proper substances in the correct quantity and at the right time, in order to function properly – that is to say, to be healthy. Your body cannot function properly in inedia if you have not modified your programs. You must eat so that you do not harm your body. If you force your body to non-eating, you may harm it. If you push it too much, you will kill it.

The full secret of inedia and non-eating is the proper modification of these programs so that they function differently. For example, you can modify the programs responsible for the processes of eating, digestion and excretion in such a way that the body will not require food for proper functioning. Then, according to these modified programs of instinct, the body will always function properly, regardless of whether you give it any food or not.

Inedia and non-eating are not possible without the modification of programs and data in instinct.
How is the program modification achieved? I will discuss that topic later in this book. However, in order to grasp the concept, one needs to fully comprehend the information given here, about the Consciousness, IAM, mind, instinct, intellect, intuition and man.

The Consciousness creates IAM, IAM creates the mind and the mind creates the rest, that is Life.

THE INTELLECT

The intellect is the part of the mind that creates. The intellect works in this way: first it creates a question, next it contrives, calculates, analyses, tries, projects, solves etc. and so on, in different order, until, finally, it creates an answer (solution). This answer can contain the next question.

The thing which passes, from the moment of having a question until finding the answer, is called time. Time exists only in the intellect. The intellect cannot exist beyond time. The intellect has been creating time so that it can exist and function. Beyond the intellect there is no time, hence it can be said that time is an illusion of the intellect. The same is with space.

The intellect perceives and builds the world as bi-polar that is the world in which everything has two opposing sides, at the same time there exists something and its opposite. For example: question and answer, good and bad, light and dark, cold and hot, easy and difficult, hope and doubt, man and woman, perfect and primitive, love and hatred.

The intellect creates something by, among others:
- giving answers to questions;
- building, in the imagination, something which did not exist there before;
- modifying things taken from memory (that is, from the instinct data base) or from senses.

The intellect, contrary to the instinct, does not accumulate data that is the intellect does not remember; it only thinks (re-arranges and creates the data).

The intellect is a part of the mind, a tool used for conscious programming of the instinct, for finding solutions and for creating. Your life is created in your intellect. Your decisions are created there. You bring problems into life and get rid of them also in the intellect. Using the intellect, you may or may not think logically, communicate with beings, explore, learn, solve tasks and answer questions.

If you were not using the intellect, you would behave as a thoughtless animal. Your body would not behave according to the decisions of your intellect; it would merely follow programs of the instinct. This is what happens to man, especially to those with weakly developed the intellect. Their body is more ruled by instinct than by intellect. You have probably observed this kind of behaviour in man. The less intellect and the more instinct ruling the body, results in man being reduced to providing more for his basic needs and satisfying his cravings which are examples of instinctive behaviour.

Man's intellect is a very useful tool. Without using the intellect, people would still be living like animals in nature. Their technology would consist of the level of their muscle strength and the speed of their movement. Or, that level could be developed further to using wooden blocks, stones and sand.

However, using the intellect can cause man's suffering. Some examples include using intellectual power to destroy nature and making tools to kill people. Some people use their intellect to manipulate others in order to enslave and reign over them.

Man can unknowingly use false information to develop their own world in the intellect. Such man creates problems and thereby unconsciously programs their instinct, which brings sufferings caused by man's own wish. If you do not wish to suffer, do not blindly believe all information. All that is written, spoken and seen is only information. It can be true or false. If you believe without thinking, you are asking for suffering.

Take advantages of your intellect that you control. It must serve you because it is your tool. It has to serve you in solving problems, so that you will understand and learn efficiently. The intellect has to serve you in making efficient visualizations, so that you can modify programs of the instinct for your own benefit. The intellect must obey you.

Sometimes you need to switch the intellect off – this ability is very useful. Thanks to this ability you can, for example, fall asleep at will, cut off attention from stimuli of the environment, move into meditation. You can also hear intuition or use an almost perfect method of communication and information receiving, which is known as telepathy.

THE INTUITION

It is the part of the mind, which knows everything without any question, thinking, creating or searching. There is no question in the intuition. Even if there appeared one, at the same moment the answer would appear too. Actually, there is no such a thing as the moment in the intuition either, because the time (together with other illusions) does not exist in the intuition.

Time, space and bi-polar world do not exist in the intuition. They are the creations of the intellect which were built into the instinct as programs and now are running continuously.

The intellect is unable to understand the intuition because the intellect is a smaller sphere of the Consciousness. It follows that the intellect is unable to explain how the intuition works.

The intuition contains the intellect (think about the spheres), so the former understands the latter. Similar relation exists in case of the intellect, which contains and understands the instinct, but not vice versa.

It explains why man, who is the representative of the intellect on Earth, is able to understand and explain, for example, the functioning of the body or behaviour of an animal. It also explains why the animal is not able to understand man, if, for example, the animal is asked to solve a mathematical problem or to explain abstract things. The animal is not able to do so since the instinct is smaller sphere of the Consciousness than the intellect.

Now you may be able to conclude that man (who focuses mainly in the intellect) is not able to understand immaterial beings spiritually more developed (who focus mainly in the intuition). Indeed, people do not understand them, but they understand people as much as people understand animals.

Therefore, if one man tries to explain something coming from the intuition (so-called: spiritual things) to another man, they can only philosophize. The imperfection of this communication is similar to a situation, in which one cow tries to explain the function of man's intellect to another cow.

So whilst continuing attempts to explain the intuition in this fashion, I will add that it also serves as a kind of a link or gateway to IAM for man.

Talking about people, I also use the expressions: intuition, intellect and instinct, as definitions for parts constituting the mind (as per the above description). So 'the intellect' is a sphere of the Consciousness and also is a part of the mind with the description of its function as above mentioned.

Every being, including people, is in its essence the Consciousness which has limited itself to a determined sphere.

Intuition, which is a part of the mind, is also your tool. It is a powerful tool for communication and receiving information. When you can fully use intuition, you do not need look for information through the intellect. Consequently, schools become redundant, nothing can be hidden from you, because you know what and when anything was thought about. You merely need to turn your attention to anyone or anything, to know everything about them immediately. You learn so quickly that there is no chance for a question to be formed. If you used intuition to learn how your body can live without food, this book would be useless for you. In the time of one second, you would know everything about this topic. In fact, you would know much more.

When you intuitively contact another being, you are using a type of communication called telepathy. As a result, communication technology

37

becomes completely useless. The most sophisticated and fastest telephone or Internet connections become for your primitive tools which you even do not want to see. Instead of talking for hours with the other man, telepathically you need just a second for saying everything and listening to all. Even more, you will feel everything that your interlocutor does and you will go through the same emotions.

Man uses intuition when they want to know something immediately, things that are not available for the intellect or would require too much time and energy, like travelling, exploration, asking, or researching.

On the other hand, using intuition makes man see life less interesting. What is the fun of knowing everything about a topic or about someone, just at your wish? Then, there is no secret for you, there is nothing to look for or to research.
How can you play a lottery when you know which ticket will be drawn? How to enjoy presents when you know in advance, who is to and what is going to be given to you? How to participate in a conversation when you know who is to speak and what is going to be said because you read their thoughts?

THE FUNCTIONS OF THE MIND

The intuition only KNOWS, it does not think and does not act.
The intellect only THINKS, it does not know and does not act.
The instinct only ACTS, it does not know and does not think.
To successfully realize something, man needs to utilise
all the three functions of the mind.

MIND and BRAIN

By the way, do not confuse mind with brain, because they are two completely difference things. You already know that the mind is an immaterial device created by IAM. It does not reside in the body; on the contrary, your body is an image in your mind.

The brain is a physical organ in man's head. It is the central controlling device for electrical and light signals in man's nervous system.

WHAT IS LIFE?

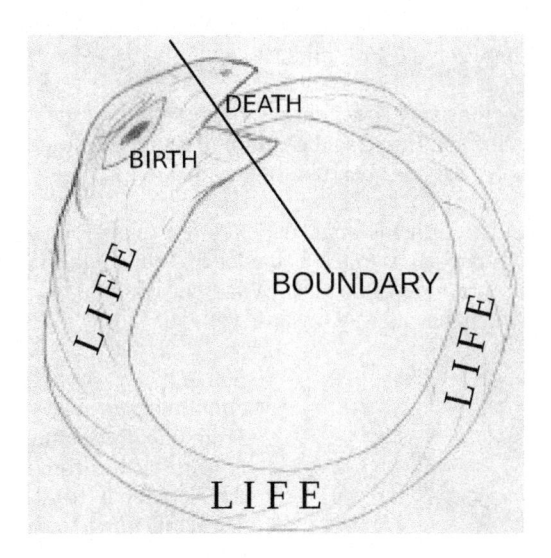

```
        DEATH
   BIRTH
                BOUNDARY
LIFE                    LIFE
          LIFE
```

Life is a transformation occurring in the movement from birth to death.

The beginning of Life is called birth and the end is called death.
Birth exists due to death and death exists due to birth. Birth and death are the same inseparable thing, but seen from the opposite sides, from different dimensions or from different worlds.
For something to be born, something else must die. For something to be able to die, it must first be born.
The boundary between death and birth is the transformation of one thing into another, but this does not stop Life, although one thing must die so that the other can be born.

The analogy of a snake eating its own tail can symbolically represent Life. Thanks to this, the snake lives. If the snake stopped eating (killing or creating death), its body could not be built (reborn or create life); it would die of starvation.

When the balance between death and birth is kept, Life never ends, that is Life is eternal.

Birth is presented by the sun because it emanates and gives life to matter. Death is presented by the black hole because it devours and kills matter.

In the universe, matter is created by suns (stars) and is annihilated by black holes. Matter lives between the sun and the black hole.

Beings choose where they stay – this defines the direction of their activity. They move towards the sun (light) and creation of matter or they move towards the black hole (darkness) and killing of matter.

Light forces create, give birth and emanate. Dark forces annihilate, kill and devour. The former is needed as much as the latter. When light forces and dark forces are in equilibrium, Life exists. When one of these forces outweighs the other, Life makes its way towards the end.

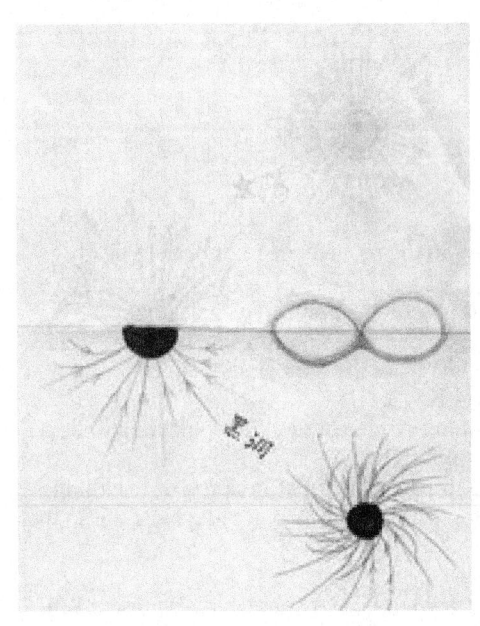

Sun and black hole connect the two dimensions.
From one dimension, the sun is seen (birth); from the other, the black hole (death) is seen. The same thing – which simultaneously kills and creates – is the black hole in one dimension and the sun in the other dimension.

The black hole must annihilate or kill matter so that the sun can give birth or create matter.

The killing creates a substance for birth and the birth creates a substance for death.

A FABLE ABOUT A FISH

Am I a fish or what?

First I am going to tell a fable or (looking at it from a different angle) a true story, which is the prologue for the subsequent description of the man.

Once upon a time I had a fish. I decided to experience the life of a fish. How is it to be a fish? What does the fish do, and why? What does the fish feel? Can it be a non-eater? What kind of emotions does the fish experience? I was interested in knowing answers to such questions. So I decided to explore it. I was curious and I wanted to have fun (to play).

First, for a few months, I daily spent a few hours with the fish. I was observing it in different situations. I found out a lot of things and I learned a lot about the fish. I could even write a book and become an authority in the field of fish life. I had observed everything that was possible to be seen in the life of the fish. That was my experience that people told me about in the past. However, only now, when I have seen it by myself, I can say that I know it.

There was nothing more that I could learn from the observation of the fish. The observation alone could not answer my numerous questions such as: How does the fish see the world? How does the fish feel the water with its skin. How do its body organs react to changes of the water temperature? How does the fish feel the friction depending on its moving speed? The observation alone could not give me answers to these questions. Other people told me how it feels, but for me it was only information about their experience of being in a fish body. Well, if I do not do it myself, I will never know, because the way to knowledge is through experience.

So I had decided to experience the life of the fish, and in order to do this I entered its body. So as for the body, I was a fish. I could feel as if on my own skin all the things that I did not know but was curious about. I could experience myself all the things that people tried to explain to me. Now I finally know how it feels to be a fish.

Actually, at that time I should not have said that I fully knew how it was to be a fish. I was in the body of the fish, this is a fact, but the thing is I knew that I was not a fish. I had experienced everything what could be observed and felt on the body, but I had not learned the emotions of a fish. Exactly, the emotions, which is the essence of the fish life. How is it, what does the fish feel when a pike is approaching to eat it? What does the fish feel when another fish eats its children?

How could I have experienced the whole spectrum of the emotional and mental life of a fish? Well, just being in the fish body was not enough, because I knew that I was not a fish, and that it was only a game I was playing. When I am playing, I know that it is only a game.

Other people told me stories about mental and emotional life of a fish, but again, to me it was, just information. I decided to experience it all, in order to know, and not just have information. I had a choice to enter the body and mind of the fish and to forget that I am not a fish, and that I am only playing.

I did that and lived through the whole life of a fish, not knowing that I was not a fish. Only after doing that (as it turned out) my experience about the life of the fish became complete. All these things, that are having done the observation, feeling the physical body and going through the emotions, constitute the complete experience. Only when having completed them all I can say that I know the life of the fish.

Now I can explain this to other people, just like others tried to explain to me in the past. However, I know that those who do not have such experience will not understand me. Even more, there will be people who will say that what I am saying is not true and they will ask for a proof. How am I going to give them a proof of all that I have experienced? They do not have such experience, they have not opened themselves to it because they have decided to only look and listen to my information. I know that they are not capable to understand me, that is why I do not intend to convince them or prove anything. I can give them just information which they can experience by themselves if they decide so.

Have you realized that with this fable I have described man – what they are and what they do here? Do you know that you are such a fish, a character in a game created by IAM?

Being man this time, you already got to know to some degree what man does and what they feel. Having defined an experience to go through, man experiences life in a chosen form (body) and circumstances (location in the space, life style etc.). Man does not know that they are not a character in a game, and that they only uses the character's mind and body in order to experience Life, in other words – to play.

WHAT IS MAN ?

The picture below is a rough visual representation of the elements making up man. Many other beings living outside Earth look similar in graphic terms.

All of the matter, including the spirit and body, is in the mind.
The mind is in IAM.
IAM is in the Consciousness.

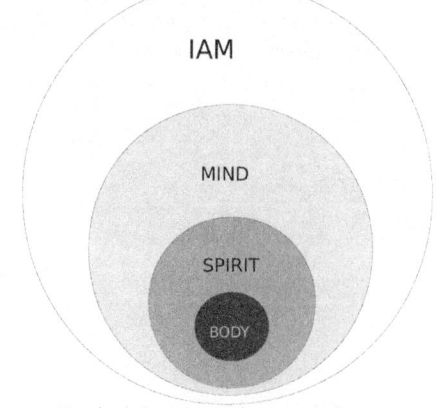

IAM

MIND

SPIRIT

BODY

Your body is an image in your mind.

IAM is the centre, the root, the first cause, the essence and simultaneously is the creator of all the other man's elements. IAM is an imagined independent and separated piece of the Consciousness. At the same time IAM contains inside itself all the elements making up man, because all the elements exist only in IAM.

Since IAM is an imagined piece of the Consciousness, IAM has all its attributes, for example, IAM is almighty and omniscient. Therefore you may ask yourself, what IAM can wish, since it is perfect, it has, knows and can do everything. Of course, the intellect is not able to understand that, it can only philosophize about the matter – like I am doing now.

What does IAM wish? The answer is simple: IAM is watching/playing a game that it has created. The mind created by IAM is running the game called Life. Since IAM has, knows and can do everything, it needs nothing, therefore it may choose to watch/play a game, for instance.

The game is called Life or 'the experience', and in order to be the most successful it should look like the real thing. The less things and situations look mock, the better the game is. IAM can produce such circumstances by making limits, that is by creating a sphere of Consciousness which is suitable for the conditions of the game in creation.

In the case of the game called: "experiencing Life as man on Earth", IAM creates the following tools which are suitable for the experiencing of:
1. the mind, which consists of the intuition, the intellect and the instinct;
2. quite sophisticated structure called 'the body', which actually consists of the material (physical) body and an invisible element called 'spirit';
3. circumstances and conditions for the experience (e.g. living in a small town on Earth)
4. the destiny, that is the end of the game, end of Life.

Having created all necessary elements, IAM is playing what can be called: 'an evolution from imperfection to perfection' or 'spiritual self-development'. It is quite an interesting game, when a being who in its essence is perfect does not know this and thinks of him/herself as being imperfect and therefore strives for perfection.

Having read the story about a fish, you get an image of what man is, what they consist of, how they function and what they do. In place of a fish, you can imagine any other being. So, you are not man, not a body or a body plus mind – these are your tools to play the game. In your essence, you are IAM, the Consciousness.

Specifically, I use other words to describe what man is, because this is important information for you. Knowing deeper what man is, what they consists of and how they function, gives you more possibilities to create life consciously.

You are already aware that nothing exists, only the Consciousness. Everything, every place and eternity are in the Consciousness. IAM is an imagined piece of the Consciousness and has the same traits. To put it more simply, let us accept that all is created in IAM; thus whatever exists, is in IAM.

IAM creates the mind. The mind consists of intuition, intellect and instinct. In the mind, all matter and entire universe exist, because they are images, as is everything else, a kind of illusion created by the mind. Part of this matter is man's body.

You can draw the conclusion from the above illustration that man's body is an image in the mind. Man's mind is a product of IAM.
The image is only an image, which is something that has no solid base; therefore, it is an illusion. The conclusion is simple, that everything which is material, universally known as 'reality', including man's body, is just an image in your mind, just an illusion.

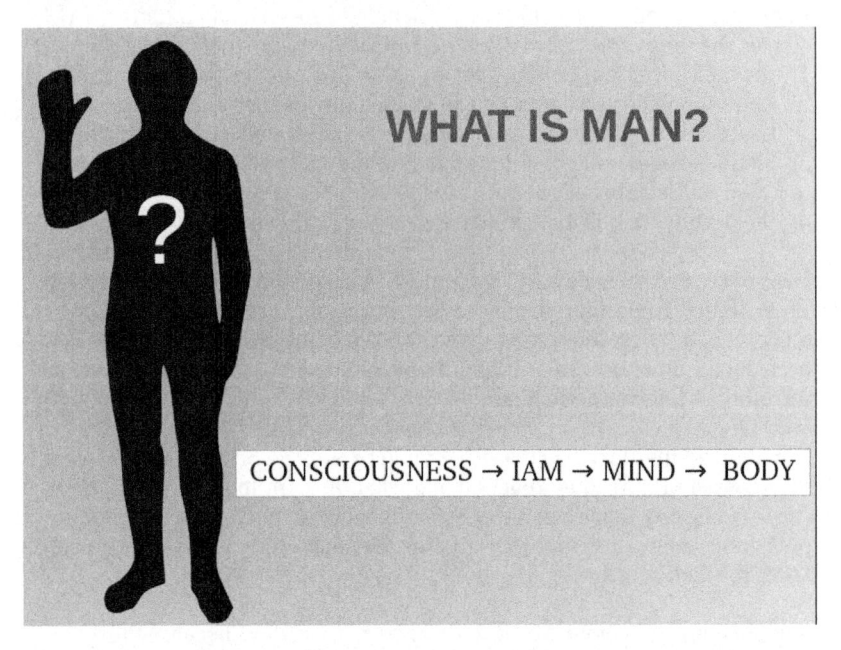

WHAT IS MAN?

CONSCIOUSNESS → IAM → MIND → BODY

Then, what is man? Man is a creature of the mind produced by IAM emerging from the Consciousness. The Consciousness » IAM » mind » body.

Viewing from an energetic aspect, man simultaneously creates and kills, according to the process shown on the diagrams in the chapter "What is life?".

Eating and excreting are processes supporting Life. Man, in order to live, eats and excretes, that is, kills and creates. Any other life form in our universe does the same, that is, transforms one form of matter to other.

This diagram shows where man is found in the food chain and eating dependencies.

Every life form on the diagram (subatomic particles, atoms, molecules,

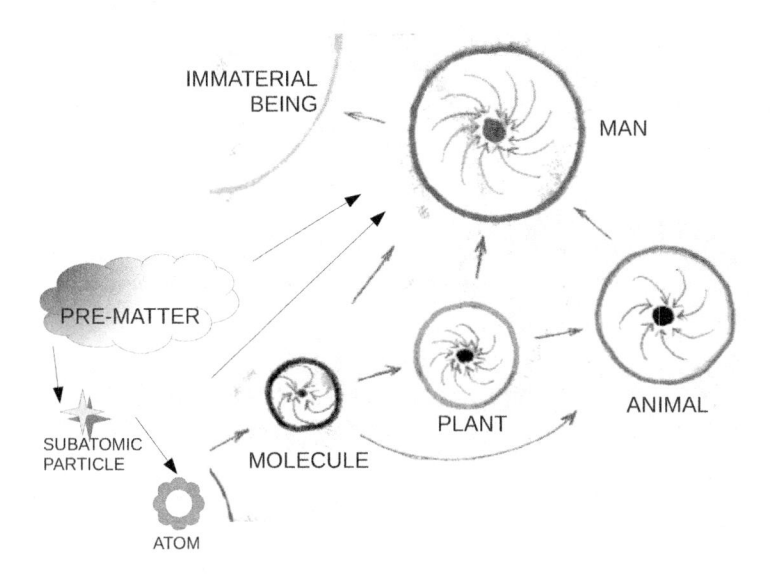

minerals, plants, animals and people) simultaneously take and create, kill and give birth, absorb and emanate.
As the diagram shows, man can absorb (consume) animals, plants, minerals, molecules, atoms, subatomic particles. Man can also use pre-matter (prana, qì, ether, vril, information field or any of many other names for the pre-matter) to create energy and body's matter.

The black hole and the sun can be found in every being. The black hole represents everything that a being absorbs, can be by eating. The sun represents everything that a being emits, can be by excreting.

THE LIGHT

The Light – written with capital **L**.

Do you know where these expressions come from and what they mean? – "living on Light", "living in Light", "fed by Light", etc.
What actually is this Light?

This Light is not the thing that human eye can see, so it is not emitted by a light bulb, a sun, fire or very high temperature. This Light is something that you can sense or 'see' with your immaterial vision ability, your spiritual eyes, your sixth sense or whatever you call it.

Now imagine that somehow you are observing what the Consciousness is doing, so, you can see how the Consciousness creates Life. Imagine that while you are floating in the total darkness, the nothingness, you suddenly see kind of an explosion of light of indescribable beauty, something that you could compare to the Big Bang – that is Light. At the same time you deeply experience something like a peaceful pleasure – that is Love.

What you see and feel are by-products of the process in which the Consciousness creates Life. The process of the Life creation by the Consciousness.

When the Consciousness creates Life, you can see Light and feel Love. These Light and Love are by-products of the process of the Life creation by the Consciousness. These Light and Love are the same thing; however, the Light your see and the Love you feel.

Every being is a manifestation of a sphere of 'the Consciousness creating Life', thus Light and Love are at the source of every being. So, you can say that you always 'live on Light and Love'.
The larger the sphere is, the more Light and Love the being is able to manifest.

The Consciousness is in the essence/root/origin of every being. It manifests itself as much as the mind of the being allows it. Therefore, the larger the sphere of the Consciousness in which the being lives, the brighter Light can be emanated by the being, lighting up the darkness around.

So you are already living on Light, actually, you always have been. If you are aiming to live on Light, just let yourself feel that you are.

It is not enough, to understand it intellectually, but once you feel it, you will know it and it will become your reality. Then you will know that you are the master and creator of your life.

Now, close your eyes. Fully relax. See and feel the complete darkness for a while. Then let yourself see Light. Once you see it, turn your attention to your feelings. What do you feel? Love. Tell yourself and deeply FEEL this: IAM the Consciousness, the source of Light, Love and Life.

> Light and Love are manifestations of Life-creation process.
> They are the same thing but Light you see and Love you feel.
>
> Every being is a manifestation of a sphere of 'the Consciousness creating Life', therefore Light and Love are at the source of every being. You can say that you always live on Light and Love.

The following is another, complementary explanation.

Light is what is seen at the moment when Life is being created. When the Consciousness creates something, for example, an atom, the sun or the universe, Light is seen. The Big Bang is a huge flash of Light, which is sensible when the universe is created. The Consciousness is creating energy and matter.

When you close your eyes, withdraw reception from the senses, deepen yourself in a state without thinking, that is when your intellect becomes passive and you are entering meditation. When this happens, the first thing you see is Light. Your eyes are closed, darkness surrounds you, but you see bright Light. That comes from you, from your essence which is the creator of your mind and body. You are creating them all the time, that is why Light is there all the time.

Man and every other creature have this Light inside them. It is a manifestation of Life. The life of a creature is being created all the time, that is why every being shines with light.

SUGGESTION BY THE SOCIETY

Once, at the beginning of my first non-eating experiment, my wife told me: "What you are doing is against nature." Before answering I suddenly realized that there was a lot of truth in her statement. Why? Before I answer, please think about the three cases below.

1. When a baby is born in a society of people who eat, he demands food from the moment of the birth. The baby has to be fed because if he does not receive any food for too long, the body will stop working (die). Not giving the baby any food would be acting against nature.
2. When a baby is born in a society of people who eat, but the parents are inediates, the baby will demand food in less quantity than the one in the above example.
3. When a baby is born in a society of inediates, he will refuse to eat from the beginning. Then the baby should not receive any food. Giving the baby food, would be acting against his nature.

Do you already know what causes these differences? You can guess that it is about programs in the instinct of the baby, the programs which are responsible for the relation between man and the matter called food.

From the moment of the conception every man is under the influence of the society suggestion. In the womb the mother has the biggest influence on the baby's instinct, next are the father and the other family members and then the people with whom the mother spends most of her time. If they all are people eating 'normally', one should not expect that the instinct programs of the baby in the womb would be different from those prevalent in the society. Therefore the biological nature of the baby born will be also alike, resulting from the influence exercised on this man during their entire stay in the womb. The eating habits of man are being created already in the womb.

Similar processes are taking place during the whole time after the birth. Until the baby becomes an adult, his diet depends on the society in which the child lives.

A new born baby has the instinct sufficiently programmed in a way that allows his body and mind to function properly. A set of these programs constitutes his nature. Acting against this nature causes disorders or even death in extreme cases.

The conclusion is simple: next time when you decide to be born on Earth as an inediate, first choose the parents and society suitable for the occasion.

The society suggestion is not limited to the influence of the parents and all the people which man is in contact with. Man is also influenced by education, environment, colours, sounds, temperature, food consumed, games and so on. All that and even more continually program man's instinct.

You probably guess how useful a tool, which is the knowledge about the society suggestion, in hands of manipulators is. Understanding the mechanisms of reactions (programmed answers) to specific stimulations (data) in a chosen society, it is easy to manipulate the people (primarily their emotions) in a manner, that their thinking, talking and acting are in accordance with the manipulator's expectation. Fear, desire to feel love, envy, compassion, want of power, desire to punish and other factors causing emotional reactions are used in carefully a planned manner, so that people, according to their own will, do exactly what the manipulators expect.

The instinct is programs and the manipulator is a programmer who knows how to program man in a manner that is not noticeable to man and that often results in man being thankful for the manipulator's work.

Often the voting people are a good example of this. Also look at the advertisements, films, wrapping of merchandises, arrangement of shops or offices, declarations of politicians, and so on and so forth. Listen and feel what they evoke in you, what emotions? Do you think that it happens by coincidence?

The more you think for yourself, that is the more consciously you do something and the more you pay attention to the society suggestion – the more you discover the underlying suggestion and the more you understand how strong an influence it has on the thinking, talking and acting of people. Then you can say that you think by yourself, not according to the patterns built in your instinct. Then you act more and more independently, you become more independent man. Also then the emotional states emerging in you are becoming of the kind that you decide to have, not of the kind that your instinct was programmed to produce in response to specific stimulation (data).

Please, be aware that man who does not understand or control their instinct, regarding the programs governing the matter called food, is not able to become an inediate. Such man is still a slave of their instinct's programs.

REPROGRAMMING

The instinct is the part of the mind, which creates matter (therefore, also human body). How the body functions depends on the instinct. Among other things in the instinct there are also relations between the body and the external matter, of which food is a part.

The instinct of man who 'eats normally' has a set of programs running all the processes related to eating and food. How does it work in case of average man? – I think there is no need to explain.

Knowing this much about the instinct, you can easily come to the conclusion that in order to become an inediate (non-eater, breatharian) the main task to be done is to change the functions of programs related to eating. For the average inhabitant of Earth the result of the programs' work can be described as follows:
> If proper substances (defined as 'food') are delivered in human body, through the digestive system, in proper quantities and at proper times – the body works. But if something changes, for example, the quantities decrease too much or the timing is wrong – the body does not work properly, and in extreme cases the vital functions stop.

Therefore, in order to make the body independent of any food, time and quantity, the programs need to be modified, so that they work in the following way.
> Regardless of whether substances are put into the body or not, regardless of the time and the quantity – the body works properly. The instinct constantly keeps the human body working properly and man can be called an inediate.

Man who prefers to start from diet modification and who has not decided yet to become an inediate, may change the programs so that they produce the results as described in this sentence: If the body receives only plant derived food, it works properly. In such a case man may be called a vegan.

Another man may decide to make some other changes. This man will change the programs governing the structure and functioning of their body, so that the result is described in this sentence: Only if fruit or vegetable juices are drunk by the body, in proper quantities and appropriate times, the body works properly. Such man can be called a liquidarian.

How to change the way in which a program works? How to delete a pro-

gram or data that I have decided to get rid of? How to build in new programs and data?
The methods used for realizing such decisions are visualization, hypnosis and suggestion.

It is worthwhile to be aware that a large part of instincts consists of beliefs. Man is a powerful being with potentially limitless abilities but man is limited by beliefs. Beliefs are barriers or limits that man does not cross. The more beliefs man has and the more limited they are, the more man has to release in order be free.

If you believe that the body needs to eat to live, then you have to eat. If you do not eat, you will destroy the body. With this belief you also can give up aspiring to inedia or non-eating.
Those, who believe that the body functions because it is built and energised by consumed matter, are not able to keep the body functioning properly.

The belief, that a body has to eat in order to live, is a barrier that cannot be crossed by man aspiring to inedia. Man needs to remove this barrier. Then, reprogramming in this area is required. I wrote about it in earlier chapter called "a secret".

It is the same with other beliefs. Every belief is a limit. You cannot cross a limit because if you do, you suffer. But you can remove limits, this gives you more and more freedom to act. Reprogramming is a process of removing beliefs from instinct and opening a way to freedom.

When you are releasing beliefs, then you are also leaving those who manipulate you. The master, guru, spiritual guardian, adviser, pastor, priest, teacher and so on, are all your barriers you do not want to cross. They also are sources of your beliefs. When you decide to become more free, you will leave them, that is, you will remove these barriers, you will stop believing them. This reprogramming also releases your belief in manipulators.
Be aware that the author of this book is also a kind of a manipulator. Later you should leave him, stop believing in what is written here, so that you can grow and move farther.

Beliefs are also found in religion, philosophy, various systems and 'isms'. They contain useful information that you can utilize in your life. However, when you blindly believe them, again, you fall under barriers not to be crossed. Only after removing these barriers, can you feel relief. When the burden is removed, your mind becomes lighter and you can move farther, and grow, that is, expand the sphere of the Consciousness that you live in.

Reprogramming, or the removing of beliefs, may not be easy. When you decide only: "I do not believe this any more." or "I am leaving this church." or "I abandon this master.", etc., it is not enough.

Instinct requires a complete decision, image, and energy, in order to be reprogrammed. I wrote about that in the chapter "visualization".

POWERING THE BODY

Shortly and simply, considering it mechanically, energetically and chemically, it can be said that the human body is being built, sustained and powered in 5 different ways:
- digestive tract – consumed food;
- breathing – inhaled air;
- skin – sun light and cosmic waves;
- movement – electricity;
- the will of life – imagination in the mind.

In other words, the body, to function properly, needs:
- proper diet, which is individually selected proper material food;
- to breath air which is used to build body proteins;
- the sunshine to fall on the skin and into the eyes;
- to do physical and energizing exercises to produce electricity;
- the will of the body owner to keep the body to function perfectly.

All those five needs are needed in different amounts, individually tailored for every man. When you spent more time doing mind exercises, you wanted to eat less. Similar thing happen when you are doing energizing exercises or you spend much time on a sunny beach. During sunny summer man wants to eat less than they do during cloudy winter.

When the will of the body owner to keep the body to function perfectly develops sufficiently, then not only food and drink become needless, also the breathing, the influence of the sun radiation and the temperature also become less needed.

You already know what man is. From that you can easily conclude that man's body is also powered by actions that occur in the imagination. Since man's body is just a picture in the imagination of the mind and all matter is just a picture as well, powering of man's body is also a picture, the same kind of illusion.

In reality you may think that this appears different. Man eats material food so that their body has building material and energy for living. Sure, in that reality, which is only an image of the mind, an illusion, such a thing is really happening.

When you shrink your view to the intellect sphere of the Consciousness, you may not see other possibility. However, when you view this from outside the intellect sphere, you begin to see how matter and energy function and what they are. You can see the illusion.

Knowing what man is and how they function, you also know that man's body is powered in such a way that is pictured in their mind. Knowing already what instinct is, you probably guess that man's body needs powering, that is, food according to man's belief. I wrote about this earlier.

DIGESTIVE TRACT

The digestive tract transforms eaten solid and liquid substances, generally called food, nourishment or feeding. It makes man feel a contentment caused by the look, smell and taste of the dishes, and mainly after making the stomach full. Also hunger and thirst disappear after some eating.

So called scentific understanding and explanation of how the consumed substances build and power the body, is as this. The consumed food is disassociated (by e.g. the enzymes) to simpler substances (mainly chemical compounds, e.g. glucose, amino acids). Next, these things are used by the body for synthesizing (building) what it needs and for extraction of the life energy (to be used for e.g. moving, thinking, body heating). The resulting conclusion seems to be simple, that the consumed substances give the body energy and building matter. So considering the energy, the body can be compared to a car or a locomotive in which fuel is burned for energy that moves the whole machine.

Some people wonder if really the eaten bread or drunk fruit juice builds human body and can be burned (like coal or wood) for energy. And why different people, although they consume food which differs a lot by the composition and amount, are quite similar in their stature and weight. This happens even if the daily lives (environment, work and, physical activity) of these people are very similar.

Another real example; man who weighs 120 kg eats two slices of bread and drinks two cups of coffee a day only, but he does not lose any weight. On the same day his peer eats six loaves of bread, two sausages, half litre of milk, three cups of tea, biscuits, fruits and something else, and he remains slim. They are of the same stature and have similar amount of physical activity.

You probably could give more examples like these, if not then it would be enough to look around and compare people regarding this matter. Such examples make it clear that there is no absolute connection between the amount of eaten food, its composition and the body appearance or how much life energy man has.

Why does it happen like this? If bigger quantity of eaten food gives more life energy, then people who eat more should feel more energized. There is even so-called 'energetic value' of food. An amount of grease has this many calories, of milk has less and of saccharose has more calories, and so on. But why eating bigger amount of sugar with fat causes man to feel worse than when they drink the same quantity of fruit juice or just water? Why after a big and satiating meal man, instead of radiating with energy, feels lazy and weakened?
Since our childhood we have been under this suggestion: "Eat more to be stronger." It is a pity how children are being programmed by the use of this and similar harmful suggestions, which later in their life results in so much suffering: diseases, ageing and earlier body death.

By the way. One of the most serious harms that can be done to a child is to force him/her to eat. Carefully watching the child to make sure that they finish eating everything from the dish, harms the body of this small man that you do love. That causes, among others, changes in the psychical and physical structures of the child, which are difficult to reverse. Such changes affect the psychical and physical health of man during their whole life. Shortly, forcing children to eat more than their body really need, causes wounds to children's body. These wounds may not be recoverable.

Let your children decide for themselves. Do not worry, your children will not starve and will not overeat (unless such a program already has been built in). You only need to protect them against poisons like sweets, fries, chips and all fried, fumed or grilled food, and also against animal milk including all its products. By the way, you cannot buy milk in a shop any more. It was possible in the past, but not any more in this degenerated civilization. Even if the label says "milk", it is a different substance from the viewpoint of physics and chemistry. If you really want to have milk, you need to go to a female animal directly.

Going back to the above questions – the answer is simple and for many people astonishing. Eaten food does not give any energy to the body. Eaten food causes the opposite reaction, it forces the body to spend energy for decomposing, neutralizing and excreting all of it. The human body uses its own energy for transforming and excreting what man inserted in the digestive track.

The other answer can be also astonishing. Eaten food does not build human body cells. It has an impact (information of programming) on how they are built and how they function but it does not build them. The body does not directly build its cells from eaten food. However, the body utilizes information and life energy of the eaten food. That's why the eaten food should be living, taken directly from nature, eaten without any processing.

What does the body do with the consumed food? The body get rids of the food completely if it works properly. The body removes the superfluous, poisoning substances with faeces, urine, sweat, saliva, sebum, blood, breath, hair, nails and epidermis. But if the body does no function perfectly, then it deals differently with part of the consumed food. Part of it is stored (eg. as fat or glycogen), other part is put aside for later removal. In the present civilization this became normal, in other words, there are almost no ideally healthy people.

It seems that the human body is a machine producing and removing a waste polluting the environment. With this action it follows the law of changes in nature. The more man eats, the less life energy man has, the faster man ages and the sooner the body wears out (is killed). Every machine wears out, the human body, an electro-biological machine, is no exception to this.

Continuing, what is happening to the eaten matter? It is decomposed into different chemical compounds. These compounds enter the blood and circulate in the whole body, reaching the cells. Every chemical compound created in this way contain information. This information affects the work of the cell because information is a program and data. The cell, being affected by this information, can produce what it needs for living, e.g. protein, minerals and water.

In this way, the chemical compounds, originating from what man eats and drinks, reaching the cells play the role of catalysts that cause specific reactions. This is why the appearance and behaviour of man depends on what they eat. A substance reaching a cell is a catalyst causing reactions which are beneficial for the life or are not. The bigger amount of harmful information, the earlier the cell dies.

The body of man needs a few thousand chemical compounds a day in order to work properly, every one must be delivered in proper amount and time. If the body does not receive them in the right time and amount, it starts to work improperly – this is called an illness. This makes the body wear out (death) faster.

Do you think that with food you can deliver all these substances to the body in the right time and proportion? This is practically impossible; isn't it? Fortunately the body can synthesize them, but under the condition that man does not interfere.

Man in natural state does not need to eat anything. In the distant past, when people on Earth were more developed, living more consciously than now, they did not need to eat. They could do that for fun of experiencing matter. Similarly, at present times, people do not need stimulants but use them for pleasure.

Then, why does man have teeth, a stomach, intestines, which is a sophisticated digestive and excreting system? The reason is to deeply experience matter. As much as 90% of experiencing life on Earth is somehow related to eating. Think about it, if man did not have a digestive system, they would have foregone the possibility to fully play in matter.
The digestive tract is a sensing device of the nerve system, which allows you to fully experience the external matter, matter that is not your body. Once you put this external matter in your body (you eat), it circulates in your blood system and fills your body with information. Then you feel deeply what it is, as if you become that matter.

Many inediates and non-eaters return to eating after some time. For some, the reason is that they cannot keep the body functioning properly any longer. For others, the reason is boredom. They feel that to live like that is senseless, since the 90% of life's possible experiences have been removed. They still desire to experience matter and all associated things. After all, there is enormity of them.

BREATHING

This is, of course, about the lungs which provide the body with air and remove gaseous substances that are products of matter transformation. The lungs have another important task, they provide the body with protein. The protein of the body is produced from air that contains all the elements N, O, C, H constituting the protein molecule.

There are breathing exercises, where proper breathing is to charge the body with more life energy. These exercises, if properly done, have the power to heal the psyche and the body. Some of them are beneficial during fasting and non-eating.

QÌ or PRANA DRAWING EXERCISE

The following describes the secret of how to efficiently draw in qì/prana with breathing. You can use this method to energize your body. It may be very useful during fasting or transitioning to non-eating. Do this exercise whenever you feel low level of life energy and you do not know how to increase it with your will.

Stand astride comfortably with bare feet directly on the ground. Let your arms hang freely on your sides or. you may like to move your hands a few cm in front of your thighs. Feel how energy is freely flowing through the entire body.
Next, close your eyes partially and inhale deeper than usually but do not exaggerate. Stop the inhale when your lungs are fully filled with air. Do not block the larynx or nose. Simply, when the lungs are fully filled, stop inhaling and hold your breath.
Now imagine that there is an invisible and imperceptible inhale occurring. Imagine a stream of 'energy' (let us call it 'qì/prana') flowing from the sun, through the middle of your head top, continuing inside your body and accumulating in your belly, below the umbilicus (dān tián).
Keep holding your breath while imagining that the stream of 'energy' (qì/prana) is flowing into your body. After a while, you will notice that you want to yawn. Do, yawn deeply and let your tear come out – that really energizes your body.
When you feel saturated or you cannot hold the breath any longer, freely release the air out of your lungs and breath normally several times until you are ready to repeat this exercise effortlessly.
Repeat all of this effortlessly but do not force the body to withstand without breathing longer than it is comfortable for you.
Remember the order of this exercise:
1. inhale;
2. hold your breath and start imaging the energy stream inflow;
3. stop imaging and exhale and breath normally.

What you do may be called the 'qì/prana inhalation'. As you know, qì/prana is not air and it has no mass and does not occupy space. However, qì/prana follows your imagination, your will. Hence qì/prana obeys your imagination/will, it is enough to think that qì/prana flows into your body in order to make this really happen. You really feel the effect of this exercise, you feel more energized.

Know that qì/prana can be drawn from the sun/sky or the Earth/ground. Your imagination decides that because you are directing the drawing of qì/prana. When you chose to draw qì/prana from the sun/sky, you will feel it flowing through the middle of your head top. When you chose to draw qì/prana from the Earth/ground, you will feel it flowing through your feet and legs.

You can also draw qì/prana simultaneously from the sun and Earth. This is the most efficient way to energize your body with qì/prana. In this instance, you are directing the qì/prana flow from above, through the middle of your head top and from below, through your feet at the same time. You have to clearly feel it. Both streams of qì/prana, the upper and the lower, meet in the area of your dān tián (the second chakra) or in any other region of your body that you choose..

When you feel weak energetically, you may want to accumulate qì/prana in the "solar plexus". When you have a sore throat, just direct qì/prana there and imagine it healing your throat.
You can direct qì/prana to any part of your body in order to energize it or heal it. You can also draw qì/prana in and distribute it throughout the entire body, without focusing it in only one region.

If you heal others with touch, you can draw in qì/prana and concentrate it in your entire body or only in your hands. Then, you can transfer it to another man, through your hands. Do not use your own life energy to heal others.

This qì/prana drawing exercise is especially efficient if it is done in a place that is saturated with energy like the seashore, a mountain peak, a forest, desert at sunrise or power spots. When you draw qì/prana from the environment in the rays of the rising sun, you receive additional energy.

Drawing in qì/prana at the peak of the inhalation is an efficient method of nourishing the body. Some people use this method to fully power the body. By simply drawing in qì/prana, they give the body enough energy to live without food and keep the body functioning properly. Air is food.

This exercise can be modified in different ways in order to stronger feel the energy in the body. For example, when drawing in qì/prana, you can slowly rise your hands, moving them up in a semicircular manner. When exhaling, you can lower your hands in the same semicircular manner.

Be aware that in this energizing exercise, the imagining of how qì/prana flows into the body is much more important than the breathing. Qì/prana is neither breath nor air, but holding the breath can be utilized for drawing qì/prana into the body more efficiently..

SKIN

Man's skin absorbs the radiation coming from the sun (sunshine) and it also breaths. The skin needs sunshine to synthesize some substances for the body, for example vitamin D. Your skin needs the sunshine, especially the ultra violet light. You can say that sunshine is food for human body. When insufficient sunshine falls on your skin, the immune system become weaker and you body deteriorates. Man's body will not be in perfect health when the sunshine falling on the skin is insufficient.

Gases and liquids can enter or exit the body through the sin. In this case, the skin functions in a similar way as the intestines. Superfluous substances are removed from the body through the skin, so it functions also as an excreting organ. Gases, perspiration, mucus and sebum excreted through the skin may contain toxins that the body removes.

You can conjecture that cosmetics (cream, shampoo, lipstick, powder, soup) applied on the skin are absorbed into your body. Then they circulate with the blood and may poison the body. Some of these chemicals may remain in the body for longer time causing illness. Therefore, before you put any cosmetic on your skin, be aware of this fact. In other words, if you can drink a shampoo without suffering any body problems, probably it is suitable for washing the hairs. The same is with a cream, if it is not edible, it also is not suitable for the skin. In order not to poison your body with cosmetics, use products made from nature. Ultra violet sunblock lotions are especially harmful.

Sunshine falling on the skin is one of the most important foods for man. Lack of this food weakens the body's self-defence system so much that the body is not able to protect itself against illnesses.
The visible sun light and invisible cosmic rays fall on the skin. They are essential for proper functioning of the body. For this reason, man should stay without clothes in nature so that the skin can see the sun and sky as much as it needs.

Allow your entire skin to be exposed to the sunshine. Walk barefoot and naked whenever you can in 'the bosom of nature'. However, be aware that the sunshine, as any other food, cannot be taken in too big doses. If you expose your skin to the sunshine for too long, it will be burn and damaged. Especially if you have light skin colour, start from just 10 minutes in the first day. You can extend your sunshine expose of the skin by 5 minutes every day. Never allow your skin to become pink or, even worse, red. This is a harmful burning.

Also allow the sunshine freely fall into your eyes, on the retinas. Do not use any sun glasses unless it is so light that your really cannot stand the brightness. However, do not look directly on the sun, this may burn your eyes. Read more about it later in the chapter about sun gazing.

Walk barefoot and naked in forests, on mountains and on the seashore. Swim in natural waters if they are clean. When getting out of the water, do not towel the skin, let it dry in the wind – in this way the skin adsorbs energy from the moving air.

Emanations from the sun and cosmos, plus wind and water in the air, are food for the body, which the skin adsorbs. If the skin of your body is insufficiently exposed to sunshine, do not wonder that the body becomes unwell – it simply lacks food.

Mark Adams has written in his health Internet portal:

www.naturalnews.com/046638_ebola_immunity_antivirals.html
„Vitamin D is a powerful immune booster as well as a natural pathogen destroyer. It increases the body's production of a class of proteins called antimicrobial peptides, approximately 200 have been identified thus far. They are known to directly and rapidly destroy the cell walls of bacteria, fungi, and viruses and play a key role in keeping lungs free of infection.

The best form, by far, of Vitamin D is naturally occurring Vitamin D3, which is produced by sun exposure on the skin. A single, twenty-minute, full body exposure to summer sun will trigger the delivery of 20,000 units of vitamin D3 into the circulation of most people within 48 hours."

MOVEMENT

You need to move in order to keep the body in good shape. The body needs movement of all muscles. It is through stretching and relaxing that the muscles produce electricity which is necessary for the proper functioning of the body cells. All the body organs slow down and later decay when the cells do not have sufficient charge of electricity. The human body is an electro-biological machine. Move yourself but do not exaggerate, do not force your muscles to exercise excessively.

You can consider heartbeat as the determinant of sufficiency of physical activity for the body. When exercising physically in nature, you should keep the heartbeat at the rate of around 130 for a few minutes, then take a rest. When you exercise at least 3 times a day for 3 to 5 minutes, you give the body the minimum of movement. Depending on how advanced you are in exercising, this guidelines may be too much or too little for your body. Therefore, adjust the amount of the exercising.

It is most important for those who fast or aspire to inedia or non-eating, that they regularly expose the body to sunshine, wind and water and also exercise in nature. Then the process of cleansing and repairing the body progresses more efficiently and man suffers less from symptoms.

Stay in nature not only during warm and sunny days. The skin needs the radiations from the sky and the wind every day. If it is cold outside, windy, rainy, etc. do not spend much time outdoors. Even if you run barefoot and naked on the snow only for one minute, at the temperature -20°C, your health will benefit.

Sun and cosmic radiations, wind, water and vapour contain life energy, that is why they are food for the body. When you are thinking slowly or are tired due to long sitting at a desk or watching TV, take off your clothes and run at a trot half a mile or so, outside. After you return home, take an alternating hot and cold shower – you will feel vigour. You will have much life energy again. Thanks to this self-treatment, you can work intellectually at efficient rate again because your thinking is fast and sharp. The body will be stronger, more resistant and persevere. The ageing process will slow down, so life will be extended.

THE WILL OF LIFE

To have a human body, you need to have the 'will of life' for it. You can keep your body alive as long as you have this will of life. Once you withdraw it, your body will deteriorate, probably become ill, processing towards death.

What you do is you see in your imagination that, according to your will, the body is self-powered automatically. This means that you have decided that the energy necessary for the proper functioning of your body is being created automatically.
You have decided this; therefore, according to your will, all energy required by the body is provided. This happens because energy follows your will.

In this case, you do not have to focus on any nourishment or the source of life energy for your body, you just imagine that it manifests through your body naturally. You clearly feel this energy flow, whenever you focus on it. You can also freely regulate and direct it, if you notice a need to do so.

Having sufficiently expanded the sphere of the Consciousness in which you live, you know that everything is a picture in your mind, an image that is an illusion. So is also energy. In this illusion, the matter of your body is created from energy.

The 'will of life' also works for people who have strong/deep faith. These people believe deeply that God ordered them to live without food. In that case, God provides their body with everything that they need.
The unshaken belief and emotions of man constitute efficient visualization. Visualization is a technique used for materializing a picture from the imagination into the reality. This is a mental technique. It is efficient even when it is done unintentionally. You will read more about visualization later.

BODY CLEANSING, PURIFYING

The human body has a sophisticated cleansing system. Removing the redundant and poisoning substances is done with the faeces, urine, exhalation, mucus, sebum, perspiration, blood, lymph, tears, hears, nails and epidermis. The human body can be compared to a machine excreting waste, which is produced mostly from what the human consumes.

The functioning of this electro-biological machine depends on efficiency of its self-cleansing system. When the body is working properly, it is being fully cleansed an the current bases and it does not store anything redundant. When the body is unable to transform and remove substances inserted into its interior in too big amounts, then the body accumulates them. It accumulates them in forms of, for example, glycogen in the liver, fat under the skin or between the muscle tissues, gunge of unknown composition in a cyst, heavy metal chemical compounds in the bones, bone marrow or brain.

The body of man eating a lot of food, breathing poisonous gases contained in the air, and drinking poisoned water has a serious trouble because the body is unable to sufficiently cleanse itself. In this case the body is accumulating everything that it is not able to remove on current bases. In such a case the cleansing and excreting system is overcharged. Then, if from time to time you let the body rest, in other words, you breathe clean air and fast long enough, the body removes the harmful toxins.

These accumulated toxins often weaken the body's self-defence system which results in more illnesses. In case of body poisoning causing illnesses, fasting is the most effective human body physical curing mean known on Earth. Properly conducted fasting produces 'miracles' because it removes some of so-called "incurable" diseases.

This simple information can be understood by elementary school children. I wonder, why so many doctors do not know about it? When they do not know how to cure an ill man's body, they say that it is an incurable, but the fact is that incurable diseases do not exist. There are people who do not know how to cure an ill human. If these people form a majority, if they create a strong suggestion group and if instead of admitting their inexperience they talk about incurable disease, then the myth about incurable diseases is created.

You do not have to be a scientist, doctor or philosopher to be able to understand the simple fact that a body full of toxins needs some rest from eating.

Give it some rest so that it can use its energy for removing poisons. Giving the poisoned body some chemical compounds called 'medicines' is one of the most common errors made by people due to their insufficient knowledge. Eating these chemicals further poisons the body.

How does the body cleansing system of a statistical inhabitant of the Western World work. Actually, this question relates to people who do not starve; on the contrary, they eat too much.
Let us compare this to a car engine. If the engine's rpm is from two to three thousands, the car will serve you for years without engine problems. But if the engine constantly is forced to work at seven thousand or more rpm, it will break down in a short time.
The body cleansing system of a statistical inhabitant of Earth who eats too much, can be compared to this engine which howls at maximum rotation speed. It is a real wonder how strong the human body cleansing system is. No machine built by man would be able to withstand such a treatment.

The cleansing system consists mainly of the liver, kidneys, skin, lungs and large intestine. These are the organs which are overloaded with work caused by too much eating. This is why large intestine cancer, liver cancer, skin tumours are among the most often occurring diseases these days. An organ being forced to overwork will break down earlier, after a few dozen of years or earlier.
Those organs mentioned above, work at 100% of their capacity. In order to keep the body clean they should not exceed 70% of their work capacity.

The results of many researches about the impact of food on humans, unequivocally prove the same thing, that the more humans eat, the worse health they have, the more often they become ill, the faster they age and the earlier they die. Statistically, decreasing the food intake by half extends the biological life time by at least 20%.
If the statistical overeating man would decrease the amount of eaten food by four fold, the body life span of 120 years would be a statistical normality.

What is consumed in too big amount, is harmful – that is a fact; however, what is consumed in too little amount, is also harmful – that is also a fact. Every man needs different amount of food, at different time. Therefore, I suggest that you consider all those charts and tables, which present a relation between the body weight, amount and calories of food, with less seriousness. It is more beneficial to use the 'conscious eating' method in order to find out for yourself what, how much and when the body should eat, so that it will function properly. Giving general eating directions for all people to follow, may bring more harm than benefits.

Man can purify their body efficiently with a proper diet or fasting. The primary requirement for purifying the body is breathing clean air, drinking clean water and eating food free from toxins.

When travelling in various countries, I noticed that people living in cities do not have clean air, water, and food. The water available in cities, especially, is energetically dead and toxic, except in a few locations.
If man does not reign sufficiently over matter with their mind, they will not purify the body when drinking such water and bathing in it. As a result, efficient body purifying is difficult to be accomplished in a city.

Having decided to efficiently purify and rejuvenate the body, man ought to go to nature, that is to a forest, mountains or the seaside where air and water are clean. The cleanness of water is particularly important.

The lack of proper water for drinking and bathing is presently one of the biggest health issues for people living in cities. I am going to delve into this matter, in another book, in order to help people to protect their body from the constant poisoning.
If you have information about this topic, please let me know. Water is a large topic – where to get clean water from, how poisoned tap water can be purified for drinking, how to produce properly structured water for consumption, and so on.

Be aware that your body, particularly the brain, consists mostly of water. The water you consume, directly impacts your body. This happens continually, even when you do not feel this any more.

For now, provide yourself with efficient filters, which remove the fluorine, chlorine, bromine, lead, platinum, cadmium, coper, aluminium, iron and many other substances that harm the body. Fluorine and chlorine are particularly dangerous when added to drinking water. Fluorine, aside from harming bones and teeth, badly affects the pineal gland. That stultifies man and thus makes it much more difficult for man to grow mentally/spiritually, therefore man becomes more and more like a machine in their thinking and acting.

Store drinking water in containers made from silver of purity 999, at least. Learn how to treat water by using vortex movement and magnets. Find information about water electrolysis using a semi-permeable membrane; this makes water alkaline. Many people need to consume slightly alkaline water.

You should study the works of *Masaru Emoto* to learn how shapes, sounds, words and thoughts affect water. Using his information, you can restore proper structure to water. In this way, you can program any drink while holding it in your hands, before consuming it.

Your body is mostly water. Your words and thoughts program body's water and the water which you intend to drink. Being aware of this fact, talk and think about yourself only in positive terms, even when joking.

Apart from that, I suggest disposing of all water containers that are not made of glass, porcelain, silver, gold, enamelled or stainless steel, stone or wood. Never use plastic or rubber bottles unless you really have no choice. Water solves plastic, then it goes into your body, poisoning it. Even so-called "food grade" plastic is a poison. Remember, plastic should never touch any food.

NON-EATING or STARVING

I hope that you do not force your body to fast. Fasting should be done properly, if not, it becomes starving. Fasting is a body healing procedure. Please, consider it deeply and make yourself aware of the following facts that are not known to many people.

Food and eating are neither bad nor good. They are essential part of experiencing life in our universe. When the experience associated with food and eating becomes useless for you, they will naturally detach from you effortlessly. By forcing yourself to discard food and eating, you create limitations that do not allow you to fully experience your life.

Inedia or non-eating are not about compelling the body to become adapted to living without food. The true state of inedia appears by itself as a result of expanding the Consciousness sphere in which man lives. In this case, inedia is a by-product of conscious self-development.

First of all, inedia or non-eating gives you the freedom to choose. In inedia or non-eating, you can choose to eat or not to; your body does not need any substance called food. If you eat, you do this because of other reason, not in order to deliver building material or energy sustaining the body's life. You eat for a company or because you wish to savour something or because you have decided to experience a new taste, etc. When you are in inedia, you really have no will to eat and you clearly feel that food distracts your comfort, then you eat and drink nothing.

Although the natural ability of non-consuming foods is the main attribute of inediates or non-eaters, this should not be the main goal. This also means that an inediate or non-eater is not an ascetic man mortifying the flesh by refusing the body what it really needs. The real inediate or non-eater is man whose body naturally does not need to eat at all, to remain in perfect shape. Still, the inediate or non-eater has the choice, they can remain absolutely without food and drink or they can eat for a pleasure, for a company; not because their body needs food. The most significant difference between a non-eater and an eater is about the ability to choose.

You can understand now, why some inediates or non-eaters sometimes drink water, tea, coffee etc. Some of them, once in a while, eat a piece of a chocolate, biscuit, cheese, horseradish etc. They know that inedia or non-eating is not about ascetic flesh mortifying.
When you smoke a cigarette once in a month, are you a smoker?

When you drink a glass of vodka once in a year, are you an alcoholic? Therefore, when you eat a biscuit once in a while, are you an eater?

Besides this, even if you are an inediate, there is no guarantee that you will remain one forever. It may happen that after a few months or maybe a dozen of years, or after longer time, an inediate unexpectedly comes back to 'normal' eating. It may also happen that within many years of inedia man may have periods of eating for days, weeks or longer. Like an average man may fast from time to time, an inediate may eat sometimes.

From the point of view of man aspiring to inedia or non-eating, this state can be regarded as freedom from the most powerful terrestrial bonding of man to the matter. This bonding, called 'eating', can be also considered as the strongest addiction of man. Then, the process of becoming an inediate ot non-eater is very similar to liberating man from a drug addiction.

Inedia or non-eating is only a stage, a place which man passes by while walking consciously on a path of conscious self-development. Therefore, inedia or non-eating should not be forced on the body as the ultimate goal; they appear as by-products on that path.

According to the definition, man who regularly nourishes themselves with liquid foods, e.g. juices, bullions, milk, sweet coffee with cream, is not a non-eater. In this case we have a liquid diet, thus we call that man a liquidarian.

Fasting, starving or refraining from eating in other ways, all in order to achieve a specific goal (for example, to lose weight, self-healing or religious ritual) are not inedia or non-eating. During these activities man does not consume food for a period of time but later resumes normal eating. Normally, man feels hunger during that time. In inedia or non-eating there is no feeling of hunger.

Also, man who forces their body to fast for too long time (for example, to prove that they can live without food) is not called a non-eater or an inediate. Harming the body in such a way can emaciate it or even cause death from starvation.

It is worth remembering that the way to becoming an inediate leads mainly through conscious self-development. There are many auxiliary methods for people who decided to realize this goal. I wrote more about some of the methods later in this book.

I often reiterate that inedia is a by-product that comes when man has sufficiently expanded the sphere of the Consciousness in which they live. There are exceptions such as primitive man becoming an inediate. I have written very little about these exceptions because this book is dedicated to those people who are on the path of conscious self-development.

I suggest that you focus on expanding the sphere of the Consciousness in which you live, instead of focusing on inedia. When you expand your sphere sufficiently, that is, you develop yourself spiritually enough, then things like inedia will come along just as an act of your will. You simply decide to be an inediate and you will then be one.

When you force your body to non-eating, you harm yourself. If your goal is to harm yourself, I will not support that, but I do not criticize your choice to experience life on Earth. You have free will, so you can choose suffering.

You can recognize the full power of inedia only after you have achieved that state. Then you can truly say that you conduct a lifestyle without eating. But when you force inedia on yourself, you are far from the reality created by an inediate. Forcing inedia on yourself causes a deeper descent into the illusion.

When guided by common sense, you can try many times to live a lifestyle of non-eating without harming your health. Every attempt can be a valuable lesson for you. But when you forget about the common sense, then experimenting with inedia may damage your body. This is why I often repeat, "Let common sense guide you".

The fact that you do not eat or even are a non-eater or inediate, does not make you better. You do not have any reason to feel proud and superior. You are still neither better nor worse than other people.
It is the same with eating. The fact that you eat less or more, lighter or heavier food, follow this or that diet, does not make you better or worse.

Different states of the body, fasting, diets, eating, non-eating, inedia and other things are only your choices to experience life on Earth. You do not become better or worse just because of your choices. You simply walk a different path than most others.
If people judge you because of your food choices, it is their problem, not yours. Therefore, you do not have any reason to worry.
Allow your Inner Joy emanate so that you and other people will feel Love.

HOW IS THIS POSSIBLE ?

An answer to this question could occupy a whole book written from the philosophic, religious, esoteric and strictly scientific points of view. So-called scientific explanation of inedia, how and why man can live completely without food, qualifies for the Nobel Price. When and which scientist will be brave and independent enough to undertake this task for the good of mankind?

How can man live without food? What about the law of energy conservation? What new cells are build from to replace the dead ones? These and similar questions are asked by people who want to find out how inedia functions in human body, or by people who want to prove that living completely without food is impossible.

Let me answer frankly, I never had an intention to prove that man can live without food. First of all, the only man who can prove anything to you is yourself. What does it mean to prove something to you? It means to make you believe or know that something is a fact. This means that you would have to believe it or know it. Who can decide about your faith or your knowledge, if not you?

How many times have you met people who were provided with absolute proof of some fact, yet they still refused to believe it? Those people who decided to prove something were sure about their poof, but they still did not succeed in convincing others.

If you want to prove to yourself that inedia or non-eating are real facts or that they are false claims, you are free to go ahead. You can explore and experience it for yourself. I have done this.
In the past I believed that man could live without food but I did not know it. That was one of the reasons why I decided to check it out and to conduct the two-year experiment on myself. That made me sure that I could live without food. I now know what non-eating is. I have built my knowledge by experiencing non-eating.
In more than a dozen of years that followed, I met many people who were fasting, trying to live without food and others who were non-eaters. They have shared their experience with me, asked for advices or talk about their endeavours.

FOR THE OPEN-MINDED

The reason why the science exists is because not everything has been discovered and described in theories yet; thanks to this fact the scientists can conduct their research. This also means that there are things that even "the philosophers have not dreamed of". Regardless of whether we believe it or not, the phenomenon exists and it does not care about our ignorance or beliefs.

In the past people believed that Earth is flat, that the sun orbits Earth, that an object heavier than the air cannot fly, etc. People who were saying that it is not true and it works in a different way were believed to be unwise, ever worse, sometimes they also were persecuted. Nevertheless, the phenomena did not care about what people were thinking, the phenomena just existed, they were functioning in the way that they were created according to the laws ruling the universe. People did not know these laws so they were saying that such things were impossible.

Exactly the same happens in the present time, people do not believe something that they do not know. Once they get to know something, they change their thinking. This is neither good nor bad, this is man's attitude to things that deny their beliefs. Inedia or even long fasting are not exceptions to this attitude.

It is a fact that since the beginning of the human civilization on Earth there were, are and will be people who did, do and will not need to eat. So this means that potentially every man is able to live completely without food. Of course, a potential does not automatically mean a skill; first, a potential has to be drilled and developed.

FOR THE ESOTERIC

The omnipresent pre-substance/pre-matter, that everything is built from, known under many names, e.g. pre-energy, prana, qi, orgon, ether, vril, quantum field, keeps alive the body of man who does not consume food. IAM is the source of this pre-substance. Everything that man needs for their body and mind to live is created directly from it.
On the other hand, an important requirement for the human body to work properly without the material food is proper modification of some programs in the instinct. The instinct controls the whole metabolism and it forms the physical body of the human.

Man's body is an image in the mind created by IAM. This image is automatically created and sustained in the instinct, in other words, this image is a set of programs in the instinct. Some programs creating the body are dealing with eating and food. According to these programs, the body needs to eat 'normally' in order to work properly. If the body does not receive any food, it will deplete energy and food and in extreme case it will die.
When the 'eat/food' programs function in this way, living without food is against nature.

Modifications can be made in this programs, which will enable the body to receive everything that it needs for normal functioning from other sources than the digestive system. Having gone through this kind of program modification, man's body is created from matter directly emerging from the pre-substance/pre-matter. This is the same process that is called the creation of the world by the Big Bang.
The Consciousness » IAM » mind » body.

FOR THE SCIENTIFICALLY MINDED

What does an electron eat so that it has lots of energy and it can live forever if nothing destroys it? How about the atoms of the human body? What do they eat?

Man who sufficiently understands physics, knows that all of the matter and energy are derived from a common source, Matter is influenced by thinking. The result of an experiment depends on the experimentalist's expectation. Thus, the creation and behaviour of energy and matter occurs in the mind.

The human body is a very sophisticated self-running electro-biological machine. It remains a largely unknown structure, run in/by the mind. You may need to study physics, sacred geometry, chemistry, electronics and informatics to better understand the body. On the other hand, the more open minded the scientist is, when engaged in his research, the more he is willing to acknowledge "I know that I know nothing".

The mechanisms of powering the body, transmutations of elements and energetic processes taking place in the body remain largely incomprehensible. However, the modern physics, with its theories and hypothesis often more fantastic than science-fiction stories, brings the researchers to the understanding that the body is an energetic creature controlled by programs or, be it said clearly, it is a very large and sophisticated structure of programs.

Once I read an explanation in a popular science magazine with articles about quantum physics, that from an informatics point of view it is not possible to prove that our universe is not a program structure. It is easier to prove that the universe is a program structure. You see, it is coming out more and more to the masses that a human being is just a set of programs created and controlled by the mind.

One of the sources of the construction material and energy for the body are substances produced by the body chemical-physical-electronic plant that is the digesting and breathing systems and the skin. Beside this the atoms consisting the human body are build by quantum field (other name for: qì, ether, prana, etc.) transformations which produce the solid matter.

You can find the research made by Nobel Prize winner, Alexis Carrel, who experimented with the tissues of a chick heart that he kept alive for 34 years. Alexis concluded that a cell is immortal if it is kept under the proper conditions, but it can be killed.

I would be interested in participating an a scientific research. Take someone, for example me. Let me give up food and observe my body in order to see what happens during one year. How does the body is adjusting itself and what changes are taking place in it? That would be interesting. Perfect topic for a PhD degree, isn't it?

FOR THE BELIEVERS

God is everything, knows and can do everything. Nothing can exist without God. Every thing was created by God. Inconceivable and omnipotent God is the only one and the highest perfection. Since God has created everything, knows everything and can do everything and is the highest inconceivable perfection, God can decide and choose people who will be able to live without consuming food.
Man does not have to know how and why God decides to do something to man. God can give people the ability to live without food. Also, man can ask God for the grace to be an inediate or non-eater, because God grants sincere prayers for the fully devoted children.

WITHOUT PHILOSOPHIZING

For a long time I was going to write this, but how to describe something that cannot be described with words and the intellect does not comprehend it. This can be understood only by feeling it, at least telepathically. Any attempt to describe it would be ... philosophizing (wasn't it supposed to be without philosophizing ☺ ...?).

Nevertheless, as you can see, I have decided to describe this. Let this text to be a contribution which brings the understanding of what is the source of life closer to your mind and body.

When I am asked, what I nourish the body with in inedia, my truest answer is that I nourish it with ... nothing. I know, I clearly see and feel this, that in inedia I maintain the body in perfect condition, just because I am being conscious that **IAM is the creator of Life**. Do you understand? – the creator of Life. By simply being aware that **I create Life**, I can maintain the mind and the body (that is, my tools) in any state I wish. I see and feel this. At the same time, as I turn my focus inward myself, I feel IAM which creates Life and maintains its creation.
I am the Master Creator of my life.

I know that until you feel IAM, you will not be able to understand my explanation, although this is the simplest one I can write down. I know what I am, I feel this thing and I can see how I am creating Life by just being aware about this fact.

Once you know what you really are, you see and feel what you would describe as "IAM is consciously creating life", then you need noting more any more. Your true self-awareness and feeling of this fact causes that you do not ask question any more.

Then you also know that when man says: "I am nourished by prana", "I live on Light", "God gives me this grace", this man either cannot explain better, does not understand or does not feel what he really is in his essence.

This or that way, why would you want to limit yourself? Why would you want to be dependent on qì/prana, Light or God? Of course, you can nourish yourself with these things, if you decide so. You can also give up these things, once you feel IAM which is what you really are in your essence. Then, not only food and water, but also God, Light and qì/prana will not be needed by you for living. You will not be limited by "living on Light", "nourishing the body with qì/prana", "God's love or grace" because you

will feel the power of creation within you. You will have the choice, not only 'to eat or not to eat'; you will be also able to choose between nourishing yourself' with qì/prana, living on Light, living on God's love, or non of these things.
Whether you are aware of this fact or not, you create the world in which you live according to the principles and beliefs created by you. You are the Master Creator of your world.

IAM is the creator of Life, Light, Love, qì/prana, breathing and food. IAM also created and constantly modify these mind and body which are tools for experiencing or playing a game called Life.
IAM can enjoy whatever IAM has created, that is food, water, air, qì/prana, Light, Love, God. IAM can play the game of nourishing the mind and body. IAM can also throw this concept away, as not needed for the playing and, simply, live just by being aware that IAM is the creator of Life.

So do you now understand more how this is possible that man can live without food? Do you also understand why the real Masters leave and do not teach people? How can they teach about something that the intellect is not able to understand? How to explain something that man does not feel yet? And how to make you understand that, in your true essence, you are just playing a game. And, you are the Master Creator.

The clearer you feel what you are, in your essence, the more inedia and other, so-called, impossible things will be something natural for you. At the same time, less and less often you will try to find something outside yourself, because you will feel more and more that all things always have been in you, actually, you have been always the source of them all.

"The truth will set you free."

People ask me about 'my method' for living without food. How do I do that so that I can keep the body in perfect state without eating? How did I do that for the first time between 2001 and 2003?

Let me repeat it again. I can explain it and deliver an enormous amount of information, but how much does that help you if it is not the intellect that decides about our possibilities? To describe something clearly enough for intellectual understanding, is something very different from the experience itself. And in this case it is about feeling.

I do not have any method. I simply know that I could do it. When I decided to give up eating, I knew that I could live like that. At that time, there was no fear in me that something bad could happen to my body due to not eating.

How can I explain to you what I felt at that time? What did I feel when I gave up food, since I know that this was simply a matter of a decision made by my will?
In general, the body is to follow the mind, because it is just a picture in the mind – this is how I see it.

Imagine that you asked me what I felt and what I saw on a top of a mountain that was difficult and dangerous to reach, where I lived for two years. I can tell you what I saw and felt on the mountain top. I can also tell you what was on the way while climbing the mountain and later on my way back. I would be talking and you would be listening carefully.
Even if you intellectually understand my story, you would still not know because it was not your experience. You would only have some information, provided by someone who went all the way to the mountain top and returned.
Only after you start on the way to the top, reach it, watch everything around you, feel it, absorb emotions and go all the way back, will you know. Then you knowledge would be based on your experience. It will not be just some information from someone else.

Inedia is like such a top of a mountain difficult to reach. Only after experiencing the way to inedia, living it and returning, will you know what that is. Then you will be able to talk and explain about all of that. People will listen and remember your information but they will not know because it was not their experience.

When I focus on what I am in my essence, which I call IAM manifesting Inner Power, then I feel that power, that energy, that source of my mind and body. THAT is sufficient for keeping my tools (mind and body) in the proper condition.

Therefore, to make it simple, I can say that my method consists of focusing on IAM, which allows me to feel the manifestation of the Inner Power, that creates everything in accordance to images in my mind.

WHY INEDIA

First of all let me emphasize that the purpose of this chapter is not to encourage anybody to non-eating, but to give some objective information only. The subject 'why to live without eating' is not intended to convince you about superiority of non-eating, it is to inform you about the aspects and influence of inedia or non-eating on individuals and the society.

If inedia does not interests you, if you feel that eating is a pleasure that you are not going to give up, then for sure non-eating is not for you, so you can stop reading here. What you feel is the most important thing for you if you have decided to walk consciously, that is, to choose your path of conscious self-development.

"Why should I live without food if eating is a big pleasure?" – sometimes people ask me this question. First of all, you should know that you do not 'have to', because nobody is going to compel you to do this. However if you would like to know why some people chose inedia or non-eating, you can read what they most often say about it.

Probably every non-eater has their own answer to this question, however some answers are frequently repeated. Hereby I have listed some facts and most often given answers. The descriptions of individual feelings come from people who do not force their bodies to live without food and whose bodies function properly when this style of living is applied.

MAN IN NATURAL STATE

A long time ago, man on Earth was in natural state. For the people living presently on Earth, it is difficult to imagine what the characteristics of man in the natural state would be. The following are some of the characteristics.

The body of such a man never needed any material food. People did not eat although they could because they had a digestive tract. However, they played by tasting different things. The digestive tract functioned as it should do, that is, as a sensing device for the nerve system. What we now call 'eating food' was known as 'heavy drug addiction'.

Those people did not need electronics to communicate and machines to move from place to place because intuition was commonly used and flying was as normal as running is today.

Creating matter from thoughts with the use of visualization was something normal. This is why industry, as known today, did not exist at that time. Recall this: when you think about something during night dreams, that happens – man in natural state can do something like this in reality.

During the time that people lived in the natural state, there was no job as we know today. Present jobs, which can be compared to slavery, were completely useless in that time. Everyone could do what they wished to do by using visualization. People created and modified matter according to their needs and for pleasure.

Illness did not exist unless someone desired to create it out of curiosity, just to experience it for fun. Later they released it instantly just by an act of their will.

Man in the natural state was full of joy and therefore emanated Love. If you saw such a man, you would see a light aura around them. These days, the aura of a man is invisible unless you practise the ability to see it.

Such a man lived as long as they decided to. The body did not degenerate; these days it is called ageing. Men who were a thousand years old, looked like children who were a hundred years young.

Presently there are a few people living in the natural state on Earth. They, certainly, do not make themselves known. If you do not ask such a man about their age, you may not know it. Some of so-called 'big spiritual masters' sometimes learn from people living in the natural state.

Potentially, every man can regain the natural state. Inedia is one of the side effects of such transition. The process of regaining the natural state is commonly called 'spiritual development' because it is happening from the spirit into matter. Aspiring to inedia may be a manifestation of the return to the natural state.

PERFECT HEALTH

Imagine your body working perfectly, without a vestige of an illness. No cold, rhinitis, cough, pain, fatigue or lethargy. You body is healthy and clean as if it belonged to a perfectly healthy baby of a few months young.

When reading this you may think that you feel good and are healthy as this text presents. However, if you have not positively experienced non-eating or fasting, you probably do not know and do not feel what I am referring to. Regardless of how much one would try, it is impossible to explain with words this state of perfect health and well-being, compared to what you can deeply feel by experiencing it.

Majority of 'healthy' people do not know what perfect health is because they have not experienced it. As long as you have not experienced it by yourself, you can only imagine that during inedia one feels better than in the time period when they were feeling 'perfectly' when eating.

The immune system functions so efficiently that even when you stay with a group of people suffering cold, influenza or other contagious diseases, who sneeze, cough or blow their nose around you, it has no effect on your health.

One of reasons of this high immunity to infection, which in fact is a truly natural body state, is the absence of toxins in the body, which are being introduced with food and accumulated in the body for years by people eating 'normally'.

Industrially produced food is contaminated with many agricultural toxins and other poisoning substances which are added in order to increase the food production, make it look or taste better, remain fresh longer etc. The amount of these poisons, which are regularly introduced into the body with food, exceeds the body's ability to remove them. This is why the body is cleansing itself for the first few weeks or even months of non-eating, which can cause different symptoms. This cleansing and health recovering process clearly brings increasing well-being which makes you feel the mind and body becoming lighter.

FREEDOM

Enjoying perfect health, with no need to eat or drink, I am free from the common belief about the constraint of acquiring, preparing and consuming food. This means that hunger, starving and problems related to them does not concern me regardless of my living place.

It does not matter whether they are a rich or a poor man without so-called 'means for survival', their body is alive and functions perfectly and they enjoy well-being. Inediate's life does not depend on food and all the troubles associated with acquiring it.

The inediate can choose – they do not need food to function properly but they can eat something for pleasure, for company or for other reasons. This is the freedom of choice which other people who eat 'normally' do not have. People eating 'normally' do not need to drink coffee or eat chocolate, but they are free to enjoy them – that's the freedom of choice they have.

Inedia or non-eating are steps on a path to regaining full freedom by man. When you are aware of this you experience more often that man can be free also from other things, which are commonly believed to be necessities without which the man's life is impossible.

Freedom from food automatically means freedom from, among others, buying food and associated articles, most illnesses, kitchen and toilet.

ECONOMY

Think how much time, money and energy an average man spends on the following activities related to food.

1. First they work as slaves in order to make money.
2. How many hours a month do they spend on buying food with hard earned money?
3. Next, they prepare the food for eating, so they cut, peel, cook, bake and fry it, etc.
4. Then they eat it with or without appetite, believing that man has to eat in order to live and there is no other way.
5. Having eaten they wash the dishes, clean up and think about what to prepare for the next meal.
6. Man is unwilling to work with a full stomach because the body has less energy, which was directed to digesting. This influences the mood disadvantageously. In this state watching TV, reading news papers or sleeping is preferably chosen.
7. A few times a day the body needs to excrete all the things that were eaten and drunk because otherwise the body would become poisoned to death.
8. When the body does not stand overloading it with food and poisons, and becomes ill, people spend money and time on doctors and medicines instead healing the body by fasting.

How many times a day, a week, a year and in your entire life do you repeat the same above things? How much money and time are used (wasted)? You would wonder if you have calculated it.

Regarding all these things, inediates save a lot of money, time and energy. It is a big difference to live without food or to eat normally, as people who have experienced non-eating feel. It is quite interesting to experience both life styles in order to compare these differences.

For some people it is important that inediates usually need less sleep so they can save time on it. Depending on an individual the time saved on sleeping ranges from one to six hours per night. However there are inediates who almost never sleep or others who sleep ten hours every night.

Beside the above factors, have you already calculated how much money an inediate can save for not buying kitchen equipment and cleansers, plus how much water and energy can be saved? Let me give you my example from time period when I was a non-eater in year 2002, I summed all above factors and got 800 PLN of saved money per month (the average salary was ~ 2000 PLN at that time).

Some people buy books and magazines about cuisine and diets or self-healing and slimming down by following diets. Money spending of this kind is history for inediates.

Talking about these factors of saving money, time and energy it is easy to notice how much man made themselves dependent on food as well as on food and pharmaceutical industries. How much man is enslaved by them? How many people complain of this situation believing that there is no other way of living?
Do you know that the freedom lies no farther then in your mind? At any time you can decide to change your life style and its circumstances.
You are the Master Creator.

ECOLOGY

Practising inedia or non-eating I noticed that the amount of my rubbish decreased fivefold. 99% of the things that I continued throwing away were recyclable materials (paper, metal, plastic). Collecting and selling them I could make money, however I usually donate them to people collecting recyclables. Therefore I can say that when I practise inedia or non-eating I pollute nature approximately hundredfold less.

Really, is so much rubbish produced by man at home associated to food?

Yes, it roughly looks like this. It is easy to see that most rubbish thrown away by a family consists of food package and meal leftovers.

Also, it would be an error to not calculate the global amount of faeces and urine which enter into the ground and water. Multiply what the statistical Earth inhabitant excretes by seven billion and add billions of kilograms of this matter coming from industrial breeding. How big is globally the daily produced mountain of faeces and urine?

One can fantasize in order to imagine paradise on Earth inhabited by inediates only. Here are some details that show huge nature saving on this planet compared to our present Earth.

1. Average man throws away many-fold less garbage.
2. The industry uses many times less natural resources. Thanks to this the amounts of burned coal, oil and gas are many times smaller. Consequently smaller pollution of soil, air and water occurs.
3. There is no industrial breeding so nature is not destroyed by pasture, agricultural chemicals, hormones and antibiotics. Earth is free from billions of tons of industrial animal excretions.
4. There is no industrial production of vegetables so Earth does not suffer of forest grubbing, soil impoverishment and huge amount of chemical fertilizers.
5. Production of paper, plastic, glass and metals is much smaller, which translates to slower depletion of natural resources, less trees cutting and less rubbish from packing.

Practising inedia or non-eating is associated with big nature saving – it is easy to imagine and experience this. So inedia or non-eating are highly ecological.

The above picture of Earth is just a fable for the time being. This fable tells about a paradise to be built in future. It is possible that this paradise will be built much earlier than some people are expecting now. The Consciousness sphere of average man on Earth expands faster these days, which also influences eating.

Bigger part of Earth industry is associated, more or less directly, with eating. One industry branch depends on other, a change in one branch causes changes in others. Along with diminishing of food industry the entire Earth civilization will be changing, sometimes revolutionary. There are only a few people who can imagine the result of this change, which is caused by freeing man from food.

LIFE ENERGY

Most inediates, compared to people eating 'normally', feel much more life energy in themselves. It lets them keep higher physical and psychical activity for many hours a day without even feeling tired, like it happens to an artist under inspiration.

Higher level of life energy in intellectual sphere often manifests by higher creativity. In this state it is much easier for man to create, invent, teach, learn and work.

Many inediates experience higher level of life energy as decreased need for sleep and rest. Some inediates sleep a few hours a week only. An inediate who after travelling for a few dozen of hours, takes a shower and without feeling tired starts working, this can be a good example of resistance to tiredness.

In periods of non-eating I experience myself that after ten hours of mental work with a computer (which sucks energy from man) my thinking power is as good as it is when I start the work. I only feel a little muscle stiffness so I think about doing more physical activity like, for example, swimming or jogging. In periods when I was eating "normally" I was tired and had conjunctivitis at midday, I had headache in the evening and my thinking was so inefficient that I made too many errors to continue working.

High level of life energy in inediates is not an extraordinary phenomenon. The body uses up to 90% of its energy for digesting and eliminating. Inediate's body does not digest, this is where the surplus of usable energy comes from. Thinking mathematically one could say that an inediate has up to nine times more energy compared to the time when they eat normally. If man has not experienced this difference on their own body, it is difficult for man to believe and comprehend it.
Really, what has happened to the divine being called man, who has made their body a digesting and eliminating machine?

It is easy to experience the fact that the more the human eats, the weaker they become. Having eaten a large meal, are you willing to work? Do you feel energized or weaker? Many people notice that the more they eat, the weaker and lazier they become. This common saying: "eat to be strong" is actually opposite to what people experience.

It happens like this because the more food falls into the stomach, the more work the body has to do which means the more life energy is used for digestion and elimination. Eating something may take just a few minutes but digesting and eliminating it takes a few dozen of hours. When the body cannot stand the overload, the body starts to function unwell that is, it becomes fat, gets ill, ages and finally dies. This is why fasting is one of the most efficient healing methods widely known on Earth.

This is a new, true saying: Eat less in order to have more life energy, more creativity and cleaner body, then most of common illnesses making people suffer will not harm you. Of course, limiting food intake below the level of the RNB (real need of body) also is harming because it weakens and deprives the human of energy. Body and mind function best when the RNB is followed.

CREATIVITY

It is a common knowledge that the acts of working, studying or thinking are less efficient with a full stomach. Having eaten a heavy dinner man is less wiling to think creatively or study. People fall asleep if they are not physically active. Digesting eaten food takes proportionally most energy from body.

When body is not digesting the human can use the spare life energy for other activities. Mind and body are so closely connected that they create a union, thus they affect each other. The cleaner and less loaded with food is the physical body, the easier, clearer, faster and more creative is the thinking. Even fasting people enjoy lightness of thinking after they have gone through initial body and psychic cleansing. The majority of inediates enjoy permanent lightness of their psyche.

When the activity of digestive and cleansing systems stops, the human has several times more energy, which then naturally flows to higher realms called mental, spiritual or psychical. Pituitary and pineal glands become much more active, the senses widen their perception range and thus man finds more interesting things in spiritual area of life. This is why more new ideas appear in the mind and the thinking occurs more efficiently. One feels like man whose mind was cleared of fog, dark mist or mud which covered it before. Then man sees mental world much clearer and lighter.

The above things make the inediate's creative will bigger. This may manifest as writing, painting, composing, founding an organization, giving seminars or lectures, doing research and so on.

My story can serve as an example. From the beginning of my non-eating I was clearly feeling much increased psychical activity and psychic sensitiveness. In any moment of day or night I could start to write or speak about any subject and, what I felt, to do it endlessly. The topics were appearing in my mind, so many that I could compose a brochure containing only the subject titles. Sometimes I wondered that I know so much about subjects in which I previously considered me a laymen. I realized many things of what I call knowledge, because my perceiving from the intuition was much more effective; it was enough to turn my attention to a subject.
Having returned to "normal eating" (after almost 2 years without food) I noticed that my mind lightness and creative will decreased , although they were and still are more intense than before I started the non-eating period.

SPIRITUAL GROWTH

A long time ago man noticed that there is a dependency between decreasing food intake and so-called spiritual growth. This dependency is so important that it is being emphasized by many teachings, religions, beliefs and schools whose purpose is spiritual growth of man. Restraining periodically from food is often practised by many people who are on a path of conscious self-development.

This dependency is clearly felt by fasting people. Its mechanism can be easily understood by people who know that eating is a factor that weighs down man to the ground, I have described it before. Some people decide to practise inedia or non-eating so that they can permanently dwell in the state of so-called 'high vibrations'.

Inedia or non-eating are one of many possible by-products on the path of conscious self-development. I have mentioned that linked things affect each other and that body and mind are unity. Therefore, decreasing activity in the physical area (mainly digesting and elimination) will enable more life energy to be used in the mind area. During fasting and inedia or non-eating the mind activity increases because life energy naturally flows into this area.

Neither inedia nor fasting is necessary on the path of spiritual growth; however, many people consider experiencing these states a significant help. Biography of many so-called 'spiritual masters' include fasting or long periods of significant decrease in eating, which they did in order to attain specific goals in their mind. Many of them eat just for social reason, not for the need to feed their body.

Food is the strongest material link that connects man to matter. When this connection is broken, many other material dependencies automatically break. 'Earthly concerns' which have been important until now (games, news in the mass media, disputes and many other), become unimportant and daily life becomes simpler, easier, happier and more tranquil. Man more often and with stronger intensity directs their activity into their inner world, to IAM, to God, etc. That is why man becomes less influenced by suggestions from the society.

During this time, doing energizing exercises is easier and gives more pleasure because man better feels energy. Concentration, contemplation, visualization and other mind exercises are better performed, intended results are achieved sooner and easier. Also making the mind passive is easier. It is easier to feel your Inner Joy which feels you with Light and Love.

If you can see the aura, you will notice that it glares more around man living without food. It has symmetric shape, pulsates life and, describing briefly, is beautiful. The energetic centres called chakras look similarly. If, before starting inedia or non-eating, there were any dirty areas or disorders in the aura, they completely disappear.

REJUVENATION

If mind activity is not considered then it can be said that the main causes of human body biological ageing are contamination by toxins, too much of consumed food and low energy level. Many people practising inedia or non-eating or sufficiently long fasting feel their bodies rejuvenate. This is the main reason why some people decide to start inedia or non-eating.

The process of biological age reversion caused by fasting or inedia is a known phenomenon, which is proven not only by body appearance but also by results of clinical research. Evelyn Levy, who underwent thyroid examination after she started inedia or non-eating in 1999, can be an example. The result of the examination suggested that the thyroid belonged to a woman 15 years of age while Evelyn was 38 at that time.

To make sure that you understand me well, let me emphasize that long fasting or inedia or non-eating do not guarantee the age reversion in every man. Forcing the body to live without food longer than it needs, causes the opposite result, that is, the ageing process clearly accelerates.

When your RNB corresponds with complete lack of the need to eat, the biological body age reverses to the limit defined by your mind, because in this case toxins, eaten food and low level of life energy do not accelerate the ageing process. In every other case forcing body to fast results in harm, which visually manifests in body rapidly changing to looking old.

Immortal man, that is one who knows how to keep their body in good condition as long as they decide, can live completely without food. Of course, this does not mean that every immortal is an inediate or the contrary.

CURIOSITY

Among many reasons why people decide to start inedia or non-eating there is also curiosity. "How is it to live completely without food for many weeks, months or longer?" – people may ask themselves this. "If I do not try this, I will never know, because only my own experience gives me knowledge. Other people experiences can give information, not knowledge." This is what man can think, if they are deeply interested in inedia and decide to experience that state.

For example, for me the curiosity of experiencing something is one of the main reasons why since I was sixteen I have been experiencing with diets, fasting, living without food, obesity, slimming, emaciation, illnesses, (self)healing, ageing and rejuvenation. Results of these experiments are side effects of my curiosity. Thanks to this I am building and remembering my knowledge. I am using this knowledge to write this book and advise people who ask.

It is worth remembering that doing experiments on yourself can harm the body or mind. This can cause illnesses or even death. Some experimenting people reach a place where harm done to the body or psyche is so serious that reversing it seems impossible. This is why I advice you not to follow me or other people who do similar experiments.

PREPARATION FOR A CHANGE IN YOUR LIFE STYLE

Approximately 90% of man's life on Earth is somehow related to food and eating. Of course, this is not only about sitting at the table and chewing food but includes all activities related to eating.

Now, imagine that when you give up food and become an inediate, you immediately lose the 90% of life related to eating. Do you know what that means? If you are living alone, far from people, this may be a small change for you. But if you are actively involved in society, this may be a revolutionary change for you. You may suddenly face situations which you never expected.

This is what may happen – some examples taken from the lives of those who gave up eating, depending on the society in which they were living.
Death.
Illnesses.
Loss of job.
Rejected by children.
Doctors, assisted by policemen, came and took them to a hospital.
Family members, especially hopeless parents, accused and attacked them.
Acquaintances and friends considered them mentally ill.
Strangers, who received false information from the mass media, attacked them.
They met new, wonderful people.
They changed their profession.
They were now considered masters, gurus, sages, etc.
The mass media become interested.
They fell in love with humans and animals.

Of course, if that happened to others, it does not mean that this will happen to you. However, it is worth to be aware of the possible changes.
Are you ready for such possible changes? Do you know how to find a remedy if you do not want to accept these changes?

Have you ever noticed how often man makes a decision while having no idea about what the final result will be? Man not only does not know the final result, they also do not know what is the **real** reason of their decision.

Man decides something under influence of emotional stimulus; this can be compared to acting as a machine which was made to function by just pressing a button.

Every change of life style reflects on man. Every change which man makes in their physical or psychical spheres reflects in their life style. When man starts inedia or non-eating, the changes in their life may be felt so strongly that their results become unbearable. The behaviour of the non-eater, their relations with people, objects, places and situations as well as their attitude to everything. become very different.

If you decide to experience inedia, non-eating or long fasting, it would be worthwhile for you to first deeply consider and make yourself conscious about what is the real reason of your decision. Consider whether you are ready for different circumstances awaiting you, because they will change your interpersonal relations.

The personal survey and analysis technique called WSW, described below, may help you to find out what the real reason of your decision is and what may be the outcome. These two methods are useful before making any decisions in your life. If you are using these methods before making decisions, you will notice significant favourable changes in your life. One of the things that you may notice is that you become more and more free and self-confident because you will be less and less influenced by suggestions from the society.

PERSONAL SURVEY

Before you decide to adapt your body to living without food, it is worth asking yourself sincerely the following questions. Before answering any of these questions remain calm in silence in order to better feel the true internal answer.

In this case it is more advantageous to tune to answers coming from the intuition. Answers and the excuses found by the intellect have less importance. Either way it is not worth cheating or making excuses for yourself, because the true picture of the matter consists of facts only and of what you feel.

Consider doing the personal survey with the WSW analysis so that you will have the fullest picture of yourself in relation to the decisions made. The full analysis may take anywhere between a few hours to a few months.

So sincerely answer to yourself:

1. Why do I want to start inedia or non-eating? What is my main and the deepest held goal?
2. Will my hitherto conducted life style be an obstacle?
3. Am I prepared for the big changes which will occur in my relationship with my family members, friends, colleagues and other people? Can I foresee what kind of changes will take place?
4. Does the state of my psychical health allow me to do this?
5. Does the path of my spiritual growth include inedia or non-eating?
6. Do I really know that I can and I know how to do this?
7. If problems arise whom will I ask for advice?
8. Have I talked it through with my close relatives, so that I know their true opinion about my decision?
9. Am I afraid? Of what?
10. Am I fully aware that the adaptation to inedia or non-eating is mostly a spiritual rather than physical process?
11. Am I under an influence of the society suggestion and thus somehow forcing myself?
12. Actually, what for do I want this?

Why? So What? **ANALYSIS**

The main purpose of the "**W**hy? **S**o **W**hat?" analysis is to realize the true reason of a decision that you make. WSW can be called a psychological method of intellectual analysis, during which you make yourself more self-aware in relation to a decision you make. The final result is that you realize the primary true reason of your decision.

This analysis works best when done by and on yourself, because sincerity is the basis of finding the final right answer. If someone is sincere with you as much as with themselves, you can do WSW analysis for them.

It is best to make the WSW analysis on paper. You can get yourself a big piece of paper. Write the statement of your decision in the upper left corner. Then make the 'Why ....' question.
Now, answer the question. Write down all the answers that may appear. You can draw arrows, from the question to the answers, so that you can better visually understand the course of your thinking.

Then, for every answer you give, make a question starting with the word "why". Having answered to one of the why-questions, continue asking "why ...". Carry on like this until you run out of answers. When you do not find a logical answer to the question "Why ...", ask yourself: "So what?".

Having asked yourself "So what?", do not answer intellectually, instead tune yourself to receiving the answer though your feelings. Be mentally passive, do not do any thinking; then feelings, emotions or pictures may appear as the answer.

The instinct and intuition are best perceived when the intellect is passive, that is when it does not create thoughts and is not tuned to receiving stimuli from the senses. When the intuition or instinct answer telepathically though feelings, emotions or pictures, then the answer is the fullest.

The picture you have made with the questions and answers written on the paper may be similar to a tree. Instead of drawing this picture you can use one sheet of paper for a group of answers or one sheet for all answers to only one question.

In Polish the question "So what?" (*No i co z tego*?) contains the truest intellectual answer: nothing (*Nic*). If you do the WSW analysis you will find this answer at the end of it.

Here is an example of the WSW analysis.

I HAVE DECIDED TO LOSE SOME WEIGHT
Why have I decided this?

answer. 1.
- So that people like me more.
- Why do I want people to like me more?
- When people let me know that they like me, I feel better.
    - Why do I expect (need) someone's favourable opinion about myself?
    - People's judgement of me determines how I feel.
        - Why does my mood depend on someone's judgement?
        - My self-esteem is not strong enough.
            - Why do I have such a low self esteem?
            - ... and so on.

answer. 2.
- So that X will see me as more attractive and he will like me.
- Why do I care if X likes me?
- Because I love him.
    - So what?
    - ... and so on.

answer. 3.
- So that my body fitness improves.
- Why do I want my body fitness to improve?
- Because then I feel better and am more attractive.
    - Why do I want to be more attractive?
    - Because then people will like me more.
        - Why do I want others to like me more?
        - Actually I care more about X, if he feels more attracted to me.
            - Why do I care about X?
            - ... and so on.

answer. 4.
- So that I can save money on food.
- Why do I want to save money on food?
- I think I have too little money.
    - Why do I want to have more money?
    - It makes me feel more secure.
        - Why do I feel financially insecure?
        - I am afraid that one day I will have no money for living.
            - So what?
            - Then I will live in poverty?
                - So what? ... and so on.

FAMILY MEMBERS

Family members that you daily live with in the same house are the people who have the biggest influence on your life. Their attitude may help you or make it from difficult to impossible for you to proceed with the preparation for inedia or non-eating. It is worth to consider their opinion and possible behaviour concerning your decision to change the life style.

At the beginning your main task will be to explain to them what you will be doing and why. Their cooperation will be beneficial for you, hence the better they understand you, the less obstacles will be created by them.

It is worth that you be aware of the fact that becoming an inediate may cause many changes in your attitude and understanding about the matters of this world. At the beginning this may worsen your relationship with your kin and friends. In the extreme case, if the desire to understand one another is insufficient, isolation from the family members or divorce may happen.

The energetic structure and emanation of your bodies will change significantly. This may cause disharmony between you and your spouse, children, parents and other family members. If they do not understand you and do not support you, it is almost certain that unpleasant situations will occur among you all. In such situations the disharmony becomes unbearable because fear, irritation, hate, anger and similar unpleasantness occur.

Instead of this, the opposite may happen, the energetic structures of your bodies will make the people, who live with you, feel that they grow spiritually. This is called "raising the vibrations of other people". As a result they will become more interested in the immaterial sphere of life. It may change their attitude toward eating.

If however, despite the objections expressed by the family members you will decide to begin the adaptation to inedia or non-eating or long fasting, a better solution would be removing yourself from them for a while. You can live in another place for a month or so or you can send the family members on vacation so that you will be at home alone.

It is worthwhile remembering that support or obstructions from family members is often the crucial factor in whether the decision is accomplished or whether man fails or not. This is why, in case of non-supporting attitude from the family members, it is worth to consider deeply whether to begin at all.

COLLEAGUES

Most of the above written about family members is also valid for colleagues. Working in the same place often and for a long time creates special family-like relationship between people.

Even if you have made them believe your story of why you have given up the lunch break, which you all used to eating together, then for how long are you going to hide the truth? Is cheating them worth it? Your look and behaviour will change so sooner or later they will find out.

Depending on your relationship with the colleagues, you may become the focus of their admiration, imitation or envy, jokes, hatred. So, before you begin, try to imagine how they can react. Anticipating their reactions will allow you to plan in advance how you will respond, or you may decide whether to give up the idea about inedia or non-eating, at least for some time.

Your imagination, thanks to which you will be able to foresee possible reactions of the colleagues and superiors in your workplace, may help you avoid undesired situations. An example of such situation may be losing your job because your superiors may suspect that you have become mentally ill or a member of a dangerous sect.

Therefore how things develop will depend on your behaviour, the type and place of your work, reactions of your colleagues. For you these may be favourable, insignificant or devastating. When you can foresee these events and people's reactions, you can prepare yourself for the change, modify them or give it up.

FRIENDS

Your acquaintances and friends belong to those people whose behaviour you may want to consider, because the change of the life style will influence the relationship between you. The more food is involved in your meetings, the bigger the changes will be.

If you are used to meeting over a table full of food, then your non-eating state will be noticed soon. Imagine what will be their reaction to your new life style. They may support you, they may also get involved or they may break the contact with you. So you may lose your friends (which, of course, will prove that they were not really your friends).

ADDICTIONS

If you know that you can live without any food, then you are probably free of addictions to sugar, salt, nicotine, alcohol, drugs, overeating etc. But if they continue to tie you down, it means that you are not ready yet. It does not mean that you cannot try or that you will not be successful.

Addictions do not make fasting or non-eating impossible although they usually become quite an obstacle on the way. It is a fact that thanks to fasting or even attempting to start inedia or non-eating man may succeed to free themselves of addictions. Heal fasting is one of the most efficient methods to free man from an addiction especially if it concerns food.

In case of non-eating, statistics show that man with an addiction has not attained the ability for inedia or non-eating. The existing addiction proves that the sphere of the Consciousness in which man lives is not expanded enough. It results in one's inability to make the right changes in the programs of the instinct, which are necessary for inedia or non-eating. If despite the existing addiction man keeps the mind and body working properly during inedia or non-eating, this man is an exception to the statistical rule.

Man tied down with an addiction needs to consider freeing themselves from the addiction as the first step towards attaining inedia or non-eating. First of all this is about working with emotions. Later the liberation from the need to feed the body comes.

Addictions are a complex topic for a separate book. Here I emphasize just one thing that an addiction is a program in the instinct, which enslaves man for as long as man allows the program to function.

HABITS

A habit can be distinguished from the addiction by the emotional reaction of man. When man gives up the habit, no emotions arise. Self-liberating from an addiction is difficult and often causes unpleasant emotional reactions, but giving up a habit is not felt as something difficult and unpleasant.

During the adaptation for inedia or non-eating some of the habits are stopped or changed, especially those related to eating. For example, if every morning you buy food and then eat the breakfast with the family, be aware, because you may want to give this habit up. Think how the family members will react and how you will feel about this. Will you first talk to them about this?

Perhaps you have other habits, so it is worth to think whether changing or stopping them will influence your life. Some examples of habits include meeting with friends in a bar, eating dinner with clients, picnicking, fishing, stockpiling, buying food every Friday in a supermarket or baking cakes for holidays. When you give up all these habits, how will this affect your family life, time planning and comfort?

In addition, new habits may arise because, for example, you may find more free time, which previously was used for eating matters. Probably you will not want to prepare food, sit at the table with others when they eat and to wash dishes like before. How will you use the time? Will a new habit be born?

The fact that your habits will be changed is not usually a sufficient reason for giving up long fasts or initiating inedia or non-eating. On the other hand, it is worth considering what changes may occur in your life and whether disappearance of habitual actions from your life will prove advantageous. How far can I go and how much will I move in the direction of these changes?

DIET

This is about the diet man had just before becoming independent from food. Looking at it and explaining it from a different angle – the ability of non-eating is a result of the aggregated increase in frequency of human body. This is why what you eat just before starting non-eating may either ease or harden the adaptation process.

In general it can be said that the so-called "low-vibration-food" (e.g. fried, smoked, grilled or containing a lot of chemicals) puts man in a harder position on the way to the high vibrations. On the other hand, the so-called "high-vibration-food" (such as whole raw fruits without toxins) gives much stronger position. So depending on man, the material side of starting inedia or non-eating may be easy, more difficult or turn out impossible.

The human body does not usually like sudden or big changes. When changes are very small, the body does not feel them. This also goes for the diet of man endeavouring inedia or non-eating. For the body it is more advantageous if the change to zero-food-diet is occurring slowly enough, so that the body does not feel the change as unpleasant.

One of the most frequent problems arising particularly at the beginning of inedia or non-eating, is the taste. The non-eaters do not insert anything into their bodies and so they have no way of tasting any food. For some people this becomes as tiresome as a bad dream. This is why it is worth to first consider the matter and ask yourself this question: How big a problem would it be for me, not to be able to enjoy the taste of food.

VISUALIZATION

The instinct builds the human body, keeps it working, controls the data (e.g. eaten food, memory), reacts to psychical and physical stimuli, and so on. Any activity of the instinct is just a program, automatic reaction to instructions.

I have mentioned before that programs can be modified. If I do not like a function or a reaction to a stimulus, I may decide to make modifications. The purpose of making modification in the instinct is to change the result of instinct's activity.

If I decide that my body will react in a specific way to, e.g. heat, darkness, wounds, food or noise, I can achieve it by changing the corresponding program in the instinct. By 'reprogramming the instinct' I mean any modification, removal or insertion of at least one program in the instinct.

Firstly, it is worth to remember that the instinct requires loving care. The more you love your instinct, the better it serves you. You can treat the instinct as if it was your beloved child or pet. Often focus on feeling how much you love your instinct.

Your beliefs and programs in your instinct create the needs of the body and its reactions to situations. Man's habits are manifestations of pictures and programs built in the instinct.

Man who knows how to reprogram the instinct is able to change any outcome of instinct's action. This also goes for the needs of the body regarding its nourishment.

So when you are ready to make yourself independent of eating, one of the things to do is to reprogram the instinct's programs related to eating. Depending on your reprogramming skills, it may require from you any period of time from one second to several life times.

Visualization is an efficient method used for reprogramming the instinct. It is a conscious action which brings planned changes in the work of the body and in life circumstances. You can use visualization to materialize your dreams.

If you want to make the body ill or healthy, make yourself rich or poor, if you want to posses things, develop certain ability, change relationship, etc., you can use visualization. If visualization was compared to programming and you were compared to the programmer, then life is a game which you are writing according to your preferences.

For the visualization to be effective, a picture or film has to be created properly in your imagination and saturated with energy.
There five conditions which must be fulfilled, for the visualization to produce the desired result.

1. Make a clear, realistic and vivid picture or film, in which details are perceived by all the senses.
2. Make sure that it is in the present time, now and here.
3. Feel that the result has been achieved.
4. Know (not just believe) that it is your present reality.
5. Saturate it with the energy of Love and accompanying joy.

Re. 1
First and foremost, know what you want, what is the final result that you have decided to achieve. See all the details of the thing that you have decided and which is going to be produced as the result of the visualization. Create a picture in which the senses also work. The more senses take part in the picture and the more realistic, vivid the picture is, the easier it is to accomplish the visualization.

For example, if the result of the visualization is to have your own house, imagine yourself living in this house with your family. See all of you speaking (the sense of hearing) near the house and how you invite friends to visit it etc. Let the smell of the freshly painted walls, flowers of the garden, be around there (the sense of smell). You can also taste a freshly prepared drink in the kitchen (the sense of taste). Outside the house you feel the nice warmth of the afternoon Sun. All those images becomes a film in your imagination.

Create only those details in the picture which are important for you. The rest of the details will be created accordingly, so you do not need to care. For example, if the location and the shape of the house are important to you, then clearly create these details in the picture. If the number of the windows and the colours of the walls are not so important to you, do not create them at all in you picture.

Do not include the way of achieving the final result unless it is this way that interests you the most. The picture itself, that is the final result of the visualization, is important, not the way of achieving it. If you are creating in the picture a way of achieving the final result, you are limiting yourself by this way. There are other ways that you are not aware of, which are more efficient, easier and advantageous. So you would be better off creating the final result in your imagination and not thinking about the ways of achieving it.

For example, if you have decided to heal your body, then see yourself full of joy, happy and completely healthy. Do not imagine any method to heal yourself. IAM has much more efficient methods, compared to what the intellect is able to imagine.

Re. 2
The result presented in the picture created in your imagination has to exist in the present time. If in the imagination you say, for instance, will have, will become, will receive, will buy, or any other 'will' (the future tense), it will become a fact. Therefore, today it 'will' be to be attained, tomorrow it 'will' be to be attained, after a year it still 'will' be to be attained, after twenty years nothing will be changed because it still 'will' be to be attained ... Remember, 'it is now realized'.

The visualization gives you what you have created. Since you have created 'it will' (future happening), you will always have the thing in the future, never 'having done' it. In other words, the result of the visualization will never be attained in the present time. Since you are living in the present, always, you will never receive what you visualize to be realized in the future.

Re. 3
The picture created in the imagination has to present the result already realized, the goal already attained. For you it is already the present reality. In case of the above example, you see and feel yourself in the house as realist-

ically as if you were living in it. You **are** living, sleeping, working, resting in the house. You treat everything as really existing, occurring in **the present time**.

The instinct is not very good at dealing with the illusion of the intellect called 'time', it does not know what time is. It understands and reacts as a small children. If you tell children "later", "tomorrow", "after one week", they will not distinguish the significant difference because their intellect has not learned to create time.

This is one of the main reasons why the picture has to present the desired state as already materialized. You are already now seeing and feeling it as realized in the present reality.

Re. 4
Do you remember what is the difference between 'to know' (knowledge) and 'to believe' (belief)? I have already mentioned this. Well, when you know something, you do not believe it. When you believe something, you also doubt it because you do not know it.

Not clear? Let me ask you. Do you know or do you believe that you are reading this book? What is your answer? "I know that I am reading." or "I believe that I am reading." Do you now comprehend the difference?

Looking for advices about how to do visualization, one can find information that says "you have to strongly believe", because "believing can move mountains". Well, no matter how strong you believe something, at the same time you also doubt it. But when you know, you have no doubts.

Another example. If someone now called you and asked what you are doing. You, according to the fact, may answer that you are reading a book. You know it, but the other party may only believe or doubt what you said. If the other party could see you now, they would be able to say: 'know'.

"How can I know, not just believe, the picture or film in my imagination?" – you may ask me. Well, you remember that in your picture or film you must activate all your senses. Knowledge is based on experience gained through your senses. When your senses are active in your imagination, you know, not just believe, so you have the knowledge.

Properly done visualization requires you **to know** that the picture in your imagination presents reality already materialized in the present time.
If you still do not know, you only believe, then do believe it strongly. In

this case, believing is more advantageous than doing nothing.

By the way, have you seen man materializing an object, e.g. an apple on their outstretched hand? You have seen an example of visualization in which man already knew that the object was there.

Re. 5
Without sufficient amount of energy visualization will not produce the desired result. When I talk about energy here, I do not really relate to the known definition of physics stating that 'energy is the capacity of a physical system to perform work'. What I mean by 'energy' is the thing that man feels under the influence of an emotion. An emotion is a reaction of the instinct (so it is a program), occurring when energy is suddenly released or blocked.

Do you recall any past moment when you were 'hair-raising' frightened and your heart almost 'jumped out'? Then, recall the energy which captured you at that moment. Also recall the energy which stirred you, when you were feeling the strongest love affection of your life. Now you probably know what I am referring to, when I say that the visualization needs energy.

You have the **picture** ready, which is totally **real** and exists in the **present time**. You also **know** that the picture represents your **present reality**. Now you only need the **energy**, in order to manifest the picture in this material reality.

Allow yourself to feel the most powerful energy, the energy appearing when emotions accompanying Love arise. First allow Love to manifests itself through you. Allow this to happen naturally. You need not to do anything except allowing, because you are the source of Love.

In visualization, the picture can be compared to a seed inserted in the soil. The energy arising with the emotions is compared to water. The seed without water would never grow to become a plant.

How to do visualization practically? First relax your entire body and psyche. Allow Love to manifest through your mind and body. When you are feeling the rising energy accompanying Love, bring the picture (with all the attributes as described above) into your imagination. The more Love manifests through you, the more efficiently the visualization produces result.

The efficiency of visualization depends mainly on two factors: the picture and the energy. The picture in your imagination has to be as real as if you were seeing it in front of your eyes. It has to show the final result which you have decided to materialize from your imagination into the physical reality. It is better to imagine the final result as already achieved, rather than imagining the methods of the picture realization. In this way, you do not limit yourself about methods of achieving the final goal.

The picture has to be powered by energy so that it can be realised. This is as important as water is for a seed thrown onto the soil, so it can grow to become a plant. Sowed seeds must be watered regularly. The same process applies to the picture – it has to be powered with energy regularly.

Create positive emotions when you are imagining a picture that is the goal of your visualization. Allow your Inner Joy to emanate. Emotionally move deeply through your image and see the final result as already manifested in your physical reality.

Visualization is a powerful mean to realize goals. If you are using it properly, according to the description above, matters will move in the direction of your goal. How far and when the picture will be realized depends on energy which you emanate into the picture in your imagination. In other words, the final result depends on your emotional engagement.

Man is constantly visualizing, even when asleep. You can see in your dreams, that visualization is realized much faster, almost instantly. Often it is enough to only begin thinking. Dreams occur in a world which is much less dense than our daily material life. Therefore much less energy is needed in that world to realize a picture.

Man almost always visualizes unintentionally. Man visualizes without being aware of it; they also do not realize that their life is a result of their visualization.

I sometimes meet people who complain about their life. I see a lot of fear and negative emotions in their perception of the world. Those people suffer due to their own desire, although they are not aware of it. Most often, unpleasant situations happen to them which cause their suffering.
Those people have used the visualization technique very well. Some of them are real masters at this but they do this unintentionally. Having a negative picture in their imagination, they evoke emotions associated with fear, anger and hatred. Therefore, what would be the result of their visualization?

It is worthwhile to be aware that instinct has no idea about what is a joke and what is serious matter. So, when you are speaking jokingly about yourself in a negative way, emanating emotions at the same time, you are doing visualization, which is going to be realized.

You have probably met people, who jokingly were saying sentences like: "I am old", "stupid me", "I am blind", "I cannot afford it", "I am too poor for this" and other negative expressions. When you look at those people, you can see that they see their lives unhappy. They encounter much "bad luck". By now, you probably know that all of this happens according to their own desire. After all, they have visualized these events themselves.

Therefore, I suggest, talk about yourself positively even when joking. Instinct, which brings pictures from the imagination into the material reality, does not distinguish between a joke and a serious matter. Instinct always realizes your visualization, whether it is done consciously or not.

Those, who really stand behind the education systems and the mass media, know the power of suggesting with emotions. They are very aware of the power of suggestion and visualization. They use this knowledge to manipulate people. They instil in people the notion that people are something less than perfect beings. They promote violence, anger, hatred and death on TV, Internet and in computer games. All of this arouse negative emotions in people. Negative pictures connected with negative emotions lead people to suffering and cause them to see themselves as less worthy beings.

You are already a perfect being. Regardless of what you do, you are the Master Creator of your life. Every being is perfect, although they may see and experience the world differently.
Do not allow anybody to instil in you the notion that you are something less than a perfect being. You can freely reject those suggestions contained in the education system and the mass media, which suggest negativism, or that you are small, poor, or that you have to serve and work, or that you need to be saved. As long as you follow this kind of harmful beliefs, you will be a slave.

Knowing that man is almost always visualizing, you can use this to your advantage. You can see yourself as a perfect being because in your essence, you are one, you are the Master Creator. Even if you consider yourself an imperfect being, and others instil in you such a picture, the fact is that you are already perfect.

I suggest, imagine and feel yourself emanating joy naturally. Hold this picture in your imagination. This is the most benevolent picture that you can

imagine and hold in mind, unless you choose suffering.
Here is a description of a sample picture, or feel free to create another.

I ..(your name).. feel joy naturally and without a reason. I am joyful. Joy.
I ..(your name).. am always filled with joy. Joy is in me.
Joy is emanating from me so everyone around me feels Love.

Of course, this description of a picture is just one of the five requirements of visualization, which I described earlier. Combine the picture with the remaining four elements so that your visualization will be efficient. Thanks to this, you will become a joyous man. The other things will follow to support your joyfulness. Everything in the entire universe will arrange itself so that your picture will be realized.

Scientific confirmation of visualization is found in frozen water crystals. Water is known to to create many structures depending on the factors influencing it. Molecules of water are arranged in specific structures depending on peoples' words, thoughts, feelings and emotions.

Search for *"Masaru Emoto"* and his "Messages from Water" on the Internet. See how clearly water is influenced from everything that man says, write, thinks and feels. See how beautiful, bright and orderly water looks when someone says words like "love", "thank you", etc. Look how disgusting water looks when words like "I hate you", "I will kill you", etc. are said.

The human body consists mostly of water, especially the brain. What you think, say and feel creates immediate and direct physical reflection in your body, especially in the nerve system, which programs your body. What would you want your body to look like?

CONTEMPLATION OF PASSIVENESS

Contemplation (sometimes erroneously called meditation) is a type of a mental exercise in which the intellect is focussed on a concept, idea or thought. The concept can be a material thing (e.g. painting, man, scenery), an idea (Love, Light, trust, true) or a thought or nothing.

Contemplation is one of those mind exercises which widen the sphere of the Consciousness in which man lives. Thanks to contemplation, expansion beyond the sphere of the intellect happens. This comprehensively develops man and makes them feel the growth in their conscious self- development. As result of contemplation, problems disappear, body illnesses are eliminated, knowledge manifests itself giving man more possibilities and power.

"The simplest solutions are the most efficient ones." – I often say this. Contemplation of passiveness confirms this statement because the exercise is very simple, easy and efficient. Without any preparation, every man who understands the instruction, is able to contemplate.
Contemplation influences children's mind in very positive way. If a child, even as young as two years of age, understands how to contemplate, it is worth to encourage them to practise. The intellectual, psychic and physical growth of a child using the contemplation of passiveness is much broader.

Contemplation of passiveness is advantageous and useful for every man practising conscious self-development. Being a member of a religious or philosophical organization, a social group or similar formations is not an obstacle to practising contemplation of passiveness.

Contemplation of passiveness individualizes itself, that is it gives you what you need in your conscious self-development. As you grow, this contemplation modifies itself in order to serve you the best. The modification is happening naturally and automatically in a way which produces results best suited to your needs. That is one of the reasons why this mind exercise is so powerful from the beginning.

Because it individualizes itself to man, the course and the results of this contemplation are different in case of every exercising man. Therefore, it does not make much sense to compare the course and achievements of your contemplation with those of other people, unless for learning purpose or curiosity only.

Sit down in a comfortable position with your spine naturally erect. You may sit on a chair with the feet on the floor and the knees at right angle; on the floor with the legs crossed; or on the floor with the feet put on your thighs. The important thing is that you should be in a position which will allow you to contemplate for a few dozens of minutes without feeling any discomfort.

The lying position is also suitable for this exercise, if you prefer it; but then it is easier to fall asleep. If you choose to lie down, you had better not lie on your side. It is better to lie on the back, without any pillow, with your hands and legs spread apart. Make sure that nothing causes any discomfort to the body.

This exercise contains in its name the most essential instruction – passiveness. The intellect has to be passive, that is not to think but not to fall asleep either.

The intellect of an ordinary man, when not asleep, is usually quite active with thinking, creating, solving, analysing data from the senses, etc. Man's intellect can also fall asleep, that is to be kind of switched off, when it is not active. These two states take almost all of the intellect's working time.

There is a third state, into which the intellect seldom enters, the total passiveness. In this state the intellect is not active, that is it does not think and does not process any sensory stimuli. This state occurs, and last for several seconds, at the boundary between the daily activity and dreams. Maybe you can recall what occurs when you are awakening. On the one hand you find yourself still dreaming, and on the other hand you know that, although it is still a dream, you are awakening because the daily consciousness is appearing. This state of mind is similar to the passiveness of the intellect.

To generate and to maintain the state of total passiveness of the intellect seems to be difficult at first. An inexperienced man would say that this is almost impossible because man either thinks or falls asleep. It is a fact that for a beginner an attempt to make the intellect passive will most often result in falling asleep, especially when man lies down. However, man exercising regularly achieves the goal because "practice makes master".

Close your eyes and turn your attention to thoughts appearing in your mind. However – this is the most important thing in this exercise – do not follow the thoughts and do not create them. Do not think at all. Keep focus on not thinking (but do not think this). In your intellect, be completely passive. Be kind of totally indifferent observer of the flowing thoughts and all the stimuli coming from the senses.

Whenever you notice that you are following a thought, that is you are thinking, detach yourself from the thought, leave it instantly to restore the passiveness. In this passiveness, you are aware that there are thoughts in your mind but you do not follow them, you stay totally indifferent, really zero interest.
This can be compared to the vacant looking at a river flow. You know that the water is flowing there, because you are looking at it, but it does not attract you at all. Just, let it be with no interest from you.

At the beginning, when you start to do the contemplation of passiveness, you may notice that you can make the intellect passive for a few seconds. Then you notice that you follow a thought, as if it was pulling you. Later, as you continue exercising, the time without fallowing a thought and paying attention to stimuli from the senses will be longer and longer.

At the beginning the intellect is full of thoughts which appear and disappear chaotically. As you are practising, the number of thoughts in the intellect decreases. The sensory stimuli will be evoking less and less attention in the intellect, so it will become more and more tranquil. You will reach the state of the intellect in which there will be only one last though left – "do not think and do not pay attention to any sensory stimuli". Actually, it is more advantageous not to use any expressions containing the word "no", thus better use this: "the intellect is totally passive".

When this last thought disappears, Light of the knowledge from your intuition becomes clearer noticeable. Flashes of Light may appear earlier at any time. Some people, especially those who earlier practised something similar, may see the flashes of Light much earlier.

When exercising contemplation of passiveness sounds may be heard but not with the ears. These sounds, same as Light flashes, are data from the intuition. The intuition is present all the time but the intellect, being occupied with its activities, usually does not notice any data from the intuition. When the intellect becomes passive, data from the intuition becomes noticeable. The first data received by the intellect are the above mentioned sounds and Light.

The more passive the intellect becomes, the more data it is able to notice from the intuition. The deeper passiveness the intellect maintains, the clearer it feels the manifestation of IAM, through the intuition, in the form of Light and Love.

Now you are doing the same contemplation but not of the same kind as it was in the beginning, because now it is transformed to meditation. When the intellect steps aside, Light and Love appear, then you enter the state of meditation (no thoughts, no illusion). If your brain waves were checked, it would show that you are in the *Delta* state.

Meditation begins when the intellect completely ceases its activity but does not fall asleep. The intellect remains totally passive but it is aware about what happens in the mind.
It is impossible to intellectually explain in detail what the meditation is because the meditation happens beyond the boundaries of the intellect.

Even though initially, you may not consider contemplation of passiveness worthwhile, I suggest that you do it regularly. The more you practise it, the

bigger the changes you will experience due to enlightenment. In other words, you will enter enlightenment more and more often.
Enlightenment is a state of the intellect which is transparent and aware of information coming from the intuition. Knowledge is like light, it shows truth. When the intellect is in this light, it knows the truth. Therefore, enlightenment occurs when the intellect is in the light of the knowledge from the intuition.

Calm intellect can be easily focused, giving you the power to control your life, which not many people possess. Visualizing becomes much easier in this stage of the intellect calmness. Then man also attains ability to enter into meditation, something that many mystics pursue for decades and cannot achieve.

The goal of contemplation of passiveness is to bring the jumping intellect under control, because normally it is not able to focus enough due to its restlessness. Getting the jumping intellect under control is the key achievement on the way of conscious self-development. When man acquires this key on the way of conscious self-development, they can open the gate to meditation, intuition, telepathy and many abilities, commonly regarded as extraordinary or miracle.

"Then I experienced such kind of vertigo that tears involuntarily came out.
I was overwhelmed by happiness, joy and inexpressible love, and integrated with all the existence.
I was feeling such big joy and light heart as if I was living in another reality.
Let me say this: to love, it is much less compared to what was flowing from my heart."

Jarek

CONTEMPLATION OF INNER JOY

This exercise truly evokes a blissful experience. Feelings gained by this simple exercise bring you closer to the mighty being, that man is in their natural state. When you fully allow your Inner Joy to manifests, you reach the state of natural joy and you emanate Love and Light. When you maintain in this state, inedia is a by-product.

People usually feel joy when they are under an impact of external factor, for example, when they rejoice at happiness. The power of joy initiated by external factor can be compared to barely a particle of natural joy.

Think about it. You have probably experienced moments when you felt tremendous joy absolutely without any reason, just like that, it occurred, you did not know why. Do you recall such situations?

Close your eyes, relax and go back to your early childhood when you were not yet thinking. You can probably recall moments from that time. When you recall that state of rejoice or you experience it again, you can imagine that the Inner Joy is felt much stronger.

One way or another, the joy that you have recalled is merely a particle of Inner Joy emanating from man living in natural state.
Man in natural state is full of joy. It can be seen from a distance that they emanate a kind of invisible light and a pleasant attraction, and you can feel Love from them. Those people do not even need to smile or laugh, they talk in a normal manner and still, you will feel pleasure and joy arousing in you for no reason.

Can you imagine that situation? Have you ever met such man? Probably yes. So, can you imagine what Inner Joy is, that naturally exists in man? In fact, emanating Inner Joy is natural for man, so you do not need to create it, just return to your natural state.

Here is a description, an example of an exercise which helps you to return to the state in which your Inner Joy is manifested.

Sit or lie down and loosen up the entire body. Enter the state of total relaxation. Move away all thoughts at the beginning of this exercise and proceed as you do in contemplation of passiveness.
Having calmed the entire body and intellect, focus on feeling joy which is deeply within you. Inner Joy is the source of Life manifested from IAM through your mind and body.
Remember not to create joy. Inner joy is one of features of you in the natural state. You can feel Inner Joy when you do not cover IAM with restless activity of the intellect.
This is why it is so important for you to make the intellect passive and to focus on feeling things which are beyond thoughts, pictures and the senses.

The key in this exercise is 'allowing'. You allow your Inner Joy to freely emanate. Allow and wait with our feeling. Do not think, do not force any feeling, just allow and wait. Keep full relaxation of your body and intellect.

What you may feel cannot be successfully explained and comprehended intellectually. This has to be felt individually. Even if you read a thick book about feeling Inner Joy, you will still not comprehend it. This joyous state has to be felt.

When the first feeling of Inner Joy appear, you will immediately feel them. You will feel this power manifesting itself as joy without any reason. At the same time, you will feel Love. It is quite possible that tears will well up in your eyes, because you will feel IAM again, this Thing that you really are in your essence.

Remember, do not create anything but only **allow** yourself to feel. Inner Joy is always there, it always was and always will be. You only need to allow and focus on feeling it. Therefore, allow and wait. Feel it, do not create it, do not think about it and do not imagine it. Practise, one day you will feel it, for sure.
Allow your Inner Joy to emanate, so that it fills you with Love and Light.

FOCUSSING ON YOUR INNER SUN

This exercises is similar to the above you. You can focus on your Inner Sun when you find it particularly difficult to feel your Inner Joy.

First, fully loosen your body and bring it to full relaxation. Silence the intellect and move away your attention form the senses. Sit in a comfortable position.

Focus on feeling the sun, which is in the area of your heart. Feel how this sun grows, extends its radiation to the entire chest and then the entire body and beyond. You are feeling this because a wonderful sense of warmth, joy and Love spreads within you and saturates every cell of the body.
You see this Light under the closed eyelids and you can feel the growing joy and Love.
You see and feel how the sun is still expanding. You sink into it and then you become the sun yourself.
Now, being the sun and feeling your Inner Power, you emanate joy, Light and Love.
Remain in this state, keep it effortlessly. This is a perfect food for your body, which cures and strengthens it. The joy and Love remain, even when the sun retreats into the centre of your chest, in the area of you heart.

Some people let their Inner Joy to manifest so much that they become similar to a sun in their activities. It is clearly sensible from them, how they emanate Love, warm, safeness, etc. Around the body (especially the head) of those people a kind of light can be seen (aureole). Those people do not feel cold and warm more or less than they desire it.

CONTEMPLATION or VISUALIZATION

Learn the differences between contemplation and visualization. These two exercises require an opposite kind of actions. In general, contemplation requires passiveness whereas visualization requires the intellect to be very active.

The intellect should remain passive during contemplation, so that only one idea is present. This idea should fill the entire non-thinking, passive intellect which should act only as a passive observer. The intellect, as silent and non-creating, can notice information and flashes from intuition and instinct.

An entirely opposite action is performed during visualization. The intellect should be fully engaged in its thoughts, entire imagination and all senses around the picture. It must create a fully live picture, so that if people watched it, they would believe it is real. Also, the intellect has to rouse the instinct with emotions, which emanate energy.

ENERGIZING EXERCISES

These are the type of exercises which cause sensible increase in man's life energy. After doing an energizing exercise, you can feel that tiredness, sleepiness and weakness leave you. Exercises of this kind enhance circulation of energy and information in human body and spirit, as well as also between man and the environment.

When doing an energizing exercise, contrary to a typical gymnastics or power exercise, man does not diffuse the body energy to make the muscles work and tire them. On the contrary, man delivers energy to the body. Sufficient amount of life energy in the body is especially important in the initial stage of the adaptation to living without food.

There are many energizing exercises. Most often one can hear about and practise the Indian hatha yoga and *pranayama*, the Chinese *qì-gōng* and *tàj-*

jí, the Tibetan rites, the Western isometric exercises and different visualizations. There are many systems and they have schools, masters teaching energizing exercises.

Energizing exercises, if performed regularly, beneficially influence man's body.. Man's body becomes free of illnesses, age much slower and die much later. Being hundreds of years of age, full of energy and high physical and mental capacity, looking like in their forties – masters of energizing exercises testify that this kind of activity has much to offer.

Many regularly exercising people feel decreasing need for eating. In case of some regularly exercising people hunger completely vanishes when their energy level becomes high enough. Among the Chinese exercising *qì-gōng* or *tàj-jí*, you can find people entering *bì-gǔ*, This means that man does not feel any hunger and therefore they do not eat anything for weeks, months or years. Such man remains in perfect condition and their body almost does not age, the biological age even regresses.

For man who is fasting or pursuing inedia or non-eating, this information means that regular practice of the energizing exercises is strongly recommended especially during the entire time without food. Practising gives measurable advantages. In most cases, if not doing the energizing exercises, man aspiring to inedia or non-eating is not able to keep the body working properly.

Having decided to practise energizing exercises, you may choose one of the schools and follow their instructions. Additionally you have another choice; you can work out, by yourself, the best set of movements that suit you. It is easier than you may think. If you want, start doing it now.

Stand up, half-close your eyes, relax and focus on yourself. First of all, feel how your body reacts to the energy flow in your body. Feel the body, not the energy flow. Do not focus on the movements or the muscles of your body.
Forget what you have learned while practising *qì-gōng*, *tàj-jí*, hatha yoga or any other standardised exercises. The most important things are to become silent, relaxed and focused on **feeling** of the energy flowing in your body. Remember, focus on feeling, feeling caused by the energy flowing in your body, what does the body feels. Do not focus on the energy, energy flow or on your body movements.

While you remain focused on **feeling** of the energy flowing in your body, you may notice that some muscles want to move. Let the muscle decide for

themselves, let the body make its own movements. What kind of movement it will be, it does not matter as long as you remain focused on feeling of the energy flow. The body will choose the movements according to its own needs, so let the muscle to move by themselves.
At the same time you will feel that the energy level of your body increases. You can think about this exercises as contemplation of feeling.

Contemplations, visualizations and energizing exercises are important elements on the way of conscious self-development of man. Practising them regularly makes man bloom comprehensively. As a result thinking becomes lighter, more creative and peaceful, and the body returns to its perfect state, which is manifested by its recovery and rejuvenation. One of results of such activity is a change in dependencies between man and the matter called food. This may cause your need to eat to vanish. Food becomes useless.

Exercising man becomes a being of so-called higher vibrations, which makes man to naturally emanate more and more Love and Light. At that point there is no discussion about eating or non-eating. Eating and food lose its power over man, they becomes insignificant.

If you have decided to keep your body in a perfect shape, possibly even without food, do energizing exercises regularly. As a result of these exercises, you will learn to move energy consciously in order to build, maintain and power your body.

Sensible energy and power given to man by this type of exercises is difficult to explain in words. It has to be felt. Once you feel it just once, you may long for this energy and body power. Some masters can use this energy for killing, resurrecting, healing, nourishment or materialization.

A sparrow once hit the window glass of the balcony door of our house. It probably wanted to fly into the lighted room but did not notice the glass. Having hit the door, the sparrow was lying on the floor with no movement as if it were dead.
I picked up the sparrow, enclosed it in my palms and focussed on transferring life energy to its small body. I felt Love naturally emanating from me.
After a while, I sensed that the sparrow moved. I opened my hands and let the sparrow sit on my palm. I then felt that the bird was filled with energy and quite healthy. I extended my palm and said to the sparrow: "You can fly now, you are healthy."
The bird did not want to fly away; it was sitting on my palm looking at me. It turned its head to the left and then to the right, looking into my eyes. Only after I fully extended my hand, shaking it a little to encourage the sparrow to fly away, did it finally understand. The sparrow flew away, full of energy and strength.

If I was a master at controlling energy, I would not have to hold the sparrow in my hands. It would have been sufficient to only look at it. The result would have been the same.

Well-being is important for man who is fasting or aspiring to reach inedia or non-eating. One of the symptoms that occurs most often after giving up food, is weakness of the body. In this case, energizing exercises are efficient means. Remember this! Exercise for a healthy body and psycho-physical efficiency.

ENERGIZING BY SOUND VIBRATION

When you emit a sound from within, you cause vibrations in different regions of the body. When changing the emitted sound, you can cause vibrations, among others, in the sinuses, the entire skull, and also the windpipe, the lungs or the spine.

If you know what mantras are and probably have chanted them, for example, OM, you may probably guess how to energize the body with the sound.

When you are learning to energize the body with the sound, pay attention to what you feel. Where do the vibrations appear and how do they radiate? How do you feel these vibrations? Are they pleasant, refreshing, healing and strengthening?

The following is an example of how you can learn to emit your proper sound. Let us call it your resonant sound.
Stand or sit comfortably without any support. Relax unnecessarily strengthened muscles. Breathe deeply and freely a few times. You may close your eyes.
Relax the muscles of the jaw and open the mouth slightly, not too large. Now, when exhaling slowly, emit the sound, which is somewhere between the vowels „a", „o", „u" and „y". This can sound differently in every body. You will know it, feel it when you hit you right resonant vibrations.
Try different positions of your lower jaw, tongue, windpipe and nose and also the mouth opening. Let a part of the sound / air exit through the nose – regulate it with your tongue and windpipe.
Experiment emitting the sound from you in different ways. You need to cause clearly sensible vibrations. Focus on feeling these vibrations, where they appear and how they change. Then feel which body regions need these vibrations, and move them there. They bring energy, which can be utilised

by the body. You may feel surprised by the amount of energy that your sound has, when it is causing resonant vibrations in the body.

You can modify this exercise. Find the resonant sound of a specific place in your body. For example, focus on your chest and emit sound trying different frequencies. Change the frequency of the emitted sound, go from low to high and the opposite way. While changing the frequency, feel your chest. Feel, at what frequency your chest is vibrating at the largest amplitude. This is the resonant sound of your chest.

Do the same with your nasal sinuses. Emit sound trying different frequencies till you feel the largest amplitude of vibrations of the sinuses chamber. This time, probably, most or all air making the sound will exit through your nose and the resonant frequency will be much higher compared to the resonant frequency of your chest.

The emitted sound needs to be louder than your normal talking. Make yourself comfortable with the loudness. Feel whether louder or softer is more pleasant to you.

ALTERNATE SHOWER

Alternate shower is started with warm water. Gradually rise the temperature of the water to the hottest that you can withstand. Then quickly switch the water temperature to the coldest you can stand. Let the water fall on your entire body for more than ten seconds. Next, switch the water temperature again, to the hottest that you can withstand and let it flow on the body for a few tens of seconds. And again, switch the water the coldest you can easily stand.

Repeat this switching a few times. Finish with cold water in order to close the skin pores and activate the self warming mechanism of the body; this makes you feel warm.

The alternate shower cleans the capillary blood veins and the skin. Due to the quick changes in water temperature the capillary blood veins alternately expand and shrink. This causes the sediment covering the internal side of the capillary blood veins, to peel. Blood can flow freely through the veins again.

The same quick water temperature changes make the skin pores expand and shrink alternately. Such movements eject excess sebum with the dirt.

Thanks to this, there is no need to use soap or other skin washing substances. You do not poison the body and nature.

Ending the alternate shower with hot water is practised in cases, when man goes to bed,even without drying the skin. directly from the shower, in order to make the body perspire a lot. Normally, finish the alternate shower with cold water.

Most people feel cold, having finished the shower with cold water. However, very soon the cold causes higher energetic activity in the body. Just a few moments after drying the skin you can feel the energy warming the body. This can be felt especially well if you do energizing exercising or just some gymnastics after the shower. In this case it is even better if you do not dry the skin but start the exercising right after finishing the shower.

Instead of taking a shower, you can use two bath tubs. One bath tube contains hot water and the other is filled with ice-cold water. You enter the tubs alternately. Submerge your entire body in the bath tube with the hot water, for a few tens of seconds; then go to the bath tube with the ice water and do the same. Repeat this procedure several times and finish in the cold water, of course.

If hot water is not available, have the courage sometimes to take a cold shower or a bath in ice-cold water. This may impact your body very beneficially especially when you are tired or have sweated a lot. For many people, this procedure is an efficient method for strengthening the immune system. However, for some people, who almost always feel cold, this may not be the best idea.

Life energy of man, its amount and body energy flow, influence how man feels temperature. Two people of the same body size, in the same place, covered with the same amount of clothes may feel the temperature differently. One of them may feel hot and the other may feel just right or even cold. This mostly depends on the amount of life energy and the energy flow in the body.

METHODS

There are at least as many methods to adapt man to inedia or non-eating as the number of people who have tried or achieved this. Below are somewhat simplified method descriptions which you can consider as frameworks because they will give you intellectual information. Each of these methods can be a separate subject for a book or a seminar.

Non of these methods described below gives you any guaranty to become a non-eater. Below you have merely a list and description of some methods. The best method for you is the one, which you elaborate for yourself and experience it as the efficient one. Following blindly a way of other man, even successful one, may more often bring you down instead of making you successful.

- Natural.
- Spiritual (allowing your Inner Joy to emanate).
- Sudden.
- Forceful.
- 8 Day Process by Ricardo Akahi.
- 10 Day Process by Ray Maor.
- 11 Days Process by Victor Truviano.
- 21 day process by Jasmuheen.
- Hypnotic.
- Alternate.
- Conscious Eating.
- Trying.
- Philosophical-Intellectual (scientific).
- Sun-gazing.
- Alchemical.
- Seven-Week Adaptation (described in a separate chapter).
- Your Own.

NATURAL

The name of this method indicates the direction in which man is going. The final goal on this way is to bring you back to living fully in accordance with nature.
All aspects of your life should be adjusted, however, here I focus only on your eating habits and diet. You can gradually transform your diet through discipline, so that it is in accordance with what nature has given you.

This method can be also called diet refinement.

Man using this method gradually changes their eating habits in order to accomplish inedia or non-eating. The goal of this activity is to attain a diet whereby only food of 'highest vibrations' is consumed.

First of all get rid of microwave oven. Whatever food you process in microwave oven, what you take out is pure death. I guess you do not want to feed your body with death.

Second, the heaviest (referring to the digestion process and so-called vibrations) foods are eliminated from your diet. These are all fried, grilled and smoked food products.

Next foods to be eliminated from the diet are grains and milk, all products made from grains and milk. Some people claim that humans can drink yoghurt and sour milk or buttermilk because they favourably influence the intestine bacterial flora. The fact is that eliminating this food from the diet gives body more benefits. There are many researches about influence of dairy on human body; you can find them to study more. If you are concerned about the bacterial flora, you can drink some sauerkraut juice or pickled cucumber juice made without salt. Test it on your body to find out whether it helps.

The next step eliminates from the diet everything defined as sweets. Chocolates (also the bitter ones), candies, soft drinks and every thing produced with additives of sugar, honey, glucose or fructose and chemical sweeteners. Natural sweeteners, not containing these carbohydrates, (e.g. the plant *stevia rebaudiana*) can still be consumed if you really cannot live without them.

The next step is to eliminate any kind of food processing. At the beginning of the natural method, processing food by frying, grilling or smoking was eliminated. Now you are gradually eliminating all the other food processing methods. You no longer boil or steam your foods.

Look at nature on Earth. In general, washing and parting are the only food processing methods used by almost all known beings on Earth, except man. If you do not believe me, tell me, which creature, apart from man, cooks the food before eating it?

The human body is 100% compatible with nature. Nature's food is 100% ready for consumption. It is perfect, fully compatible with your body; you can not improve it. The only think man can do to food provided by nature is to spoil it.

From chemical point of view, it is a fact that temperature processed food, e.g. cooked egg, boiled milk, is a different substance compared to the raw natural product. The appearance can be the same but chemical analysis indicate a different substance. A kitchen is a small chemical plant, where natural substances are processed into artificial ones which are not normally found in nature. These chemical products are eaten by people.

Giving up all food processing is a big step towards reunification of man with nature. Being a part, a cell of nature, the human body is not fully adapted to the artificially produced substances in the kitchen. This return or reversal to eating only natural food, directly fro nature, causes very beneficial changes. Thanks to such changes man comes back to the bosom of nature, to mother Earth. Nature heals human body and mind.

Most of what is called vegetables and grains are products of genetic experiments made in the past, some of them as far back as tens of thousands years ago. Most vegetables and grains, when they are not cultivated but just left alone, will degenerate, become wild and disappear after some years. This happens because they are not part of nature, so nature eliminates foreign programming.

One of the final steps in the natural method is gradual transformation of the diet to liquids only. Chew any plant or its part till it becomes liquid. Continue chewing this liquid till it changes taste. Then decide whether you want to spit it out or swallow. The taste will indicate whether your body needs it or not.

It is better not to buy juices because they are chemically produced liquids. Their look, taste and chemical composition are quite different from the liquid you produce in your mouth by sufficient chewing. Drinking industrially produced juices would mean going back on your way of the eaten food refinement.

People, who choose this natural method needed anything from a few months to decades to achieve inedia or non-eating. It depended on many factors but mainly on their engagement in the so-called conscious self-development.

First essential comment.
When gradually removing foods from the diet, make sure that you do not

fight against your body. Fighting does hurts, so if you fight against the body, you are hurting it. For example, if you are addicted to fries and eat 3 kg of them a week, you do not have to give them up at once. Instead of fighting, you can use discipline. You can still eat fries but every week eat less by, say, 1%. The body will not notice the 1% change and gradually will become satisfied with the decreasing quantity until finally you will be able to give up eating fries. Instead of linear, you can use gradual logarithmic quantity reductions.

You may think that your body is free of a specific food addiction / craving for, let's say, fries. You will have not eaten them for months, but one day you may be passing by it and notice the smell. Then you may feel saliva coming out, stomach spasm and internal sucking hunger difficult to control. In such a case do not fight against it because it could give your body more benefit if you were to put a small amount of fries into the mouth and chew it thoroughly. If you do not do that, what may happen is that you will dream about fries at night, think about them often and day-dream about eating them, that means you will be suffering unnecessarily.

The body has tremendous ability to adapt its individual functions to changes in diet and other life circumstances.. The body is very flexible regarding this if the changes are made gradually and if allocated time is long enough. The combined effect of small gradual changes, despite them being unnoticeable, can be enormous. For example, a change in living environment from tropical to cold temperature or putting on or losing 120 kg of body weight. Such a significant modification of the diet is a great change for the body. If you do it too fast, you suffer unnecessarily. When you love your body, you give it enough time, as much as the body needs for adapting itself to all the changes without any pain.

Second essential comment.
The described sequence of changes does not need to be strictly followed. Every man is a different universe. What works and is true in one universe, does not have to be so in the other. So you can change the sequence. Your feelings and intuitive guidance are more important than the information contained herein and examples given by other people. I know people, who were following the so-called optimal (Atkins') diet consisting mostly of animal fat. They used a different way to adapt to living without addiction to eating.

Third essential comment.
Use discipline, not force. What is discipline? It is consciously planned and wisely, systematically realized action leading to achievement of the defined

objective. With discipline there is no fight because Love is leading the way. It is more beneficial to be able to distinguish between discipline and fight. Discipline leads to success, fight leads to injury.

Following the natural method, pay attention to the body. For some people this method is or may be harmful. The body suffers, becomes weaker, falls ill and ages faster. Those people force the body to follow a specific diet, so they hurt it in the process. You can easily recognize them by extremities blue from cold, emaciated body, low level of life energy as well as sadness, depression and fanaticism about eating.

SPIRITUAL

All of the matter, including your body, is an image or picture in your mind. Whatever was built in the matter, was first created in the mind. If non-eating starts to exist in your mind, then your body will manifest this state.

When following the spiritual method of adapting to inedia or non-eating, the main goal of your work is to sufficiently expand the Consciousness sphere in which you live. You know that non-eating is one of expected results of your conscious self-development. If non-eating becomes real enough in your mind, the body will manifest it.

Some people choose to stay in seclusion in propitious environment, some prefer the company of the closest family members and others lock themselves in a contemplation monastery. Some people choose a competent guru and follow their recommendations to the letter, some are guided by the "Higher I", angels, masters, guardians or other non material beings, yet others trust only themselves.

It is less important with whom, where and how, or which path you are following. What is more essential for the follower is that the Consciousness sphere is expanding, giving results which the practising man expect.

This is how the spiritual method of adapting man for inedia or non-eating can be summarized. With the growth in conscious self-development, man's diet and desire to eat are changing. Man is gradually moving to eating foods with so-called higher vibrations which cause less strain on the body. Man's daily body requirement for food is diminishing, until it ceases one day.

Man may feel that they live by the power of IAM, God, Holy Spirit, All-reigning Principle, Universal Mind, Highest Energy, Internal Power, grace of Allah, Brahma etc. You can mention many other names here, which nonetheless are not understandable by the intellect, because the comprehension is possible only through experiencing it.

The most important thing in this method is the exercise described above, focusing on your Inner Joy. **Allow your Inner Joy to emanate freely so that you can feel Love and see Light**. Once you achieve this state, fully activate the emanation, your body will not ask for food or drink.
In fact, this is the most powerful exercise in this entire book.

If you decide to use the spiritual method for adapting yourself to inedia or non-eating, you know that you will focus mainly on your conscious self-development. Although one of your goals will be to free yourself from the strongest material attachment (food), you know that it will come as a by-product of your conscious self-development. Therefore you will stay focused on your holistic growth.

SUDDEN

Actually, I it is not a method because inedia or non-eating happens suddenly and unexpectedly. That is kind of an occurrence which falls on man. Inedia or non-eating happens suddenly. However, knowing in what circumstances such sudden occurrence of non-eating appears, man can behave in a way which will invoke such a change. So talking about a method in this case refers to the circumstances of its appearance.

Most often it happens like this. One day the body suddenly refuses to accept all foods, which often surprises man very much. The refusal can be so strong that man feels inexplicable abomination for eating. Man feels nausea when looking at food and even vomit after eating regardless of food type.

The sudden inedia or non-eating most often happens among people following so-called spiritual way of life. The body of man deeply immersed in praying, contemplation and God worshipping has completely forgotten that it "has to eat".

Studying biographies of saints, regardless of religion, you can find stories describing periods of inedia or non-eating which suddenly and unexpectedly happened to those people. Some of them had not put anything in their mouths for many years. There were also "saints" who had not accepted any meals until the end of their life.

In present times, when the spirituality, that is the way of conscious self-development is spreading fast among Earth inhabitants, the sudden and unexpected rejection of food by the body happens more and more often among people living outside of monasteries, hermitages or shrines. Among so-called normal, ordinary people inedia happens much more often to those deeply engaged in creative work. It can be, for example, activity in the field of art. A painter or a sculptor can be so deeply immersed in creating a masterpiece, that they may forget about the world. During the day and night they will be completely taken by thinking of it and creating it. All their mental energy will be directed solely to the masterpiece. A musician or an inventor working on realization of their idea can behave in the same way. Not only will they eat nothing but they can also stay awake almost all the time for weeks, bursting with energy.

Do you remember the most sublime moments of love in your life? Do you remember that at that time not only you forgot about eating but you did not feel any hunger either? That was because love was feeding you. Indeed, when man lives in love, then Love is manifested. Love means that Life is created. When man allows Love to sufficiently manifests itself through their mind and body, then their body does not need anything else.

In some cases of the sudden food rejection there is no unpleasant body reaction as described above. Instead, man simply loses any interest in food, they feel no hunger, and has no appetite. Such state extends in time for weeks, months or even years.

There is a conclusion from all of the above. The more you focus on your spiritual side, the bigger is the chance to loosen the connection with food. The more you immerse in spiritual practices, the easier it will be for you to give up eating. However, it is more beneficial if you do not force the body.

After some time, it may happen in case of every man whose body has suddenly rejected eating, hunger may reappear. The appearance of the hunger can be as sudden as its disappearance previously. Then man starts to eat normally again.

The sudden method (occurrence) can be easily distinguished from anorexia, which cause lies in the psyche of the ill man. One of obvious symptoms of anorexia is emaciation of the body. When the sudden rejection of food happens naturally, the body continues to function well and does not lose weight if it did not have superfluous fat reserves.

FORCEFUL

As the name of the method suggests, in this case man would pursue the goal of inedia or non-eating by forcing the body not to eat. Some people are impatient or they just do not like methods, they prefer short cuts in order to have the results immediately. One of the things that characterizes people of this type is their strong will concerning any task they undertake. Having decided something, they do not pay much attention to circumstances, they just push ahead. Such behaviour can help achieve the desired goal also in case when they are pursuing non-eating.

The forceful method is quite simple to implement and it does not require any preparation. Even now as you are reading this book, you can decide to give up food for ever. "From now I am a non-eater" – having stated it in this way, you only need to implement this decision in you daily life.

Man who decides like that believes or knows that simply by making such a decision and following it, it would be enough to become a non-eater. Practically in most cases it means forcing the body to not consume any food. This makes man hungry. If man does not eat while feeling hunger, man is fasting.

This method for achieving inedia or non-eating is rarely successful. Having fasted for some time, man has to start to eat again, otherwise, if man is stubborn and fights against the body, man dies. If man starts eating again when it is not too late , the fasting will be beneficial for the body. Fasting may heal people who are officially considered incurable.

While fasting, the body loses weight. When the weight lose continues beyond the proper body weight, emaciation occurs. The body weight is still decreasing, man easily becomes exhausted, has little strength most of the time, is not happy and the body more and more looks like a skeleton covered with skin.

Not every man, who without any preparation suddenly decides to give up eating for ever, uses the forceful method. If the Consciousness sphere in which man lives, is large enough, giving up eating is simply a confirmation that man possesses the ability to live without food. In such a case man's body will adapt itself for living without eating in a relatively short time.

There are also people who know that they can live without eating, though in every-day life they eat normally. For them, giving up eating at any moment is a matter of a simple decision. The body will adapt itself quickly and will function well.

Let me make it clear, that none of the following "processes" described below, will make you an inediate or non-eater. It is not a process, design and commercially sold by other people, that turns you into an inediate or a non-eater.

In fact, as my experience proves, people blindly following such a "process" often harm their body. Although at the beginning they may feel improvements in their endeavours, later they had to return to eating or they will emaciate their body.

Just be aware that you are the Master Creator of our life, not a process sold to you by others. Of course, you can experience on yourself any of these processes, to check out how your body and psyche will react, and to make friends with other participants. However, think reasonable and do not hold too much hope because you may become disappointed.

8 DAY PROCESS BY RICARDO AKAHI

At the time of the publication of this book, this 8 day process is well presented on the Internet. You can receive information directly from the author of this process. You can check out Akahi's business web site: ricardoakahi.com .

10 DAY PROCESS BY RAY MAOR

At the time of the publication of this book, this 10 day process is well presented on the Internet. You can receive information directly from the author of this process. You can check out the Ray's business web site: raymaor.com .

11 DAY PROCESS BY VICTOR TRUVIANO

At the time of the publication of this book, this 11 day process is well presented on the Internet. You can receive information directly from the author of this process. You can check out the Victor's business web site: victortruviano.com .

THE 21 DAY PROCESS

Warning. Please, do not do the 21 day process unless you have thoroughly read and deeply considered the original description of the method, because if you have not, you may endanger your life. The description below is not enough to do it safely. I have included it here only for information purpose although Jasmuheen asked me to delete it (for safety reason).

A detailed description of "The 21 day procedure" by Charmaine Harley can be found in the book "Prana Nourishment - Living on Light" written by Jasmuheen, an Australian who is fed by prana and promotes the "Divine Nutrition" program in order to eliminate world health and hunger issues. Up till now this has been the most widely known method to those interested in the subject. Jasmuheen had been promoting the 21 day process around the end of the 20th century. Later on she introduced a simpler and safer long term method in her third book on this topic, "The Food of Gods".

The 21 day process is divided in three parts of seven days each. In the first week man does not eat nor drink, as is the case in dry fasting. It can be dangerous for the body if man is not ready. Apart from the fear, the main concern is that the body may become too dehydrated, which results in irreversible changes causing death.

In the second week man can drink water and 25% orange juice (3 parts of water + 1 part of juice). In the third week, besides water, man can drink 50% orange juice.
The amount of the consumed liquids depends on how thirsty man is and on other factors, though it is said that 1,5 litre a day is the minimum. People going through the process also drink other juices.

It is advisable to do the process in solitude and far from the civilization. In ideal conditions a friend should visit briefly every day, just in case. During that time physical and psychological cleansing will be occurring. Television, noise, troubles, daily occupation routine, computer etc. should not be available for man going through the process. The main point is to focus on your own spiritual sphere and on the psychological side of the process.

I have concluded from my observations of people interested in living without food, that most of them consider the 21 day process to be a kind of holy or magical initiation leading man to become a non-eater. None of the individuals known to me who had undergone the 21 day process became an inediate or non-eater as a result of it. However, I know some people who discovered, due to the 21 day process, that they could live without food.

It is a fact that the 21 day process does not turn man into a breatharian. Technically speaking, it is a dry fasting for 7 days followed by a juice diet of 14 days. It is quite an efficient method of cleansing the body and psyche from toxins. Dedicating this time to spiritual matters, to your own spiritual world, cleanses you more efficiently, as happens in other fasting practices.

The 21 day process will not make man an inediate if man is not prepared, that is, their sphere of the Consciousness is not expanded enough. Such man will be able to live without or almost without food for some time forcing the body not to eat – my observations confirm this phenomenon.

It can be a very different experience to go through the 21 day process as many individual accounts describe. Some people feel nothing, they go on living as before with the exception of eating. Others are so deeply engaged that it becomes the biggest spiritual change in their life. Some people start to contact with immaterial beings during that time. Every man is different, so going through the same experience is perceived differently.

HYPNOTIC

Hypnosis is a tool for making changes in programs of the instinct. Some programs of the instinct define and realize associations between the human physical body, the psyche and the external matter known as food. In case of an average Earth inhabitant, these programs cause the biological need for eating. Some specific substances, defined as nutrients, need to be provided for the body, in right quantity and at the right time, so that the body can function properly.

Programs of the instinct can be modified or deleted. The main goal of man aspiring to inedia or non-eating is to apply changes in the programs of the instinct, which can be described in the following sentence: The body works properly regardless of whether anything is eaten or not.

An experienced hypnotist, using individually selected set of suggestions, can modify programs in the instinct, which are responsible for the relation between food and the body. In this case the effectiveness depends on how man responds to hypnotic suggestions.

This method for achieving non-eating is risky and not fully researched. The main concern is that harmful suggestions may appear and be accepted by the instinct. During the hypnotic session the instinct can absorb suggestions like a dry sponge absorbs water. Every single suggestion may make a significant change in functions of the instinct.

It is worth remembering that not only words of the hypnotist make the suggestion. Also the hypnotist's behaviour, their emotions, aspect of the environment, sounds incoming from outside and other factors may constitute a suggestion causing unintended changes with good or bad consequences. You never know in advance.

For this reason and in order not to cause any undesirable changes in the psyche, I do not recommend this method. Rapidly introduced changes in the instinct, by using hypnoses, cause changes in man's life, which may bring suffering. Visualization is a much better method for making changes in your instinct.

It is worthwhile to know the hypnotic method for adaptation to inedia or non-eating and use it in life-threatening situations, which maybe caused by too long period without food. Such situations occur when people are cut off from the food source for a long time; for example a group of people lost in mountains, long period shortage of food during a war or large-scale natural disaster. Then the least harmful approach is chosen; it is better to hypnotize man, so that they do not feel hunger, instead of letting man think about starving to death.

ALTERNATE

Before you start eating alternately, reduce the number of meals per day. For example, if you eat five times a day, decrease it to four times. Later on, having got used to four meals a day, reduce them to three. Continue this procedure until you have just one meal per day and feel satisfied with it.

The next thing you introduce is eating only once every two days. Today you eat, tomorrow you fast, the day after tomorrow you eat, and the next day you have no meal again. The eating frequency is: M F M F M F and so on (M - day with one meal, F - day of fasting). After some time this eating frequency will become normal for you and you will feel fine with it. You will feel hungry only every other day.

The next step is to have only one meal in three days. Today you eat, tomorrow and the day after tomorrow you fast. The eating frequency is: M F F M F F M F F and so on. When this becomes so routine that you do it automatically, introduce one more day of fasting. So, now you eat only once in four days: M F F F M F F F M F F F, and so on.

Notice that on the eating day you should eat no more than the quantity you regularly consumed when you were eating normally. So once in four days you eat no more than you ate in one day when you were still eating normally. Do not eat four times more.

Following this procedure, you arrive at eating one meal only once a week, and further on even less often, e.g. twice a month. Remember that long chewing and mixing with the saliva are extremely important. Do not harm the digestive system by suddenly eating rapidly, too much or something too heavy for digestion.

When you are eating only a few times per month, it may happen that you forget about the day in which you planned to have a meal. You may omit it if you do not feel hunger, which will make for two or more fasts without a break. If from the beginning you call this kind of fasting non-eating, you may say that you are prolonging the non-eating periods.

Be careful when practising this alternate method because it may change to starvation. For the unprepared, the extended fasting can cause emaciation and other harmful results. When you notice that your body is starving, shorten the fasting periods, change the method and work more on expanding the sphere of Consciousness in which you live in. Mainly, focus more on allowing your Inner Joy to emanate.

TRYING

You may decide to start inedia or non-eating at any time, to just try whether it works for you. This decision may be, but does not have to be, preceded by preparation. Once you start, watch and feel what is happening with your mind and the body. As long as everything goes fine, you can consider yourself a non-eater. However, if symptoms indicating inability to live without food appear, you need to return to eating. If you continue, that will be forcing the body not to eat, so that will be fasting or starvation.

Return to eating. Rebuild and strengthen your body. When you feel that your body is in perfect state again, you can try non-eating again. This time you have made more research, prepared yourself better by doing mind and physical exercises.

You start again. This is your second try when you give up eating in order to adapt yourself to non-eating. The same thing may happen this time that after a period of non-eating / fasting, you discover that the body is starving. Go back to food in order to rebuild the body again. You have more experience now, you have learnt more. You can do more research, work out a better method for yourself and try later.

You can try like that many times. Every time you try, you may be able to stay without food for a longer time, without harming the body. After every try you will have more experience and will be able to work out more efficient method for ourself. Then, it is possible that in future you will succeed.

PHILOSOPHICAL-INTELLECTUAL

In applying this method, which could also be called 'scientific', you look for information and do theoretical studies, then you follow with practice. Therefore, I would rather consider it an addition to other methods. Man interested in the subject of inedia and non-eating would look for all available information in literature, on the Internet and participate in seminars, talk to non-eaters, and look for scientific research papers, etc.

In this method the subject of inedia or non-eating is considered more like a scientific research and philosophical discussion topic, with the final goal to bring practical result.

The main goal of this philosophical and scientific activity is to attain full intellectual understanding supported by evidence that man can live without eating. The second goal is to compile the most appropriate methods of adapting man to living without food.

For man using the philosophical-intellectual method, the analysis of facts and doing research is more important than the intuitive feeling. According to my observations, fasting and realization of inedia or non-eating is very difficult for these people. I have noticed that this purely intellectual approach is a serious obstacle for inedia or non-eating researchers.

Even so, I believe that in the future, using so-called pure scientific methods, man might be able to submit themselves to a surgery or drug treatment in order to become free from food addiction. Specialists in sciences like genetics, neurology, informatics, quantum physics etc. have been working on this subject for a long time; unofficially, of course.

SUN-GAZING

Sun-gazing has been known and practised for thousands of years, mainly in places where sun rising from behind the horizon can be seen daily.
In this method you gaze at the sun while standing or walking barefoot on the ground. This practice heals both the body and psyche. After sufficient practice, sun-gazing keeps man in the state of perfect health, good mood and high level of life energy. The healing factors are the energies of the sun and Earth.

The freedom from eating appears later as one of the by-products of high energy level being felt by man. This happens to almost all sun-gazing adepts, even those who do not believe it. Noticeable decrease in appetite usually appears after about seven months but it can happen after only three months of constant practice.

One of the first people who made this method widely known again in present time is *Hira Ratan Manek* from India. On his web site solarhealing.com *Hira* describes sun-gazing procedure. There is also a number of discussion forums about sun-gazing.

Here is a short description of the HRM sun-gazing method. Every morning at sunrise, you should gaze at the sun's centre. Stand barefoot on the ground. On the first day, start with 10 seconds maximum. On each following day gaze for 10 seconds longer than in the previous day. In this way, if you gaze at the sun every day, you will reach 5 minutes after the first month, and 44 minutes after 9 months. This is the allowed maximum. Do not gaze any longer.

The second important activity with his method is walking barefoot on the ground for at least 45 minutes daily, every day, even if you do not gaze at the sun.

Altogether, if you gaze at the sun every day, the whole process takes about 9 months to accomplish. After that you do not need to gaze at the sun every day. It is even recommended that you do not. You can do it from time to time to maintain a sufficiently high level of energy. How long and how often you gaze depends on your needs, the climate and life style. Barefoot walking is still recommended every day.

If you live in a place where sunrise and sunset cannot be seen every day, the whole process may take longer. If you missed sun-gazing for a few days, do not extend the time at the next session. If you had a long break (say, a few weeks), shorten the next gazing time.

It is very important for eye protection to finish the gazing not later than one hour after sunrise and start the gazing not earlier than one hour before sunset. It also means that one should not gaze at the sun during the day, especially not in the midday.

I hope that this warning is clear: **Forcing the eyes to gaze at the sun at any other time, except sunrise or sunset, can cause damage to the retina of the eye!** Too long period of gazing without preceding gradual adaptation may burn this delicate part of the eye. Because of the burns, if man is able to see at all, everything may look like an image with holes or spots. Such damage to the retina is considered incurable by the official medicine.

Another man, who promotes information about the beneficial influence of sun-gazing, is yogi Sunyogi Umasankar who "has discovered a method of absorbing energy directly from the sun, removing the need to eat, drink or sleep". Thanks to these abilities Umasankar walked 62000 km in India, without money, teaching his method to people.

According to his teaching, the first sun-gazing is started at the moment of sunrise or sunset. First it should be done for a short time, later the time of gazing is gradually extended. If gazing directly at the sun dazzles the eyes, one can look a little above it. It is very important to practise regularly.

By the way, here is important information regarding one of the biggest mistakes made by people; the use of sunglasses. There are situations when protecting the eyes with dark glasses is recommended because the eyes are dazzled by too much light. If you have not exercised sun-gazing, such situations would include, among others, electric welding, walking on snow in the mountains when the sun is shining, or on the beach, or long driving periods facing the sun.

Using sunglasses during sunny days usually increases the deficit of life energy. Getting sun rays into the eyes is an essential part of natural processes required for proper operation of the man's psyche and body. This mainly relates to the function of the skin, pineal and pituitary glands. Many so-called chronic diseases disappear when an ill man stops using sunglasses and allows sun rays to fall on their skin.

It is worth to remember that the sun is the father that gives life to all the planets in this solar system. How does a child feel and develop if the contact with their parent is limited?

ALCHEMICAL

This is the most efficient method of all known to me that makes use of chemical substances. In this case the non-eating comes along as one of the side-effects caused by strong activation of the body light/energy system. Those substances have been used for thousands of years. They are known under different names, e.g. manna, philosophical stone, Holy Grail, vibuthi, white powder of gold, orme, ormus. Most often, they are in the form of a powder. It can be a clean chemical element or a mixture of some of these: gold, rhodium, ruthenium, silver, copper and mercury, but not in the form of metals. For example, the non-metal form of gold looks like glass, and the powder is white. If you search the Internet, you may find much more information about these substances, if you use the words mentioned above.

Descriptions of a mysterious substance that has powers of healing body and restoring life are often done in a symbolic language and can be found, among others, in the Bible, Vedas, Koran, Egyptian scripts and alchemical books. This substance is given to only those people who are well prepared by a long process of mental/spiritual studies and practices. Apparently, when eaten by unprepared man, it can cause madness or death.

Here is a description of one of possible procedures. A well prepared man first cleanses their body by fasting for nine days. From day ten, man takes a powder or liquid of precisely determined composition which will depend on the planned end result. The powder is eaten every day, for a month or so depending on the substance and its composition. After forty days the body does not need any food. If the body still requires food, the amounts are decreasingly small until after a few months nothing at all is required because man does not feel any hunger.

Some spiritual exercises done during that time, intensely activate the light/energy system, and consequently, the nerves and the glands too. The powder and the exercises also cause rapid increase in brain activity especially of the pineal and the pituitary glands. It all causes a lot of changes in man including but not limited to their perception of the world, power of understanding and communication, skills and so forth.

For most people, in other words for the non-prepared people, the alchemical method is like a one way journey. Reversing such big activation of the light/energy system is almost impossible. Theoretically, before the reversion is finished, man would have died because of madness, mental illness. Serious suffering would be caused by too big intensification of the non-material senses. Man receives a lot of information. What man sees and feels can be partly compared to the mental state after taking some drugs, but it is still quite different. One of more interesting things is that thoughts of man materialize themselves much easier than is the case with 'normal' man. As a consequence, images based on man's fear create situations that are dangerous.

Starting from 1995, David Hudson talked in his public lectures about some powders discovered by him. The attributes of his powders met the definition of the mysterious substances used by alchemists. Research made by him and by others confirmed some extraordinary attributes and effects that these substances can produce on the man's mind and body.

You can buy White Powder of Gold, ORME, etc, on the Internet. People and even companies are selling them. However, I suggest you do not eat them unless you really know what is the content. Some of them may contain heavy metals, so they may poison human body.

CONSCIOUS EATING

The conscious eating (CE) method is one of the most efficient ways for people aspiring to non-eating. CE gives your body exactly what it needs in right quantity and at the right time.

The most important action in CE is to feel your body and psyche reactions. This is the key of CE, all the time **stay focused on feeling** the reactions of your body and psyche. Do **not** focus on food that you are going to consume.

Here it is how to do CE step by step.
Let us assume that you feel hungry.

1. Stop for a while, relax your body and psyche and ask yourself: "What is this?". Now, **feel** the answer, do **not** think about the reason. The more feeling there is and the less intellectual activity occurs, the more efficiently you will understand your body language. So feel the answer, do not think about it.
   It is quite possible that at this point the hunger will vanish and ... well, this is the end of CE this time.
   Another possibility is that a past memory or emotion will appear.

Blocked emotions, denied feelings, forgotten situations, etc., when they are pushed out by the instinct, they first are felt as hunger. This is done by the self-defence mechanism of the instinct. This mechanism sends harmful data and programs to the intellect for solutions. When this mechanism is initiated, man feels hunger first. That is why, when you feel hunger, do not blindly go for food. Instead, stop for a while, relax and feel the body and psyche reactions. If you did not wait and focus on the reactions of your body and psyche, but just went to eating, you would stop that self-defence mechanism. The harmful program would remain in your instinct.

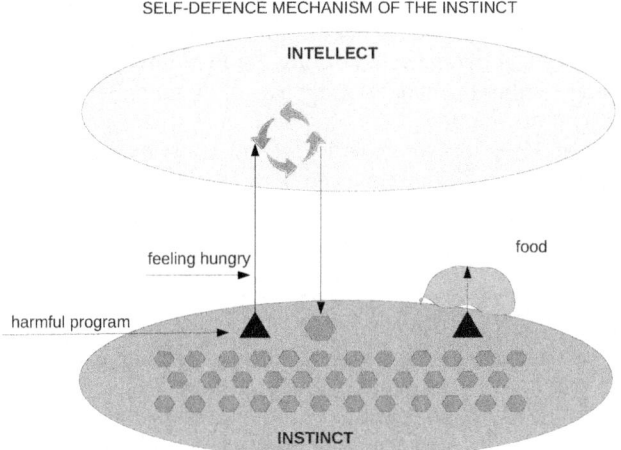

SELF-DEFENCE MECHANISM OF THE INSTINCT

2. Do you still feel hungry? There was no past memory, no feeling, no emotion but the hunger remains. Go to the next step. Ask, "What do you want to eat?" Then scan through a list of different foods and feel what food is most appealing to you. Having found it, imagine for several seconds, that you eat it. Imagine feeling it in your mouth and stomach. Ask yourself again: "What is this?" and feel the answer. If the hunger vanishes, you can stop here. Also at this moment some pictures or significant thoughts may emerge to help you understand yourself more. Immerse yourself in them, let them fully pass through you, feel them all over the psyche and body, so that you understand better what they are all about. After they are gone, they will never make you hungry again.
3. If the body really needs food, the hunger you feel will not vanish at this point, so continue the procedure of CE.
Approach food that your body wants to eat. Do it consciously, feel your

body and psyche reactions all the time. Stay focused on the feeling while you are approaching the food, approaching your hand to take it, looking at it, smelling it, biting it, slowly chewing it and swallowing. Feel your body and psyche reactions all the time. Do not pay attention to the food.

Keep this question, "What is this?", in your mind. The answer can appear at any moment. Also the hunger can disappear at any moment. If nothing happens, proceed to the next step.

4. You are now sitting in front of the food that you feel hungry for because your body needs it. Slowly take a piece, all the time observing yourself by feeling your every slightest movement and body reactions. Bring a piece of the food to your nose and smell it. Delight yourself in the smell and keep your feelings open for the answer to the question: "What is this?". You need to feel it, not to find the answer by thinking. Again, the same may happen; either the hunger disappears or emotion, image, past memory appear. If not, continue.
5. Now bite the food. Keep it in the mouth and immerse yourself into feeling it. Feel the whole intellect, psyche and body reactions. FEEL, FEEL and FEEL, observe and do not think.
6. Next, very important, chew it for a long time, never less than two minutes; the longer the better, even a few hours in extreme cases. Usually three to six minutes is enough. Swallow **only** after it has changed to liquid and changed the taste. Remember, the food you are chewing will change taste once or more. Never swallow it before the taste has changed, else it will not be conscious eating procedure.

FEEL, FEEL and FEEL, observe and do not think. While chewing, you may start to feel disgusting taste and will not want to swallow it, then spit it out.
7. Proceed this way with every bite until you feel that you are full. By doing this you are making sure that you satisfy the real body need.

With CE you are all the time making yourself conscious of the process that you are going through. The process starts by feeling hunger or thirst. As you proceed with CE, you discover what it actually is. If it is not the real body need, you will not force the body to eat what it does not need. The best care for the body is to give it what it needs, when it needs and in the right amount.

With CE you are becoming a non-eater consciously, without fighting or misunderstanding, without making many mistakes. You are discovering the real relation between your body, external matter and your psyche. When food finally stops playing its role in this relation, it will naturally becomes useless and will drop off you as an unnecessary part of this game called life on Earth.

Conscious eating, conscious sleeping, conscious talking, conscious ... whatever it is, makes you ... more conscious and allows you to expand the sphere of the Consciousness in which you live. When you expand it sufficiently, you will have no more questions because you will really know.
Then, to become an inediate, to live without breathing, without being influenced by temperature, etc. will only be a matter of your decision.

FOLLOWING A DIET

Remember this.
Whenever you fallow a diet, whatsoever it is, you harm your body, for sure. Choosing food based on a diet, means that you listen to your beliefs related to eating and food, not to the real needs of your body.
Instead of following a diet, follow the real needs of your body.

DIET FANATICS
Some people are so limited by their belief related to diet, that they are ready to defend their belief and even fight to death for it.
Then they judge all the others who do not share their diet belief, bad people. Well, it is not your diet that makes you good or bad man. It is only your judgement that makes your create, in your imagination, bad or good man. Judgement is based on fear. Fear is based on belief. Belief = lack of knowledge.

YOUR OWN

Every man is in a different universe. So how to work up a method that would be right for every man? Do you believe that someone can do the work for you?

For you the most important method is your own one. It may or may not contain the elements from all the above described methods. You work out your own method using all information you have collected and everything you have experienced concerning this matter.

Some people like to be systematic, slow working and patient; others prefer to achieve the results immediately, even using force; and still others use the middle way. Some people prefer to concentrate on the spiritual side; others 'must' have proof because for them everything 'must' be logical; the rest combine the heart with the mind.

Having information about many different methods of adapting people to living without food, you may produce your own method. As an example, this method may contain diet refinement (natural). At the same time you spend more time on mind exercises (spiritual). You notice by a chance that you can easily get by with eating every second day (alternate). You also decide to eat more consciously in order to give the body the exact substances, at the right time and quantity (CE). You also research, meditate on the matter, take part in meetings and discussion groups, read a lot etc. (philosophical-intellectual). Additionally, you regularly gaze at the sun and walk barefoot on the ground (sun-gazing). When fasting, you take white powder of gold (alchemical).

While practising more and more, at any moment you may feel that not everything in your own method works as it should, as planned. In such case you just change the method. Make a different one, also your own. The method you have created does not need to be unchangeable. What is the most important in this is that you, while experiencing, move on the way to the goal.

I have described some methods for man to use when pursuing to living without food. Let me emphasize again that every man is a different universe and has their own path. Your way to inedia is different, compared to other people. Instead of following someone else, you can work out your own method using:
- information available in my publications or that of others;
- information that people share on the Internet forums about their experiences;
- biography books of so-called saints and immortals;
- advices found in films, interviews with inediates, non-eaters and those who fast;
- a modified version of the seven-weeks adaptation described below.

ADAPTATION IN SEVEN WEEKS

The term bì-gǔ is commonly known in China. Literally bì means to avoid, gǔ means grain, food. These days bì-gǔ is understood as inedia, non-eating, fasting or the rare eating of minimal amounts.

In China, when I was talking with people who were interested in *bì-gǔ*,

I noticed that the idea itself was well known there. The people did not find it extraordinary that someone was fasting. There was a large amount of interest in this topic but there was little known about it among the people. There was very little information on the topic of adapting to living without food.

When speaking with the people interested in bì-gǔ, I was asked to describe 'my method' of achieving inedia, in detail. Those who spoke with me had read "Life Style Without Food", in which I described various possible methods for preparing the body to live without food. In that book, I emphasised that there was no universal method because every man has their own way to reach inedia.
Nevertheless, they still encouraged me to describe a method which may guide man to inedia or non-eating.

On the one hand, I know and emphasise that every man is different, hence one efficient method of adaptation to inedia that is good for all people does not exist. On the other hand, I see sincere efforts made by people aspiring to inedia or non-eating who are searching for methods to achiever that goal.

Below I described a method for adapting the body to non-eating or even inedia. You can modify this method for several reasons. First, it is not perfect. Second, your circumstances of living change. Third, you feel what suits you and what does not.

It is possible that fulfilling all the requirements and conditions described below, regarding the adaptation of the body to non-eating, will not be possible for you. You do not need to worry about that. Fulfil all requirements, that you can on a practical level. Provide yourself with the best conditions for the adaptation that you are able. Go through the preparation as efficiently as you can. In other words, do what you can, in the best way you can and do not worry about the rest.

Either way, the most important thing ought to happen in your mind. Talking theoretically, you can become an inediate solely through your decision, without any preparation or adaptation. In practice, you can never tell, for every man is a different world. Everyone has their own way which differs from all other ways.

The more conscious you are about what you truly are, the less you need from the material world and the less you will search in matter because you know that matter is a picture in your mind. If you feel that you do not know enough yet, read farther about the seven-week adaptation. However, be aware of the fact that this is information only.

SEVEN-WEEK ADAPTATION

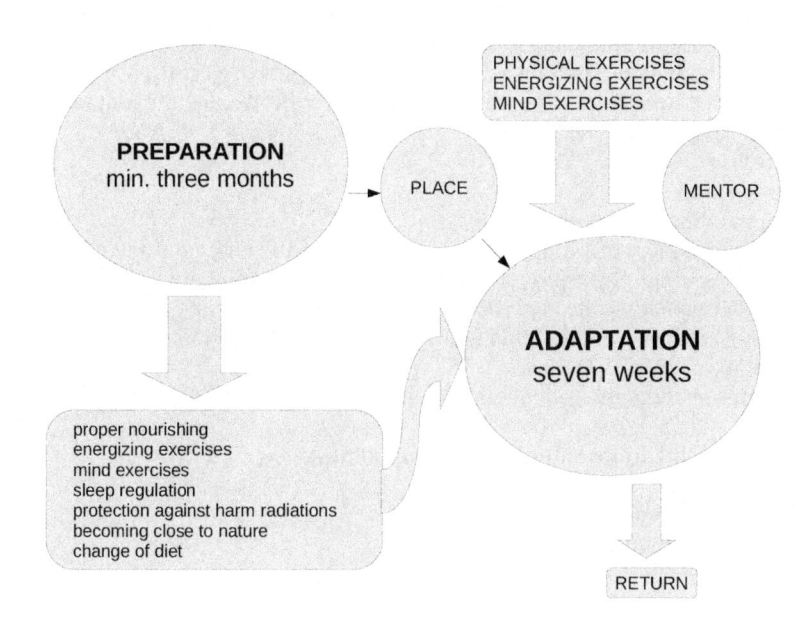

```
                          PHYSICAL EXERCISES
                          ENERGIZING EXERCISES
                          MIND EXERCISES

   ┌─────────────┐
   │ PREPARATION │ ──→ PLACE            MENTOR
   │min. three   │
   │   months    │
   └─────────────┘
          │              ┌──────────────┐
          │              │  ADAPTATION  │
          ↓              │ seven weeks  │
   proper nourishing     └──────────────┘
   energizing exercises          │
   mind exercises                ↓
   sleep regulation           RETURN
   protection against harm radiations
   becoming close to nature
   change of diet
```

I have decided to describe in detail about a series of actions which can be performed by man in aspiring to adapt the body for living without food.

Allow me to point out that this is a way for those people who are sensible enough to stop when they conclude that this way is too difficult for them, so that they do not harm the body. If you decide to follow the seven-week adaptation, you are taking responsibility for yourself.

I advise you to undertake this course of action only if you have had sufficient practice in fasting. In my opinion, sufficient practice means that you have fasted at least three times, each time for three weeks, with a minimum pause of three months between every fasting.
Have you gone through this fasting with ease? After three weeks, were you feeling well? Then, did you feel that you could fast longer to experience even more benefits for the body and the mind?
If your answers are positive, you may have the potential for longer periods of non-eating.

It is necessary to meet specific conditions related to your health. The seven-week adaptation or fasting should not be attempted if you have the following physical or mental conditions:
- a pacemaker implant or device that assists with the functioning of vital organs or substitute them;
- a body with an organ transplanted (long fasting may reject it);
- a cases in which one has to take a medicine for decreasing the immunological resistance;
- obesity;
- emaciation;
- mental illness;
- a serious illness resulting in a very low level of life energy of the patient;
- an illness requiring constant care, dialyse, surgery or other treatment, without which serious deterioration of health could occur;
- a drug addiction or addiction to using electronic devices like a phone, computer, TV, DVD player;
- serious uncertainty or doubts about success with this adaptation.

In addition, the following people should not fast:
- miners;
- pregnant women;
- breastfeeding women;
- people who perform heavy physical work;
- prisoners
- soldiers on duty.

I suggest that before you decide, it would be wise to go to a dietitian who has sufficient knowledge about healing people with fasting. Ask this doctor to fully examine you and give his consent, allowing you to fast for a long period of time.

PREPARATION

Before you start the seven-week adaptation, it is necessary to prepare the body and mind. Starting without any preparation significantly lowers the chances to achieve the expected result.

The preparation itself should not be shorter than three months in length. When the preparation lasts longer, for example, a half year or even a year, it is more of an advantages. There is no reason to haste. Many changes must be done in the body, in the nerve system and in the flow of energy.

During the preparation, man focuses mainly on:
1. Proper nourishment.
2. Energizing exercises.
3. Mind exercises.
4. Sleep regulation.
5. Protection against harm radiations.
6. Getting close to nature.
7. Change of diet.

1. PROPER NOURISHMENT

An entire chapter is written about this topic, later in this book. The reason to introduce proper nourishment is to bring the body to full function and health according to the rules of nature. Man's body is part of nature; therefore it is fully subject to nature's rules. When you align your body with nature's rules, you maintain it in perfect shape.

Absorb the information contained in the chapter "principles of proper nourishment", even if you do not intend to adapt your body for living without food. Nourishment in accordance with these principles, impacts health positively and extends the life of the body.

2. ENERGIZING EXERCISES.

I suggest that you learn this type of exercises well. I have described some of them. It is worthwhile to perform them at least once a day, the most favourable time is early morning. Make it your habit. Later, during the seven-week adaptation, energizing exercises will be one of the most necessary tools. Without energizing exercises, the continuation of the adaptation may become impossible.

3. MIND EXERCISES

Previously, you have read about the three mind exercises: the contemplation of passiveness, allowing your Inner Joy to emanate and visualization. These three specific exercises constitute the most important tools of the entire seven week adaptation. They are the kernel, while all the rest are supplements facilitating the adaptation. This is the reason why I suggest that you focus on developing the habit of doing these mind exercises both properly and regularly.

You probably recall what I often say that inedia and non-eating are by-products of expanding the sphere of the Consciousness that man lives in. Therefore, the goal is the expansion of this sphere, that is why the mind exercises constitute the kernel for the adaptation to inedia and non-eating.

LOOSENING EXERCISES

It is worthwhile to learn how to loosen your entire physical body because the level of physical body looseness can have significant impact on the efficiency of mind exercises.
Also, it is worth to make this type of exercises prior to falling asleep so that the body sleeps with loosen muscles. Thanks to this, the body's physical rest will be at the maximum. Sleeping with unconsciously tightened muscles causes illness. Man can alleviate this by relaxing the muscles.

Many people do not sense that their muscles are tight and not relaxed. Check it on yourself now and later a few times during the day. Are muscles of your jaws, neck, and shoulders fully loosen or are you tightening them unintentionally?

There are many descriptions of relaxation exercises found in the literature. S*awasana* (also written *shaw... shav... sav...*) which is derived from yoga, is one of the most popular relaxation exercises. You can easily find instructions about how to do it. Here is an example short instruction.

Lie outstretched on your back on a flat surface with your feet 30 to 60 cm apart and hands 10 to 30 cm away from your body.
Loosen the entire body. Take a few deep breaths to further relax your body. Next, subsequently scan your body observing if there is any remaining tensions to release. You can begin from the top of the head. Feel the top of your head and release any possible tension in that place. Next move your attention to the sides of the head, ears and the back of the head. Remove all the tensions subsequently.
Continue in this manner on your face, from the forehead to chin. Notice any stretched muscles of the eye globes, tightened jaws or other muscles of the face, and consciously loosen them.
Then focus on the front and back of your neck. When you feel any tension, release it by loosening the muscle.
Continue relaxing muscles in this manner, from the shoulders to the fingers, then from the shoulders, across the chest and the abdomen. Do the same for

the muscles of the back, going from the top down to your buttock. Continue like that, loosening the muscles and removing even the slightest tensions, until you reach the toes.
Next, do the releasing of the tensions starting from the toes, going upwards till you reach the top of your head.

After this or other exercise for loosening muscles of the entire body, you should feel comfortable, heavy and pleasant. Now imagine that warmth is spreading freely all over throughout your body, relaxing it even more.

When you are performing a muscle loosening exercise, it may take twenty minutes or more before your body is fully relaxed. Exercise regularly every day so that later you can easily enter the fully relaxed state. After many repetitions, you will achieve the ability to enter the state of total body relaxation in a few minutes; later, even in a few seconds.

It is all right if you fall asleep when performing a relaxation exercise. Thanks to this, the body is resting very well and you sleep soundly. Usually, when you go to bed tired and then do this exercise, you will fall asleep. A solution to falling asleep is to do this exercise in a sitting position. When sitting, relax all the muscles as described above. Only stabilize those muscles which are holding the body in sitting position, of course.

Now, let us return to the mind exercises.

It is easy to do the mind exercises immediately after waking up, preferably before sunrise. Usually people wake up with their bodies relaxed. It is a pleasure to stay in warm bed at that time. It is also advantageous to use that situation to do mind exercises because they succeed well in that opportune time.

If you are planning to do mind exercises in a fully relaxed state, do them immediately after waking up or better yet, before sunrise.

Mind exercises are usually done in a sitting position so that you do not fall asleep. Also, at that time, the flow of energy through the exercising man is better.
If you are tired when performing a relaxation exercise, you can fall asleep even in a sitting position. Before beginning to exercise, make sure to take precautions that you do not hurt yourself if your fall.

4. SLEEP REGULATION

It is best for man to live in accordance with nature's rhythms. Biological rhythms of the human body are closely aligned with the rhythms of nature. The timing and the phases of sleep are also subject to these rhythms. There are processes taking place in the organs, the nerve system and man's psyche which cannot be performed outside the time spent sleeping. If the sleep time is disrupted, these processes will suffer. When sleep is too short or takes place in time other than biological rhythms require, it is disturbed.

From a practical point of view, one has to remember to go to sleep early and get up early, preferably with the sunset and sunrise.
When you live far from the equator, you are experiencing big changes in relation of the length of day and night, depending on the season. In this case, you will probably not want to adjust your sleep time to the length of the night for that would be too long. However, you can decide to go to bed before 10 pm and get up no later than 7 am in Winter.

If 10 pm is too early for you, then you can decide to go to bed between 10 and 11 pm, but not later. Going to sleep later than 11 pm disturbs the biological process of body's self-maintenance, in which the liver plays a significant role. After the body's self-maintenance period, the liver requires some rest as well. If you go to sleep after 11 pm, you are taking valuable rest time from the liver. As a result of treating the body in this way, the ageing process accelerates and the immunity system weakens.

When preparing for inedia or non-eating, one ought to bring the body and psyche to the best state. To become an inediate, one ought to be healthy. Sleep plays an essential role in this preparation.

The other extraordinarily important factor is darkness. The body ought to be in complete darkness during sleep. The deeper the darkness, the better the body rests. If the body sleeps in semi-darkness, or even worse, in the presence of light, this causes backwardness. This affects mainly the pineal and pituitary glands, the functions of which are essential on the way of conscious self-development.

The pineal gland especially needs total darkness during sleep, then it can function well. When the eyes are deprived of darkness during sleep, the pineal gland develops less and may even degenerates. This causes spiritual development difficult or impossible.
The pineal gland plays a key role during mind exercises, which are also called psychic or spiritual. The results achieved using these exercises

depends on the health of the pineal gland.

Silence is the third important factor to observe during sleep. The quieter it is in the room where you sleep, the better for the nerve system to rest. The more noisy it is in the room, the more serious the problem is for the nerve system and the psyche. Instinct uses energy unnecessarily thus the sleep phases are disturbed.

By the way, let me point out that some parents allow small children to go to sleep late. Sometimes I see that parents carelessly are not concerned that their child is still up after 10 pm. Children who go to sleep late will not be fully healthy. Going to sleep late will affect children's development. Later, when the children become a grown-ups, they will not be fully developed mentally compared to their original potential at a younger age. That will be the fault of their parents.

That is why I suggest, caring about your children's health and subsequent long life. Have the children sleep in silence and darkness. Before they are seven years old, have them go to bed before 7 and 8 pm. Before the age fourteen, have them go to bed no later than 9 pm. Only when they are mature, at the age of eighteen to twenty one, can they decide to go to bed at 10 pm. Guiding your children in this way will result in them becoming strong on both the physical and mental level.

To summarize, during the preparation for the seven-week adaptation, you ought to adjust the body to sleeping in the **right time**, in total **darkness** and **silence**.

5. PROTECTION AGAINST HARMFUL RADIATION

I advise you to avoid living in places with the following concerns. Protect your living environment against:
1. electromagnetic waves and fields;
2. magnetic fields;
3. electrostatic fields;
4. ionizing and radioactive radiations;
5. geopathic stress.

Re: 1.
Frequencies of microwave ovens, transmitters of wireless telephone, radar, radio, television and wireless networks are very harmful. The health of children these days is worse as compared to the health of their parents (when

they were the same age). The life expectancy of these children is going to be shorter than that of their parents. This is due to exposure to the wireless Internet networks (WiFi), cell phones and other wireless devices commonly used.

The big density of the high frequency waves is one of the strongest factors causing degeneration of biological bodies, mainly for people in cities. This results in weakening the body's self-defence system, severely increasing the number of sick people and shortening their lifespan.

Electronic Zombies

I hope that you are not one of those electronic zombies walking around with their eyes fixed on the screens of devices held in their hands. They sleep with their telephone, still switched on, close to their beds. This is the reason that their life energy is being sucked by vampires. Those people live as if in a trance, having forgotten that they are part of nature, which has no electronics.
Electronics kill the intuition, weaken the intellect and reprogram the instinct in a way that makes man a less and less conscious slave. Look into the eyes of that man. How much consciousness and how much life is left there?

If you want to have a healthy and strong body, an efficient nerve system and if you want to develop your abilities to use intuition and telepathy, then protect your home, work place and specifically your bedroom. Use only wired electronic devices, which have good shielding and grounding. Shield the rooms in which you stay most of the time, especially bedroom, against electromagnetic waves of high frequencies.
You can use an electromagnetic field meter to check the wave intensity before and after the shielding.

If you are living in a house that is located far from transmitter aerials, maybe in nature, it is quite possible, that the intensity of the electromagnetic waves is sufficiently low and you do not need to use shielding. Just remember not to use wireless electronics unless there is extraordinary need for it.

A microwave oven is not suitable for cooking or even warming food. It destroys the structure of the food so severally that it becomes totally dead.
I suggest you do not eat anything that was cooked in microwave oven because it is not only dead matter, it also weakens living organisms. The programming of food that was cooked in microwave oven is pure death. Do you want to introduce death into your body?
If you do not believe this, water your flowers with cool water that was previously boiled in the microwave oven, and see how quickly they wilt and die.
Do you recall what I wrote about the structure of water? Microwave ovens destroy water structure that supports biological life.

Re: 2.
If you live in the proximity of industrial machines that emit strong magnetic fields, e.g. generators, transformers and motors, then the solution is to leave that place. The sooner you leave it, the better.

Re: 3.
Strong electrostatic fields can be formed around devices and cables working on high voltages. The solution is to install a metallic shield and ground it well. Leaving that place is a better solution for your health.

If you have a plastic carpet in your home, it would be best to remove it. If you do not want to remove it, at least spray it with an electrostatic agent and ground the carpet well.

Re: 4.
Ionizing and radioactive radiations can be found around devices emitting high voltages, containing radioactive elements and around X ray equip-

ment. In these cases you have to remove the devices or leave that area. Radioactive and ionizing radiations also can be found in nature. They are emitted by some rare minerals and the gas radon. Radon is found in nature quite often. Its concentration can be high in places like basements, tunnels, caves, etc. If your room is underground, it would be wise to check the concentration of radon in the air. Radon is heavier than air and for this reason one ought to sleep at least 20 cm above the floor.

It sometimes happens that a building has walls with high radioactive emittance. Most people feel unwell and may get sick in such a building. These symptoms disappear after they are outside for a few days. If you have any doubts, especially in a new building, measure the radiation level of the walls and the amount of radon in the air.

Re: 5.
Geopathic stress and radiation, these are found in many places in nature and negatively impact the human body.
This harmful radiation is found above many underground streams, underground rock formations, tectonic faults, hollows, etc.
In addition, the intersecting geopathic lines network harms the human body. This kind of radiations can be found by an experienced radiesthete (radiesthesia specialist). It is wise to have one in your home to check if there is any harmful geopathic stress.

It often happens that people are unwell because they live above a water stream or their bed / desk is positioned in intersecting geopathic lines. Moving away from this place brings back the health to those people.

It is good to remember human body is a very sensitive receiver of waves and radiation which are often called energies. Commonly known sciences like radiesthesia and *fēng shŭi*, are engaged in researching this type of radiations in the environment. Use their findings and solutions to protect your health.

6. GETTING CLOSE TO NATURE

Man is an inseparable part of nature. When man is totally separated from nature, they die. The farther man lives from nature, the faster they degenerate because life energy is found in nature.

How do you feel in a city and how in a forest, by a lake, in the mountains or at seaside?

Can you feel how much energy is in you after spending hours in an office, inside a building with artificial lighting? Then feel how much energy you have after you spend a day by a lake, in mountains, in a forest or at seaside? It is a big difference, isn't it? You can clearly feel that an artificially illuminated office in a concrete building sucks life energy from you. On the other hand, the totally opposite effect is happening in nature; you are naturally receiving life energy.

The kind of energy contained in nature is a natural food available for people, animals and plants. Earth and the sun emanate this energy and move it properly. The movement of this energy is disturbed and weakened in cities, particularly in the buildings.

If you are moving toward the lifestyle without food, it is the best to remain in a nature setting. This significantly facilitates the adaptation for a new type of powering the body. Increasing the powering of the body with food in the form of energy from nature, is a transitional stage on the way to non-eating.

7. CHANGE OF DIET

The change of diet during the preparation for the seven-week adaptation is an extraordinary process because it differs from other diet changes undergone by people for reasons of health, religion, belief or philosophy.
In this case, instead of saying 'change of diet', we can call it 'sublimation of diet'. Sublimation is a process of transforming something into a purer or more delicate form. The process of diet change is precisely about this. Consumed foods become increasingly more subtle in respect to the density of matter and become more energetic in respect to the amount of life energy.

This is all about the cloud of energy or invisible radiation around food, which is called aura. When you look at the aura of various substances eaten by people, you will notice that they differ in colours and brightness. It ranges from food that have dark, almost black aura to food appearing as a shining source of light with a white-silver-gold aura. You may probably guess that the foods with a dark aura are of the lowest amount of life energy and the foods with a shining aura are of the highest amount of life energy.

> During the preparation for the adaptation, as you are giving up normal food, you are drawing more and more food in the form of energy from the sun and Earth.
>
> During the seven-week adaptation, as you are gradually giving up the drawing of energy from around you, you are increasing the powering / creating of your body by the mind.

The resultant conclusion is that, in order to start the seven-week adaptation, your body should be powered by external energy from the sun and Earth. That is the reason why the elements of the preparation, which are mentioned above, are so important.

The change of diet can be made along the lines of diet sublimation described in the chapter entitled "methods", in the section called "natural". In short, it consists of gradually eliminating foods of the lowest amount of life energy and replacing them with food of the highest.

Let me add an essential comment.
When sublimating your diet, when you are moving to liquids, the most advantageous action is to suck juice from the plants when chewing them. Take a bite of, e.g. a fruit, chew it sufficiently long enough to take in the juice, mix it with the saliva and swallow, spiting out the reminder of the fruit.

I suggest, do not use electric juice extractors or blenders.
In the first place, the aura of the juice made by these machines looks less appealing than the plant or its fruit used to make the liquid or juice. You can see death in the aura. This is understandable as the fruit suffers agony in the electric machine. Imagine, what would you feel if you were the fruit? Fruits are living organisms which have their sphere of the Consciousness more expanded than man has.
Secondly, for the digestion process to occur properly, food must initially be mixed well with the saliva. If you are drinking a juice or finely chopped fruit, you do not tend to chew. The chewing itself is not only about mixing with the saliva, it is also an important teeth piezoelectric function, which is a part of the digestion process in respect to the nerve and energetic factor.

Here is a simplified list of foods, in the order from the most subtle, which are those of the biggest amount of life and shinning most brightly. This list is not absolute, that is, the order can be different depending on place on Earth. I have assumed that the air, water, and soil are perfectly clean, as they should be in unpolluted nature.

1. water gushing from rocks in a mountain
2. ripe flowers and fruits
3. ripe nuts and seeds
4. healthy living plants
5. naturally grown vegetables
6. raw eggs
7. young living fish and birds
8. young, living animals
9. boiled or steamed plants, vegetables, fruits and beans
10. naturally preserved foods (according to above order)
11. natural honey, glucose and sucrose
12. animal milk and products made from it
13. boiled or steamed flours of grains
14. smoked meat and fish
15. fried, baked or grilled meat, fish and egg
16. fried or baked grains or its flours, wheat is especially harmful
17. all food cooked in microwave oven

Pay heed to the fact that this simplified list of foods does **not** define the best or recommended diet. What, when, and how much your body should eat, depends on many factors. The above list is merely a general indication of the food value of the substances eaten by people. It is not dietary advice. Follow the Conscious Eating method, because it satisfies your body with the respect to the best nutritional needs.

One more significant thing is the chemically poisoned and genetically spoiled food. You probably know that it is increasingly more difficult to access food produced according to nature's laws. Nature does not practice degrading soil cultivation, where chemicals poisoning plants are used to protect them against insects and to increase the crop yield.
If you are to eat something produced with the use of chemicals, you'd better think twice if you would want to eat it at all. Many chemicals used in food production processes cause pathological changes in the human body, which may be irreversible. That kind of food is a poison. The most widely, unimaginable killing of life on Earth is by the usage of glyphosate.

For dozens of years, genetic changes have been made to both plants and animals. GMO (genetically modified organisms) have been known since the beginning of life on Earth. People experimenting in this field almost always degenerated food. Introducing more and more GMO in plants and animals is one of the most significant reasons of catastrophic degeneration of food and nature in the 20th and 21st centuries.

The extent of this destruction is little known by those who do not look for information. The destruction is seen in people's health, plants' resistance and yield, animals' fertility and devastation of huge areas of arable land. Complete repairing of the damage caused by GMO is almost impossible to be achieved by people. However, nature can manage this problem, if people immediately stop making changes in genes of plants and animals.

My advise to you is, do whatever you can in order to eat food free of poison and GMO. This is one of the basic principles for returning to nature. Without returning to living in accordance to natural laws, the body adaptation to living without food may become too difficult.

THE ADAPTATION

From the title itself, you can surmise that the main part of the adaptation for living without food takes seven weeks. Of course, this is a hypothetical number of weeks as you can shorten or extend the adaptation. An extension is required more often than a shorter duration.

I recall that I needed about four months to adjust the body for living without food. The difference is that I started the non-eating on a fixed date, as if by force. Also, I did this without any preparation of the body.

I must remind you to use your common sense to guide you. Sometimes, it is more advantageous to go back to eating instead of going forward where a danger is waiting. This way of life will not escape from you, nobody urges you and you have as much time as you wish. You can begin and return as many times as you decide to. You set your limits.

The way to inedia is not a competition, not a struggle, not an obligation and not an honour. The adaptation to inedia is like a way to an obscure mountain top where you travel by yourself and for your own purpose, to learn abilities unexplored until now. The higher you climb, the more you will experience, see and understand.

Be aware that the adapting is mainly a mental / spiritual process. Your mind is a horse that is pulling a cart (which is your body). The cart is inertly following the horse, it does not make decisions on its own. The cart moves ahead when the horse is walking, it stops when the horse is standing and it rolls back when the horse is not in control.

It is normal that the cart continually pulls the horse back, unless the horse turns back and goes down the hill. Then the horse has to brake the cart so that it will not run over the horse.

Do you understand this comparison?

You know that the horse has limited capabilities. Also the cart can break down. Therefore, do not overload the horse or the cart. Drive them with common sense on the path to the top.

MENTOR

I recommend that you be in close contact with a specialist in the field of fasting, non-eating or inedia. It would be most advantageous to be in contact with a doctor specializing in healing people by fasting.
This doctor could be your mentor. The mentor does not have to be with you all the time. You do not even need to see your them regularly but it is important that you can contact them when a need arises and that they can immediately arrive to you.

It is recommended that you can meet the mentor and talk with them whenever you need because you may have different needs, apart from possible medical assistance.

PLACE

Before you choose a proper place for you to undergo the adaptation, spend a few days and nights in this place, to feel it. Be sure that the air, water and soil are clean in this place and that there is no harmful radiation.
This place is no doubt in nature. The less this place has been modified by man, the more suitable it is for you.

It is possible that you will need a few places. For example, in the first three weeks you may feel better in a mountain forest which has a sunny clearing and waterfall. Later, you may feel that it will be more suitable for you to be in a valley near a lake. In the last week, you may feel like staying on a warm, sandy, sunny beach on the seaside.
It would be ideal to provide yourself with possibility to stay in such places during the adaptation. Check to see if it is possible. If not, choose a place that meets the following requirements:

- it is not too cold, not too warm or humid;
- there is a forest in not very high mountains or on a hill;
- where you can watch sunrise and sunset and admire the landscape;
or
- close to a sandy seashore in the vicinity of wooded hills and rocks;
- where you can watch sunrise over the sea;
- you have free access to a spring, river, lake or sea;
- most of the day is sunny;
- far from people, roads, constructions, power plants, airports, cemeteries and aerials;
- where you hear only the sounds from nature.

A simple cottage or hut built with natural materials like stone, wood, sand, clay would be ideal. It should include a bathroom and a comfortable room without luxuries and electronic devices. Avoid plastics, rubber and poisonous building materials. Also your clothes should be made from only natural materials.
The bed should not be made of plastics and metals. The bathroom should be clean and with water without chlorine, fluorine or other poisons. Drinking water and water used for bathing should not be in contact with plastics.

THE FIRST DAY

Yesterday you ate your last material meal. Release thoughts related to that meal because it is already history. Since your last meal, you are free from the strongest addiction on Earth; you probably have decided so.

Today you do not eat any more but you still power the body, so that it can function properly. You are powering it with energy drawn from the environment and produced by the mind.

For this purpose you perform energizing and mind exercises, which you have learned to do properly during the preparation. Feel yourself which exercises are advantageous for you and in what time.

Here is an example of what your day might look like.

You get up in the morning before sunrise and wash your face, neck, ears and hands. You go outside before sunrise to a place where you can watch the rising sun.

Just before sunrise, you draw in life energy by breathing (previously described).
Complete this exercise a moment before the sun rises.

You release all thoughts, stand relaxed and gaze at the sun. If this is your first day of doing this energizing exercise, the gazing can be done for a maximum of 60 seconds. Make sure that your gazing at the sun do **not** last longer than the entire time that it takes for the sun to rise from behind the horizon.

Next, you close your eyes and cover them with your palms in order to shield them from the light. You can still see the sun, as if it was inside your head now, in the area of the pineal gland. You feel the energy flowing from this inner sun in all directions. You focus on this inner vision for a few minutes until it fades away.

If you are standing a few meters from your dwelling, you can go back to your room, which should be darkened, so that you no longer have to cover your eyes with your palms.

You feel pleasant and well. You are strolling in nature enjoying the nice morning. You listen to the sounds of nature while feeling energy emanating from Earth and sun.

Before you went out for the stroll, you drank warm water with baking soda. This helps to raise pH (alkalinity) of the urine and stimulate your body to excrete more efficiently.
After coming back, you wash your intestine with water, to remove rotting remains of food from past days.

Later, you sit down in a relaxed position and do some visualization, in which you see yourself as a happy inediate. You have been practising visualization for several months since you began the preparation for the present seven-week adaptation.

You decided earlier what is in your picture, now you continue. I, or anyone else, will not create this picture for you, because it would be disadvantageous for you, since you are to consciously create your life. I am merely suggesting that you see yourself emanating Inner Joy and feeling Love to yourself in this picture.
If you have decided to put yourself in the picture as an inediate or non-eater, you are visualizing it from the first day of preparation.

You spend the rest of the day according to your needs. What is important, is that you do the energizing and mind exercises previously described, so that you keep your body in good physical and energetic health.

Energizing exercises alone may not be enough. The human body needs some physical activity to function normally.
One of the most important factors that determines the efficiency of adaptation to non-eating or inedia is the state of the body's physical fitness. Therefore, keeping the body in the best condition is so important.

You decide on the amount of physical activity that your body needs, because you feel it. For some people, long strolls are enough. Others feel the need to jog or cycle. Still others like to tire muscles in a gym or go swimming.

Do not exaggerate with the physical activity. If you tire out the body too much, it will lose too much energy, which will make the adaptation more difficult. "Enough is enough."

In the evening, you do the contemplation of joy. Afterwards you go outside and look at the stars and listen to nature. Before you are finished for the day, you read soulful literature, because you have taken a lot of books with you. By the time you go to bed, you perform contemplation of passiveness. You lie on your back in bed and relax your entire body, as in *sawasana* exercise. You fall asleep while doing it.

THE SECOND DAY

Its course is similar to the first day.

THE THIRD DAY

Its course is similar to the previous days.

If you are concerned about maximum removal of all the food remnants from the small and large intestines, then you clinse the entire alimentary canal. You can use methods described in the chapter "alimentary canal cleansing".
It is worth to be near your mentor taking care of you, so that they can help you if a need arises.

The next three days are similar to the previous ones.

THE SEVENTH AND EIGHTH DAYS

These days look similar to the previous ones. On the seventh day, you do a cleansing of the large intestine to check if there is any putrefying residue in the colon. If you see remnants of putrefying matter flowing out, you can repeat the alimentary canal cleansing. However, this time it may be unpleasant and cause pain.

THE DAYS THAT FOLLOW

Do not do a colon cleanse from the ninth day onward. Even if there is still some waist, this should not constitute a problem. You can deal with this issue after a few weeks, unless you clearly feel that something is putrefying in the intestines. If you experience flatulence, something is rumbling in the intestines or you feel that there is too much gas, then you can do the alimentary canal cleanse in the third week. Later, if the same problem still persists, repeat the cleanse in the fifth week.

It may happen that you experience a lot of gas even two months later. If this problem appears, it may indicate the presence of putrefying matter in the intestine, that has not yet been removed by the body, e.g. remnants of rotting tapeworm. Then, you can cleanse the alimentary canal again. However, you have to be very careful because the body is now very sensitive and reacts to a much smaller amount of liquids. Doing the procedure during this time may even harm the body. For that reason, stay in close contact with your mentor.

> The closer you come to the end of the seven-week adaptation, you ought to perform more mind exercises rather then the energizing ones.

Energizing exercises do power the body but they are just a bridge to transition the body to full liberation from food. The full liberation means that you also do not rely on energy from outside the body.

You can be a source of all energy and material substance that your body needs. Once you become the source of all the energy, you do not need to draw anything from the environment.

The body can function perfectly due to its owner's will. In other words, when you see, in your imagination, that the body functions perfectly due to your will, then this manifests itself in reality. This is called inedia.

> The human body can function properly due to:
> - proper diet, that is, individually selected proper material food by using Conscious Eating;
> or
> - the energy drawn from the environment, through energizing exercises, e.g. energy drawing by breathing, sun-gazing, tài-jǐ, qì-gōng;
> or
> - the energy created by the mind, through mind exercises, e.g. allowing Inner Joy, visualization;
> or
> - the will of the body owner, as the result of modifications made in the instinct through, e.g. visualization.

During the preparation, you initiated a proper diet and gradually sublimated it in order to achieve the powering of the body only by energy, which began from the first day of the seven-week adaptation.
Then, throughout the seven weeks, you are adapting the body to be

powered only by the drawn energy.
Then, you gradually increase the amount of the power received from the mind exercises, mainly allowing your Inner Joy, contemplation of IAM and visualization.

The final result is that the programs of body powering do not need anything from outside. The body functions properly because this is in accordance with your will. You are based on the Inner Power manifested by IAM. The Inner Joy emanates naturally from you. You feel Love which is the indication that Life is being created.

DURING ALL THE DAYS OF THE ADAPTATION

During the seven-week adaptation you carry on your life activities according to your likes and plans. During the adaptation you do not have to be completely isolated from the life conducted up to now.
Therefore, if you have office work to do, you can carry it with joy. However, seating for long periods with electronic devices and doing tiring work, are not recommended. Especially usage of electronic devices is harmful to the adaptation. Avoid them as much as possible. The best would be to get rid of them and do not touch them during the entire adaptation.
If you really have to work at the desk for several hours, take breaks often. Go outside to do physical and energizing exercises. Also, take breaks to do the mind exercises. Remember not to allow weariness or fatigue of the body to occur due to office work. If possible, avoid office work.
The same applies to any work that you do. Make sure that you view your work as a pleasure, not as a pressure. Take breaks to do energizing and mind exercises.

If you find that your body is becoming weaker and weaker during these seven weeks, that you are experiencing hunger all the time, that your dizziness does not pass, that your heart beats faster or you have more unpleasant symptoms occurring, it would be more reasonable to return to normal eating.

Every man reacts differently to giving up food. The body and mind of every man behave in different ways during the seven-week adaptation. This is why individual approach is important. Out of concern for your body, consult your mentor and decide what to do next, so that your body is not harmed and is provided with all that it really needs.

THE LAST DAY

The forty-ninth day or any other day that you decided to set as the end of the adaptation time, is a symbolic limit. From this time on, you keep your body functioning properly entirely without food.

> You have programmed the instinct to the degree that your body can function perfectly without you paying attention to it.
> or
> You have achieved the full powering of your body through doing the mind exercises.
> or
> Your body is in perfect shape without eating because you power it with energy drawn from the environment throughout energizing exercises.

When one of the statements above occurs, your body is healthy and you feel very well, then you can consider the adaptation completed.

THE RETURN TO NORMAL LIFE

At this time, as you return to your normal life, which differs immensely from the seven-week adaptation period, still pay attention to the condition of your mind and body. The most advantageous condition is when you are emanating joy naturally and your healthy body is full of energy.

There are many factors that can cause the body weaken. Some examples include too intensive work, insufficient physical activity, polluted air, harmful radiation, loss of energy through emotions, staying away from nature, lack of sunshine, too few energizing exercises, or unconsciously made negative visualization.
Take care of your body and feel what it needs. If you are unable to keep it in a perfect condition, even with exercising, then the only sensible decision will be to go back to 'normal' nourishment of the body.

First of all Love your body. Love yourself. Let the Inner Joy emanate naturally from you. Then you feel Love all the time. Commonly speaking, this is called living "in high vibrations".

Either way, I suggest that you do not force your body to live without food because that would harm it. Do not fight with the body. Fighting results in

wounds and victims. Who becomes the victim when you are fighting with your own body?
It is much more advantageous to go back to normal eating instead of fighting. This solution is chosen by man following common sense.

You know that living without food makes you neither worse, nor better, nor extraordinary. Although you differ from most people on Earth, because you have chosen a path that is rarely walked, still, you are one of many people.

Someone may ask you:
"You are not eating; so what?"
Well, nothing, just playing the game like that. ☺

SYMPTOMS

When referring to a symptom here I mean a usually unpleasant reaction of the body or psyche caused by the changes in nourishment. When you are changing the diet, fasting or adapting the body to living without food, symptoms may appear, especially if this is done quickly.

Writing about symptoms herewith, by mentioning the word "fast", I refer to either or all of the following situations: diet change, heal fasting or adapting the body to living without food. So when you read "fast(ing)", you will understand that it can also apply to a diet change or adapting to living without food.

The following descriptions are quite general and they have exceptions, because every man is a different world. General description, recommendations and procedures are not completely suited for most people, thus it is advisable to consider them as frames only. Treating every man individually gives the best results, conclusions and indications.

The intuition is the best adviser. If you can hear it well, you need no advices. If you cannot yet, then judgement is your best adviser. Descriptions found below may have a bunch of valuable information.
First of all, do not fight against the body. Fighting results in injures. When you fight against the body, who is injured? Instead, Love your body and keep it in discipline.

I will not describe all the symptoms here, only those experienced most often. Many things may occur because every man reacts in a different manner. If you are not afraid, there is very small probability that something endangering your life will happen. Properly conducted fasting never causes any illness.

If you have any doubts during fasting, stay in touch with competent mentor. The best is to be in touch with a doctor who is experienced enough in healing by fasting.
It results from my observation that no more than one percent of doctors have sufficient knowledge about heal fasting. Even among those doctors who prescribe fasting for healing, there are some who sometimes give harmful recommendations. Of course, it is better to find such a doctor instead of falling into the hands of another one who would know nothing or too little about this most efficient physical healing method known on Earth.

The symptoms listed below are temporary, they last from a few seconds to a few weeks maximum. They may manifest constantly or in bouts, changing intensity. Some people almost do not notice them, so they have no related problems. However there are people who feel so overwhelmed that it seems to them they may be dying. But with most people, who are generally regarded as having 'normal heath', only some symptoms appear for a short time. The observed regularity makes for a general rule that the more ill man is, the more symptoms may appear, they will last longer and be more ailing. It so happens because the symptoms are direct results of cleansing and healing of the body and psyche, which takes place during the fast.

1. fear
2. weakness
3. dehydration
4. dizziness and fainting
5. nausea and vomiting
6. weight loss
7. emaciation
8. pain
9. psychical instability
10. different reality
11. changes on skin
12. feeling cold
13. fever
14. loose teeth
15. loss of hair
16. swelling joints
17. other

FEAR

Fear may be the biggest problem for a fasting man. When fasting or in other life situations, there is nothing more frightening than the fear itself. Fear may become the biggest danger for fasting man.

If you are afraid to fast, the solution is, either do not do fast or do it with man whom you trust so much that you lose your fear. There are so many people who, having been suddenly deprived of food, died just after a few days. Forcing man to fast, when they are afraid of fasting, is dangerous for the life, not because of the lack of food, but solely because of their fear.

The more you fear for your health and life because of fasting, the sooner you should stop fasting. Fear about other things also has the power to harm. Man is more sensitive when fasting, so any fear may cause more damage.

Fear is the state of complete absence of Love. This state causes Life to vanish. Therefore, the less Love manifests itself through a being, the more the being feels the lack of energy creating Life, thus the being feels more fear. So if you feel fear, it means that you are inhibiting / suppressing Love, the only source of life for your mind and body. If you allow Love, of which precisely your are the source, to manifests itself more, then fear will vanish. Fear and Love never co-exist.

If you decide to get rid of the approaching fear, you may use this exercise, which frees Love from within you.

Sit or lie down in a relaxed position and become silent. Breathing freely and calmly, focus on feeling Love, of which you are the source and which naturally emanates from you. Feel that in the centre of the being that you are, the source of your life is present. This source always emanates as intensively as your mind allows it. So now let it manifest itself fully. Let it shine like a sun, warming the whole of you and the surrounding. Allow completely, and feel Love. Feel, feel ... how Love overwhelms you and everything around you. Do not create Love, do not create something of which you are the source. Love manifests itself if you just allow it.

WEAKNESS

A feeling of physical weakness is one of the most common symptoms. One can even say that to feel weak is normal. Some people strongly bound to eating, feel weakness after just a few hours of fasting. This feeling of weakness indicates that the body begins to feel the difference in delivery of nourishment in form of food. The rhythm is disturbed, therefore the body starts to react.

One type of people may never experience the weakness. Another type of people experience weakness once or just a few times during the whole fast. There are also people for whom the weakness is a full time companion. Regardless of the cause and duration, the weakness indicates low level of life energy.

How to deal with this? Well, it depends on the situation and man. If someone is too active physically, it is better for them to rest or even to lie down. Also the opposite may happen, that someone is resting, sitting, not moving all day; then they should go for a walk, cycle a little, swim or exercise.

During fasting time, some physical and energizing exercises are highly recommended. The movement and better energy flow allows the body to clean itself deeper and faster. Doing energetic and exhausting exercises is not recommended. Moderate gymnastics and exercises, during which the mind is concentrated on feeling the energy instead of making the muscles tired, have much better influence on the body. Isometric exercises, yoga, *qìgōng* and *tàj-jí* influence people very beneficially and are even salutary. It is worthwhile to do them everyday except the times when the body clearly needs rest through sleeping.

During fasting there may be hours or even entire days when the body feels so weak that man does not have the strength to walk and they feel like doing nothing but resting. These are the times when the body requires rest, preferably sleep. It may be caused by a toxin induced disease.

It is good to be able to feel whether the body requires rest or grows lazy and needs exercising. It would be wrong to sleep when the body needs exercising. On the other hand, exercising would be too big a load when the body needs rest.

Judgement and ability to distinguish are valuable qualities of fasting man. When the real need for resting the body appears, it is worth to go to bed and sleep. However if this state lasts for too long and you do not find any illness in you, it is worth to discipline yourself and do some energizing exercises.

Too much of lying down and sleeping makes the body weaker instead of giving it energy which man needs so much at the time of fasting. The blood pressure goes down, the blood circulates slower and the metabolism slows down. This makes both the eliminations of toxins from the body and the self-healing process slower. In such situation energizing exercises help a lot and make man feel better.

If the weakness lasts too long, especially after the first three weeks of fasting, this indicates that the time to resume eating is approaching. But not always, because there may be other reasons, for example, serious illness, lack of fresh air, too high air temperature or too much physical work. So to take the decision whether to stop the fasting or to continue it, depends individually on the cause and the health state of man.

DEHYDRATION

When you decide to give up drinking, you begin dry fasting. Statistically the human body can withstand without water for over a dozen days. For how long you can stay without water, depends on several factors, mainly air humidity, temperature, physical activity, the amount of minerals to be washed out and fat reserve. The safe period in optimal conditions is about four days.

During dry fasting in optimal conditions the body uses between 0.1 and 1 kg of fat daily to produce water. This is the approximate daily loss of weight. An overweight man can survive longer without any drinks than a thin man, assuming that their bodies are in roughly similar condition, have similar quantities of minerals to be removed and the people have the same amount of life energy. The body of an overweight man has more fat tissue which is used to produce water during dry fasting.

If man is not prepared for dry fasting or does it for too long, they may dehydrate the body too much. Excessive dehydration causes many abnormalities in the body functions which ends with death.

Therefore, while dry fasting, man needs to check often whether the body shows signs of too much dehydration. Dehydration level of as little as 2% is clearly felt as strong thirst. When dehydration exceeds 10%, it becomes life threatening and should therefore be warded off. Visions, hallucinations or faltering caused by dehydration clearly indicate that man is balancing on the edge of life. In such case one immediately needs to thoroughly hydrate the body as soon as possible.

If life threatening occurs, one must immediately drink water, take a bath, pour water into the large intestine and consult a doctor.
Dehydration that went beyond a critical point is irreversible. This means that attempt to hydrate the body does not rectify the situation and the body is incapable of absorbing enough water. This leads to the arrest of bodily functions.

If you do not have enough experience to ascertain the level of body hydration, you would not know when dehydration becomes dangerous. In this case it is more safe to stay in touch with an expert in this area during your dry fasting.

DIZZINESS AND FAINTING

These are frequently experienced symptoms. Only a few of those fasting for a long time can say that they had not experienced dizziness. Especially people with low blood pressure may experience unpleasant situations. These people need to take special care in order not to allow the blood pressure to fall too much. If you are one of these people, you would better start with some fasting training, a series of gradually extended fasts. In this way the body will partly cleanse itself and learn to react with lesser drop in blood pressure.

Another solution may be to drink herbal teas during the fasting, only when the real need arises. Much better solution is doing energizing exercises, acupressure, acupuncture, massage and similar treatments that increase the blood pressure.

Many people give up fasting because of dizziness and fainting. These symptoms look grave enough to shake even a self-confident faster and make them apprehensive about the state of their body. Dizziness or fainting is not as dangerous as the consequences they entail, so this is where attention must be directed. The most important is to make sure that man suffering dizziness or fainting does not fall down because they may wound themselves.

Dizziness, ranging from slight to fainting, is most often caused by too low blood pressure and/or too low blood sugar level. When fasting, the body undergoes many truly revolutionary changes. One of the symptoms of these changes is fluctuation of the blood pressure.

The lowered blood pressure is mostly felt between the first and the fifth weeks of fasting, with changing intensity. Later, with self-cleaning of the body and its adaptation to living without food, the blood pressure stabilizes at the optimal level. Fluctuating blood pressure may also come later. For each individual it will happen differently and will depend, among others, on the amount and type of consumed liquids, temperature, atmospheric pressure and physical activity.

Changes in blood pressure *per se* are not as dangerous as the movements done by man. For the sake of personal safety, it is very important that man avoids sudden position changes from lying or sitting to standing. When rising, lean against something or support yourself by placing your hands on chair, table, etc. and slowly erect the body to the standing position. When you feel dizziness coming, stop rising or sit back. Do not move to fast too avoid blackouts.

It is a good idea to learn how to behave at the times of experiencing dizziness with blackouts. Blackout is a symptom of a sudden blood outflow from the brain, causing fainting. In this case adopt the low bending position, that is, the head lower than the trunk and the hands put down in front of the head. If you feel worse, squatting will help in most cases, so put your hands firmly on the floor, lean on them and lower the head down freely between the shoulders.

If the dizziness persists, rest for a while. Lie down and raise the legs leaning them against the wall or a chair.

If the fluctuations of the blood pressure persist, cause frequent fainting or last for too long, consider whether you want to continue the fasting and consult a competent doctor. It is also very advisable to check your blood sugar level.

NAUSEA AND VOMITING

These are common symptoms of the body undergoing self-cleansing process. The body of fasting man does not use energy for digesting, therefore it can use the energy for self-cleansing. In the process of dissolving and eliminating dead cells, old concretions, accumulated toxins and excess fat, the body releases different substances into the blood. The blood, circulating through the whole body, passes also through the brain centre, which controls nausea and vomiting reactions. So the toxins circulating in the blood cause the unpleasant symptoms, like pain, nausea or even vomiting.

Other reasons of such acute reactions may include ulcer, abscess, cyst, not fully healed wound, accumulated and crusted (glued with mucus) substance, tumour. The body opens all such things and tries to get rid of them in different possible ways. This is the reason why it is better to help the body with fasting in such situations. Starting to eat when unpleasant symptom appears means stopping the cleansing and the self-healing.

As an example, let me tell you of the case of man, about 40 years of age, who in his childhood was treated with pills containing mercury compounds. On his ninth day of fasting he suddenly felt so bad that he fell down and started vomiting. Immediately after this he felt much better. In the vomit he collected a quarter of glass of mercury. The conclusion from this story is that the body accumulated and stored the mercury in his childhood and decades later, during the fast, the body opened the box in order to throw the contents out.

Usually there is no big need to be concerned about nausea and vomiting, because waiting from a few hours to a few days (in rare cases) solves the problem. It is helpful to walk in the woods, near a lake or to do some energizing exercises, because movement helps the body to detoxify faster.
Also, if you prefer, you can drink warm water to induce vomiting. If you feel nausea, and your intestine has not been cleaned with water, enema will probably help a lot.

If vomiting happens often or if it contains gall or blood, consulting a competent doctor could be helpful. It is worth remembering that such vomiting indicates that the body needs longer fasting.

After vomiting, man feels relief because the body has got rid of poison. Then sensible inflow of energy occurs and man feels much better (cleaner inside).

WEIGHT LOSS

Also the process of weight loss, being one of the symptoms, should be considered individually. When an obese man is losing weight, it is a very beneficial process of getting rid of the excess and restoring the proper weight to the body. However, when man who is already thin is still slimming down, emaciation may occur. In the former case, to continue the fast is more beneficial for man. For the later it is better to start eating again.

The rate at which weight loss is occurring, is an individual matter. It usually stabilizes after the first few days of fasting. The decreasing weight, occurring in the first fasting days, is primarily caused by the body emptying the intestine and removing the excess water, which is even more noticeable during dry fasting. If, for example, the body loses two pounds a day in the first week of fasting, in the next weeks it may lose only two pounds a week.

In some extreme cases the weight loss may be as big as thirty pounds a day. I know two people whose bodies responded in this way. There are also people whose bodies lost only a few pounds during the whole long fasting. So, as you can conclude, there are no strict rules about how much body weight has to change during fasting.

During dry fasting the daily weight loss of an obese man may amount to two pounds (or more) because excess fat is used faster by the body to produce water. Such rapid loss of weight in a slim or underweight man maybe hazardous for the body.

While experiencing weight loss as well as other symptoms accompanying fasting, first of all man should be guided by reason. Typically man of normal constitution is able to keep the power of life in the body for up to two months without any food. If the body weight is constantly going down during this time, it clearly shows that the instinct is not yet able to run the body properly without food.

Man who constantly sees their body as too fat despite it being too thin already, is considered anorexic. Fasting or adapting the body to non-eating is not for anorexics. These people should first address and cure their mental disorders.

EMACIATION

Emaciation can be caused by forcing the body to fast for too long. In this case emaciation is caused by too big loss of the body weight and building material deficiency. At the same time the life energy level is too low for man to function normally.

Emaciation can be compared to the state that describes man 'with one leg in the grave'. The next step is leaving the body. If man does not intend to die, then the earlier they resume eating, the less harm happens.

Statistically, in case of a 'normally' nourished, not too thin and not too overweight man, fasting for the period of up to six weeks does not cause damage to the body. But after this period the deficiency of the building material may become too big for the body to continue to function well. The process, which can be described as the body-eating-itself, begins. This means that cells die. They get removed but are not replaced by new ones. When the building material for nerve cells is in shortage, body life functions begin to switch off.

Therefore, if more than a month has passed and your body is still very weak, you have 'no strength' for physical activity, you cannot get up from the bed in the morning, you are not emanating happiness and optimism – this is a clear indication that you should end the fasting. The instinct has not yet learned to power the body from non-material sources. In this case do not fight against your body, do not harm it. A more advantageous and wiser act is to gradually resume normal eating. In the future, when you have more experience and the instinct is programmed better, you can try again.

PAIN

You may feel pain in any area of the body, although it usually does not happen all at the same time. Headache is most frequent, usually appears first. Other aches, in the region of the heart, stomach, liver, kidneys, joints, spine, intestine and muscle, may occur at any time and may last from a second to a few days (longer lasting pain is quite rare).

Pain during fasting indicates that the body is eliminating the cause of disease in the organ, that is, restores the organ's perfect state and function. This is a reason to be happy rather than to be afraid. The bigger the organ's problem, the more it can ache and the longer the repair lasts. It happens quite often that an organ aches although it was felt as healthy. Until the pain appeared man was unaware of the organ's illness.

The longer man is fasting, the fewer aches appear as the result of the self-cleansing and self-repairing processes in the body. What may also happen is that after a few months of happy life without any food, a piercing heartache suddenly appears. In this instance most often it is an indication of an energetic change taking place, reaction to higher perception in immaterial world, self-cleaning of the aura. This pain is rarely caused by a physical change in material body organ.

Other causes of frequent pain which happen during fasting are physical movements of body organs. During fasting some organs shrink and fat tissues are eliminated. This causes changes in the muscle tone and the relative position of the body organs. This may be clearly felt especially in the abdomen.

I recall having pain in my abdomen lasting for about two weeks; quite unpleasant because it was difficult for me to sit upright or lie down straight for more than just a few minutes. Only when I bent the body, the pain stopped. The cause was the increase of space under the diaphragm. This was caused by factors such as complete emptying of the intestine, shrinking of the intestine, stomach, liver and kidneys, eliminating of fat tissues from this area. The diaphragm was forced to work harder because it was not supported from below as much as before.

Apart from the pain occurring due to energetic changes or those caused by the movement of internal body organs, another strong pain may suddenly appear. In such case you may need to consult a doctor. As an example let me relate to you another experience of mine.

In the fourth month of non-eating I suddenly felt a strong pain, piercing to the point of fainting, in the right part of the abdomen and the back. I went to a hospital begging for an immediate strong painkiller. Later, after a few hours of examination, the doctor said that it was caused by something which clogged the ureter. My conclusion was that only after four months of non-eating, the stone that I had in my kidney had fallen into the ureter. Because it was larger in size, it caused so much pain when moving down.

As you can see, this or other kind of surprising pains are entirely possible. In some rare situations an unexpected thing may happen that may be dangerous for the health of the body, to which the body will react with a strong pain. In this case it is advisable to consult a doctor. But most often it is not a reason to resume eating.

PSYCHICAL INSTABILITY

Some people ask me: "Why do I feel so much anger, hatred, irritation during fasting?" They wonder where this flow of unpleasant emotions comes from and why. On the other hand, family members agree that it is difficult to bear such people. That is plausible because man undergoing fasting, going through this emotional instability process, may be unpredictable. For example, they can, as without any reason, throw a jam jar against a wall, explode with shouting or burst into tears. The mood of fasting man may change in an instant.

Other fasting people feel psychical reactions manifesting itself through sadness, resignation or lack of interest in anything. To these people the feeling of 'meaninglessness of everything' becomes familiar. On the one hand, man feels like doing nothing; on the other hand, man feels remorse because of their laziness, and also sees 'the meaninglessness of life'. Some of these people say that they have had enough of this life, they see it without purpose and they do not want to live any longer or they prefer not to exist at all.

The described reactions appear because the psyche is being cleansed. Fasting cleanses not only the physical body, it does the same to the invisible part of man. Therefore also the psyche is cleansed, its toxins come to the surface and blockages get released.

By the way, this mind cleansing makes man perceive things as they truly are. That is why man can find out the true sense of life, that is ... that it is just a game, that it has no sense unless you create it in your mind. What can man, who just discovered the true sense of life, feel?

Another cause of psychical instability may be non-material, also known as astral or mental parasites attached to man's body. Such a parasite or a vampire is an immaterial being who feeds on emotions and thoughts of man. Most inhabitants of Earth feed such kind of creatures on themselves.

Most often these parasites attach themselves to people full of fear, anger, hatred and other destructive emotions. Such a vampire nourishes itself precisely with this kind of emotions. The more often and the stronger man reacts emotionally, the better the vampire feels and the more parasites this man can feed. When man stabilizes emotionally so that they do not emanate any bad emotions and thoughts, their parasites are starving and feeling unwell. Fasting leads to softening of emotional outbursts. The parasite then will push man to manifest bad emotions, because it is hungry for them. If the fasting man will not give in for a sufficiently long time, the parasites will leave and man will be cleared. Dry fasting, combined with contemplation of Love and Light, is extraordinarily efficient in this case.

Another reason of different emotional reactions is the increase in the sensitivity to stimuli. The fasting man will gradually cleanse the body which makes the senses to be able to receive wider spectrum of data. Thus the senses are more sensitive for stimuli.
Man may not be prepared for this, the usual intensity of stimuli may be too strong. Too strong stimuli may irritate man. For example, what was perceived as conversation of normal loudness until now, may be perceived as clamour or even shouting during fasting, therefore this may be irritating,

Besides these emotions, the fasting man may experience also the opposite e.g. sudden appearance of joy and resulting happiness, feeling of ease of life and Love.

During fasting, different pleasant and unpleasant emotions, accompanied by certain reactions, may appear. It happens differently with each individual. In every case, it is a beneficial cleansing process, so it is one more reason to be happy rather than to be worried.

Some people may exhibit so-called paranormal abilities during fasting. In this case, man perceives information from dimensions other than just this material one. If man is unprepared, they may think that something is wrong with their psyche. Depending on their behaviour, others may consider man mentally ill, and even try to use their case to prove 'how harmful' fasting is.

Psychiatric hospitals are full of extra sensitive people. Doctors do not understand what is happening to those people and prescribe chemicals reducing activity of the brain. Additionally doctors make those people believe that they are mentally ill, creating suggestion which influences these people so badly. These "ill people" need instructions about the worlds (dimensions) other than this material one, not chemical and mental poisons. Many of these people are extraordinarily developed individuals, awakening Masters, who got lost and now need to learn more in order to understand and use their abilities.

Psychical instability may last for a long time, a few months or even years. Individually selected mind exercises are very useful to help man to control the mind and senses better.

If, during fasting, you experience emotions accompanied by reactions, which you want to get rid of, you can practise the contemplation of Light and Love. It is, in fact, the contemplation of passiveness, in which you prepare yourself for feeling and manifesting Light and Love. The more you allow Light and Love to manifest itself through your mind and body, the earlier so-called negative emotions will stop tormenting you and the sooner immaterial parasites will leave.

Even simpler solution is to allow your Inner Joy to emanate. When your Inner Joy emanates freely, it fills your with Love and Light. Then so-called negative emotions will have no chance to appear and all parasites/vampires will leave you in advance.

DIFFERENT REALITY

After a few weeks of fasting (or earlier) you may notice that the way you see and understand the world has changed. Also your thinking and acting in this world have changed. Some matters, objects and actions have changed their values, in your opinion, of course.

There are many possible ways of experiencing this new perception. You look at people and at what they do as if you were watching them in a theatre, because you feel yourself as if you were not present here, as if you were not partaking in the existence of this world.

Some things that you used to do and some subjects that you were interested in became unimportant or even worthless, although they used to be valuable and useful to you before. You have the impression that there are some things you are learning again from the beginning, so activities like driving a car, ironing, typing may be felt as a new experience. Things which used to be done automatically may now demand special attention, as if you had forgotten how to do them.

Other things, which used to require concentration, you can now do more easily, they become more natural. You take notice of and pay attention to sights, sounds and odours which did not draw your attention before. You can notice many more psychical changes. You may get the impression that this state is similar to being under drug influence.

Generally speaking, the perception and understanding of the reality of the world have changed. You may even suspect that something is wrong with your psyche. Your family members and friends may also notice your other strange reactions.

So what has happened? Many changes have occurred. The parts making up your mind have changed their activities, for example, the intellect became calmer. Also the endocrine glands work differently, for example, more DMT, melatonin, endorphins and less adrenaline are excreted.

This state may last for some time, the length of which depends on an individual. It is a good time for observing yourself and learning from it. There is no reason to worry, if the body is not in the state of emaciation or exhaustion. So you can enjoy the new experience.

What fallows is the experience described by Ariel after his dry fasting for 10 days. This is also similar to what people experience when fasting for a long time or when entering non-eating or inedia.
"I felt a sort of electromagnetic energy in my body and when I let it just be, it did things on its own. I was psychic at that time. People's thoughts & emotions didn't escape me. I had all the answers within me, was always in the right place in the right time, intuitively knew all the energy points in the body which led to often spending entire days just doing "reflexology" on myself. My body was in a constant state of fixing itself. Time was distorted, entire nights passed in an instant. I felt like in another dimension, like in a constant state of dream or meditation. I had healing abilities and saw the results in reality both on myself and others. I could sense sickness in any matter and attend to it. People and animals were drawn to me. I was and felt like a walking Sun. I was a living GPS, could reach any place without directions. Was connected to matter, could spot any kind of matter anywhere despite not

seen by the naked eye. My body bought and ate food by itself. I was an alchemist, used substances in various odd combinations with great effect. Drew intuitively with my hand moving on its own. My pain sensitivity significantly reduced to the point I could operate myself while awake and feel nothing. I fixed my own defected knee. I barely walked in straight lines but in waves and spirals. When about to say the wrong thing, my throat would respond by contracting and closing. In that way I knew also when the other side understood what I was saying or not; otherwise, my throat would signal me they didn't understand. I realized how little people understand one another, how rarely your real thought or idea passed to the other side the way you intended. It was possibly the biggest life experience I had at the time. I had several other bigger or subtle abilities, many of which I didn't get the chance to explore further, unfortunately. I was literally a superhuman for nearly two months."

CHANGES ON SKIN

The skin is the place where the cleansing and eliminative functions of the body can be observed. Sebum and sweat contain substances unwanted by the body, which are harmful to it and are therefore eliminated; this is where different body odours come from.

To put it simply, the skin is linked with the intestines. There is even a saying that the skin of man reflects the state of the large intestine and the liver. Of course, the full picture of skin condition consists of more factors.

When the body expels a poison, it can do so through the skin, which then reacts with reddening, rash, eczema etc. If man has skin problems, it is quite likely that they will re-appear when man is fasting, because the body is getting rid of the toxins which cause the problem.

Changes on the skin during fasting may also be caused by an activation of an old disease. However a new disease coinciding in time with the fasting may also cause skin changes. In the majority of such cases, the best solution will be to continue the fasting, so that the disease will leave sooner.

In extreme cases, when man continues to fast despite emaciation of their body, skin changes may indicate severe degeneration. In this case the body and its immune system are too weak, so the better solution would be to begin eating again.

Summing up, allergy, rash or other skin problems appearing during fasting are not reasons to stop, but rather to continue fasting.

FEELING COLD

If you or your relatives have ever fasted, you probably know what it means to feel cold during fasting. Although it is warm outside, the fasting man has cold hands, feet, nose and even ears. They may even be sniffing as if they had a cold. All this happens despite them being warmly dressed.

I have seen with my own eyes and have been told about non-eaters who were dressed so warmly as if it was winter, although the temperature was 25 degrees Celsius. Their hands were blue with cold, their face was suffering and their body was covered up because of the cold they were feeling. One of my acquaintances have even said: "It is difficult but quite usual to feel cold when fasting."

Man feels cold not because of insufficient clothes or low temperature. Of course, the society suggestion has formed some human reactions which result in the body feeling cold or warm depending on outside temperature.

The main factor in feeling the temperature is the amount and the way of using energy in the human body. To put it simply, if there is enough energy man does not feel cold even if it is frosty outside and, similarly, man does not feel hot in the heat. Man will feel well in a much larger range of temperatures. But if energy is lacking, or man does not know how to use it to control temperature perception, then they feel too cold or too hot.

You can conclude from this that if during fasting you are suffering because of feeling cold, you can help yourself by focussing on releasing your inner energy. To make it happen, things like energizing exercises, visualization and alternate shower are useful. Doing them regularly will make man free from susceptibility to cold.

Drinking a lot of hot drinks is not a good solution. At the time of drinking and shortly afterwards you feel warm, but at the same time the body is loaded with too much water, which overloads the eliminative system.
The flow of energy and resulting susceptibility to temperature causes what we call feeling cold or warm. You can easily learn that feeling cold or warm is subjective and depends on managing your internal energy. If you focus on releasing warmth, after a while you can feel a difference. So when you practise the contemplation of warmth, this will allow you to reprogram the instinct in the way that will enable you to always feel comfortable regardless of outside temperature.

The physical factors most affecting your feeling of external temperature are mainly the functions of the intestine, liver and spleen. So if these organs do not function perfectly, they block the circulation of energy. By simply cleaning the large intestine, which will help to clean the liver, makes man feel the energy better, not feel so cold in the winter and perspire less in hot summer.

FEVER

The body increases its temperature when it is coping (killing, removing) with microbes, this is one of its self-defensive functions. As happens during fasting, the body eliminates illness causing by opening a concentration of, for example, bacteria. They consequently circulate in the bloodstream through the entire body, causing fever. So a natural healing process of the human body is taking place.

If fever occurs during fasting, usually the best solution is to wait until it is gone. You may need to drink little more warm water (no tea, no coffee, no juice), go to bed, rest, sleep more. Usually the body will get well within a few days.

To take a drug lowering the body temperature is almost always a mistake, because it harms the body's natural mechanism of temperature control and poisons the body with chemicals. However, when having acute and very high fever, it is advisable to call a doctor with sufficient knowledge about heal fasting.

LOOSE TEETH

After a few to more than a dozen days of fasting you may start to feel that your teeth are much looser. It is easier to move them with fingers and, as it seems, to pull out. Furthermore, you feel that something is oozing (pus) from between your teeth and it has very unpleasant odour.

This is also a result of body's self-cleansing function. The body is cleansing the areas around/under the roots of the teeth. Also sinuses may be cleaned in this way. Many people do not even know that their sinuses are clogged with mucus, because it only shows up when they start clean themselves out.

After a few to more than a dozen days the loose teeth get back to the previous state and are fixed in the jaw even stronger than before. However, secretion of mucus and pus stops earlier and so does the unpleasant odour associated with it. So there is no need to be afraid that your teeth will fall out.

If the gum or a tooth are diseased with caries or broken filling, they can cause loose teeth with blood trickling from the gum or from inside of a broken tooth. For teeth in this case, the assistance of a dentist is advisable. For the gum it is better to wait a little longer, because it will most probably heal itself after full cleaning is completed.

HAIR FALLING OUT

This happens more often to women than to men. The concern is about losing more than 50 individual hairs a day. If in the first 40 days of fasting hair falls out more than 'normally', there is no need to worry unless the body is emaciated. Even if a lot of hair falls out, later you may notice that they have grown back stronger and maybe even thicker.

If body is thin and hair starts to fall out after the third week of fasting, it may mean that the body is in the process of emaciation. If a gaunt man is fasting and notices losing a lot of hair, it may be a clear indication that the fasting does not well benefit that man.

For an obese body, there is no danger of emaciation until the perfect body weight is restored. During this time, losing a lot of hair is a temporary phenomenon. Later new hair will grow in place of the lost one.

SWELLING JOINTS

This occurs during the first or second month of fasting. Joints are swelling up but there is no pain. This mainly happens to the knees and tarsal joints. You can also feel pain if the joint was ill before, because now it is being cleaned and repaired as much as the body can do it.

Swelling of joints may also be caused by drinking water containing salt (e.g. pickled cucumber or sauerkraut brine or fermented vegetable brine) or even by drinking too much water during fasting.

When joints are swelling even though man drinks very little or is dry fasting, it means that the body is cleansing the joints from accumulated salt deposits. So there is nothing that needs to be done, just wait, because the swelling will dissipate after several days. To take in chemicals (called medicines) against swelling in such a situation most often is a mistake.

OTHER

Every man goes through fasting in different ways. There are many possible symptoms in the spheres of psyche and body which may manifest during fasting.

It is more important and beneficial for the fasting man to keep in mind a positive picture, in which perfect well-being and health dominates. Concentrating thoughts on a symptom may exaggerate it in the mind, that is, create harmful visualization.

In case of most symptoms you may just wait until they pass, because they are caused by the self-cleansing of the body. The body needs time to eliminate the toxic material that had been retained in it. But all the time you should 'keep your eyes open', act with reason and do not allow any fear to prevail.

WHAT TO PAY MOST ATTENTION TO

I met many people who have tried to forcefully adapt the body to living without food. I often see that bodies of these people are suffering. This happens when man does not possess enough knowledge about reactions of the body. Those people do not know what forceful adaptation of the body to living without food may lead to. Non-eating is not fasting, hungry days or starvation. Non-eating is different in respect to the intention, conduct and result.

FIRST OF ALL, COMMON SENSE

To reason means to consider all 'pros' and 'contras', to anticipate all possible results and to consequently make decisions which bring benefits, not harm.

When attempting to live without food, procede with reason especially in respect of the body. Watch it objectively and carefully. When you see that non-eating causes more damages than advantages, stop trying.

Life gives many opportunities to try, you can try many times, so there is no need to force yourself on the first attempt. Every attempt gives more experience. The more experiences your have, the bigger is your knowledge to help yourself and others. When man acts with reason, man has smaller probability to make mistakes.

Life never ends – I often say it to people – so if you cannot accomplish something now, you can do it later, because you always have the time. Yes, you always have the time, you have all the time and you can decide what to utilize it for. Life never ends, so what you have not succeeded to accomplish this time, second, third or more times, you can still do it later. Every try gives a new experience, and this is why you are here.

You have decided to become an inediate? You have made up the plan, started with it, tried but it did not work? Any problem with this? Maybe yes, maybe no. So what?

Besides that, you have a new experience, you know more about yourself and about non-eating. The path is still open, the world still exists and you are still living and creating your life.

SECLUSION

Seclusion (being alone and away from people) proves to be very useful, in case of many people even necessary, during first few months of non-eating or during long fasting. It is better to find a place which is not connected to home. It is good to go into deep nature, to a place far from towns, roads, people, and not to contact family or friends, except in emergency situations.

If you decide to stay in partial seclusion, that is close to or in another part of the house (so that you are there to act "in case"), you will probably want to make a break every day in order to meet man who can advise you if needed. This man can be your link to the world if you are in need of something (a book, clothes), It is beneficial to have somebody who takes care of you.
If you decide to use help of a caregiver, first establish the rules about the details of the contacts and help etc. It is more advantageous if this man has experience in the area of non-eating and fasting, so that they can advise you when you feel such a need, because different situations, doubts, questions, needs may arise.

Many people decide to stay in complete seclusion, without meeting anybody and not receiving any help. From safety perspective this is less advantageous. Seek advice and consider it carefully before you decide to do so. If you are thinking of what to do, feel the answer from within you. If you still have doubts, first go for the adviser option.

Why seclusion is important? It is mainly about silencing yourself and turning the attention of the intellect to your inner part, to the spiritual side of life. Apart from being in silence, man in seclusion, far from unnecessarily absorbing occupations (mass media, noise of the street, chatter etc.), has more chances and time to concentrate on processes occurring in their psyche.

During the seclusion performing exercises beneficial for man, like contemplation, meditation, visualization and also energizing exercises, becomes easier. It is worth to use this time to do the exercises for of all the benefits they provide.

WITHOUT FORCING

It is better not to fight against the body because it is "the temple of the spirit" (to be exact, the body is inside the spirit). The body is an integral part of the being called man. The spirit without the body is no longer man.

Fighting causes wounds, psychical harms and even casualties. If you fight against your body, who will be harmed?

How does the body of man, who often forces it to do something, fights against it and harms it, develop? Alternatively, how does the body of man, who surrounds it with Love, develop?

The body is administered by the instinct which needs educating in the same way in which a wise loving parent educates their child. So if you do not successfully adapt the body to living without food in the time frame that you have set, you may need to do more spiritual work, and not to starve any longer.

The body informs you about its needs if you are tuned to feeling it. To be tuned to feeling what is the best for the body is more important than just thinking about that. Each body is different and communicates best with its owner through the feeling.

How many times I have seen people who convinced themselves that eating something (e.g. potato, ice cream, honey, fish) is bad because it harms the body, kills a being, etc. They were doing this despite the feeling that the body needs food.

Such behaviour was damaging to the body, therefore those people were sad, dissatisfied with their life, feeling pain and so forth.
Only afterwards, when those people gave the body what it needed, they were in a better mood and health. So when they stopped fighting against the body and dealt with it as would a wise loving parent, the body responded properly.

Advices concerning nourishment, proceeding principles, methods of adaptation, and so on are less important than the needs that you feel coming from your body. When you perceive them well and allow the body to feel your Love, it develops in the best way possible. By applying discipline to the body, you make sure that it will give you most of what it can do.

What is discipline? It is systematic activity full of reason and Love, with the aim of achieving something. The discipline does not know forcing because it only has the good in mind. By applying discipline, man can adapt the body to many things which are considered impossible.

It is an important skill to be able to distinguish between discipline and forcing, because the line between them is not clear. When you rely on feeling the body and you have the right knowledge, you know what still an act of the discipline is and what already is forcing. This skill is very useful when you are keeping the body in discipline, especially when you are eliminating addictions (eating too much is one of them).

LIMITED BELIEF IN INFORMATION

In a subject area that you have not explored enough and where information is not readily available, misunderstandings can arise. This is also true for inedia and adaptation methods to inedia or non-eating. When specific information becomes popular, most people interested in the subject believe that this information presents something compulsory for progression on the path to inedia.

One example. Information suggesting that one has to go through the "21 day process" in order to become an inediate, has been rooted quite deeply in public consciousness. This information is an example of misunderstanding of what inedia or non-eating is about as well as lack of knowledge about methods assisting in realization of the intention.

For your own security, if information is unproven by you, it is worth to consider whether and how you will use it? In this case, a good solution is to be in touch with man having enough knowledge about the matter.

Also it pays to remember what I have emphasized before, that any information is partially or wholly true or false. What is written in books (even those considered great or holy) and what other people say (even those considered authoritative, enlightened or holy) still has one of these attributes. This is why, when you do not have proven information, you would better rely more on you feeling of the intuition than on things said or written by others.

Even if something is true for one man, it does not have to be so for other people. In other words, what is true in the world of one man, that does not have to work in the same way in the world of other people. Every man is different, the world of every man is different, thus same data may have different attributes. Something can be true and false at the same time.

If you act based on false or insufficient data, you are going to make mistakes. In case of the adaptation to life without food, that can be risky for your health or (in extreme cases) life.

Let me give you an example. I have met so many people, who went through the 21 day process because they believed that the process will make them non-eaters. Even after having failed a few times they were still questioning themselves on what went wrong, instead of realizing that the way was wrong. They believed in information, which was false for them, that the process makes man non-eater.

When I look at many web sites on the Internet, those dedicated and explaining so-called spiritual teachings, I see so much false information. When I listen to so-called masters or enlightened teachers, I hear so much false information. When I read books written by famous authors who are widely advertised as enlightened teachers, I see so much false information.
Be aware, that masters and teachers, enlightened or not, also give false information.
Let me tell you straight, because this is really important, do not behave just like a sheep. Do not allow others to feed you with false information, in other words, do not believe what you read, hear and see. Consider information but do not believe it. Check it out on yourself and see how it works on you.
There is no exception. Every man in their life gives true and false information. Whenever man is a homeless drunk or the most respected teacher, they all give true and false information.
Therefore, when you blindly follow all their information, you are limiting your growth, so you may be stuck in your conscious self-development. Saying that, I do not refer to any person or any teaching. I just turn your attention to the fact that information can be true or false regardless of its source. Be aware of that fact.

ALONE OR WITH A MENTOR

Consider, whether during the time of the most intensive adaptation of the body to inedia or non-eating or during long fasting you will be in touch with a mentor (caregiver). A mentor is man whom you trust, who has enough experience, who can visit and advice you even when you are in a seclusion. If you do not meet the mentor, you can speak with them on the phone.

The meetings with the mentor are done in order to check if everything is right or if you need something like help, advice, object or passing a message.

Also consider whether you belong to those people, who do not benefit when meeting any man, even a close friend, during the seclusion. Some people need a complete seclusion. Meeting anybody, even for a short time, causes them more stress than gladness. If you feel the need to be in a full seclusion, at least tell your relatives and intimates where you will stay, for how long and what you will be doing.

Even if you have decided to be completely alone, make sure that, just in case, you will be able to contact an experienced man, because you may suddenly feel that somehow you need this.

HALLUCINATIONS OR VISIONS

The sensitivity of a fasting man or one becoming an inediate is increasing, that can cause hallucinations. If this happens occasionally, it is no problem, but if the frequency of the hallucinations increases, you might consider to go to see a specialist. The reason may be temporary harmless disorders of the nerve system, which should not pose a problem. It would be worse if the disorders were permanent. Too long fasting harms the body and nerve system, it can causes hallucinations. So this is an indication for ending the fasting.

It is worth to learn to distinguish between a hallucination and a vision wich is seeing what exists in the immaterial world, non-perceptible for most people. The self-cleansing body allows the brain and the senses to work better, which may cause the so-called paranormal abilities to appear more intensively. One of these abilities is to see other beings, dimensions and times.

Hallucinations are evidence of disorders happening in the body and they may be indicating that the adaptation process is too intensive. They also may be a temporary mind states caused by toxins being eliminated from the body.

However, if the visions are caused by the date received from the immaterial senses which become active, they are not hallucinations and are not a subject for a cure. Then you need you to learn, how to rightly use the immaterial senses and how to interpret date from them. People knowledgeable in the matter may help, so it is a good idea to stay in touch with them.

GOOD HEALTH

There are people who mistakenly think that inedia is fasting for health. They think that inedia or non-eating are methods to heal the body. Inedia essentially differs from fasting. Inedia is the state of the mind, which reflects through the body so that it never asks for food or drink. Heal fasting is a way to bring back good health to man, it is a medical procedure of a religious practise.

It is advisable not to start the intensive adaptation of the body for living without food if the health is not good enough. Propitious sequence is that man first makes themselves fully healthy and then man can start the adaptation for living without food. It is more difficult to adapt yourself if the body is not healthy enough, because the process becomes longer and unpleasant.

Many people, even if they feel well and do not notice any symptoms, are not aware about the fact that some of their organs are ill. Most often this concerns the large intestine, liver, kidneys and spleen. For example, most people of the so-called western society have mycosis of the large intestine, parasites in the alimentary canal or other illnesses, which do not cause directly perceptible suffering. Using simple cure methods man can get rid of these health issues.

One of the cases that starting inedia or non-eating should be dissuaded is mental illness. It is better never to mention about inedia to a mentally ill man, so that they will not harm themselves. But if such man decides to pursue inedia, they must be carefully watched.

BODY TEMPERATURE

When living in a not tropical climate, while intensively adapting the body for living without food, it is worth to pay more attention to a common symptom, feeling cold. Most often the hands and feet are cold, almost icy, even when the air temperature is comparatively high, say 25°C. At this or higher temperature man feels cold.

If feeling cold bothers you too much, turn your attention to the body temperature, because it is one of the indicators of man's life energy. When the body temperature falls below 36°C, it is sufficient reason for taking an action, because forcing the body to work at too low body temperature is dangerous.

If you feel cold and you do not want to start eating, wear warmer clothes and do exercise frequently. Also add visualization in which, for example, you see and feel yourself as a source of warmth, the body is emanating warmth as fire does.

If too much cold is felt for too long it is worth to check the liver and spleen, because there is a high chance that they do not work efficiently enough.

If the extremities remain too cold and blue, you can warm them somehow. It is worth to make the extremities warm during sleep even if it means to put thick gloves and socks on when going to bed.

However, wearing thicker cloths and warming the extremities are not the proper solutions for a longer time, because such remedies do not stimulate man to free sufficient amount of life energy for the body. An inediate may not feel cold in situations when a normally eating, healthy man does; on the contrary, they feel good in a large scale of temperatures.

The body, especially the one going through revolutionary changes, temporarily may need more warmth from outside. This helps the body to keep warm and use the energy for other things. That is why the adaptation for living without food, if performed intensively, goes easier in summer, if one lives in other than tropical climate.

The most important thing is, when dealing with feeling cold, to know what the cause is. Is this caused by insufficient amount or inefficient circulation of life energy in man? Until man gave up eating, they had been releasing energy under the effect of the eaten food. Now, when man does not eat any more, their task consists in teaching the instinct to release energy in sufficient amount even when the body does not receive any food.

DRINKING WHEN NOT EATING

A mistake often done by fasting people is that they force themselves to drink too much or too little water. Drink water or other liquids in quantity which is demanded by your body. If you drink more or less than your body really needs, you are harming it. When you drink too much, you force the digestive system, especially the kidneys, to deal with the overload.

The excess of water in body may cause leg or face swelling. It also may cause excessive mucus which the body removes through a rash, catarrh or cough. Water is the best solvent and energy source but it increases body energy requirement if the body is watered in excess.

People who drink a lot during fasting, think that by doing that they can better flush out toxins from the body. The body is not a toilet so one cannot clean it by flushing it with more water; on the contrary, it may result in less toxins being removed.

The best solution is to drink the amount of water that the body demands for. Drink when you are thirsty, not when hungry. Drink slowly, sipping and mixing with the saliva before swallowing it.

CLEANSING THE LARGE INTESTINE

Enema, about which many scientific papers and books were written, about which many people think with disgust, though they have never tried it, is very beneficial for the human body. I will not discuss everything about this topic here but if I was to summarize it in just one short sentence, I would say: The deeper and the oftener (of course, within the limits of the body need), the better.

The large intestine is the organ, from which different substances are being absorbed into the body, including all toxins oozed by putrefying mixtures. Everything is directly absorbed into the blood and then circulates through the entire body.

The internal side of the large intestine is covered with villi, thanks to which the absorbing process can run smoothly enough. During the passing years of life, mucus and gum-like substance precipitates on the villi. Other substances of difficult-to-assay composition stick to it. Gradually something looking like gum insulation is formed, which makes the proper function of the large intestine difficult or impossible.

Besides, this grown layer is a friendly environment for many bad bacteria, mould and parasites. Proliferating colonies of these microbes and their excrements damage the beneficial intestinal bacteria, poison the blood, thus the entire body. This is how a favourable basis for many illnesses originates, of which more and more representatives of the terrestrial civilization suffer, and which grows like an epidemic, e.g. cancer, allergy, diabetes.

The doctors applying hydrocolonotherapy know that substances can be washed out from the large intestine, which was a residue from what man ate years ago. This happens because the layer of mucus and fecalith grows thicker with the course of time, if the diet is harmufl. This layer constricts the diameter of the large intestine and gradually makes it impossible for the body to absorb anything except products of the putrefying matter.

Then the liver becomes intoxicated so much that it is unable to neutralize all of toxins. Thus, the body of such man is under the influence of poisons all the time. This can be clearly seen on the face and the whole skin. Illnesses happening often, feeling of tiredness, headaches, faster ageing of the skin, dim or even yellow eyes are all symptoms clearly indicating a poisoned body, with the origin coming from the large intestine. Cleaning the internal side of the intestine may bring back its proper functions, which in turn makes the body healthy.

When one stops eating, the intestine first slows down and then stops working. Remains of the digested food remain in the intestine, it also is the case with the mucus and gum-like substance and the fecalith. New matter does not flow into the intestine, so the old one is not moved out. The matter remaining in the large intestine changes into hard lumps, which is not beneficial for the body, for sure. It may be a nest of parasites.

The remaining matter and the mucus gluing the villi inside the large intestine can be washed out with water – a simple and efficient method. This in many cases brings back health or even saves the life of man, whose body was full of toxins, tumour and parasites. That is why flushing the intestine with water may be so important. In case of many illnesses, well done cleansing of the large intestine is enough to remove the cause of the illness and heal man.

I usually frankly tell people, especially those who consider enema to be a disgusting thing, this truth: "You have the choice – you do not have to wash the intestine. However, if you wash out its contents, you throw out the rotting matter from your body. If you leave it in there, you are putrefying from the inside."

From the day that you stop eating, cleanse the large intestine with water at least once a week. You decide for yourself about the frequency of the enemas, according to the need of your body. A good procedure is to rinse the intestine once a day in the first week of fasting, once in two days in the second week, and twice a week later.

The intestine is cleansed with water until it is completely clean inside. This may take from a week to a few months, depending on the skill and state of the intestine. Especially removing the gum-like mucus requires much work because it tears slowly and resultantly. Usually many rinses are needed in order to fully clean the internal side of the large intestine.

Of course, efficiency of the intestine purification mostly depends on the skill of particular man. Complete purity of the intestine, from the anus until the point where the large intestine connects with the appendix, requires enemas repeated many times.

People have constructed apparatuses which help wash the entire large intestine. There are efficient and usable ones among them. However, if you want to be independent from any apparatuses, you can learn to do ordinary enemas.

While doing frequent cleansing of the intestine, you will work out the best method for you. You can modify and apply the advices written here.

At the beginning you can imagine that the large intestine is a pleated and very curved tube, like the one of a vacuum cleaner, and has the form of the U letter put upside-down. So ask yourself: What should I do to wash out the contents of this tube? What to do with water and the body? What kind of movements and positions of the body to apply in order to wash out, with water, the whole tube from the beginning to the end?

The large intestine is washed with water at the temperature from about 15°C to 45°C. Try first hot and then cold enemas in one sitting, do it alternatively. Pour in as much water as you can hold but do not exaggerate. The slower you pour in the water, with breaks, the more you can hold inside. More water poured in washes better and deeper. Of course, do not exaggerate because the intestine is not a balloon. From 0.1 to 2 litres of water can be poured in the large intestine.

When the water is inside, do some movements. When you keep in mind that the large intestine is like a U-tube put upside-down, you can easily work out helpful positions and movements. For example, you can pull the belly in and out, shake it to the sides or down and up, massage it. You can also raise your heels and immediately let them down hitting the floor. You can also jump several times.

After doing these movements for a few seconds to a few minutes, push all the contents out. Your imagination can help also in case of this activity. For example, in order to let out all the water from the ascending part of the intestine, you can put the feet on the wall and then raise the belly up, even up to the vertical position. In this position pull the belly in and out a few times. Then turn on the left site and move the feet down. From this lying position (on the left), at the same time raise the buttocks and pull in the belly, but keep the head down. Then squat and throw out the intestine contents as much as possible. Repeat the procedure as many times as needed, so that all the water will flow out. Then you can, again, pour in water and repeat it all.

To master the described method of intestine flushing, man needs to practise. This is an efficient method for cleaning the intestine, removing the fecalith and bringing back the right functions of this important organ.

Some people rinse the large intestine with urine, herbal infusions, coffee, water with lemon juice or other liquids. This may be a good idea in some cases, especially when you want to give the body a painkiller, a medicine or a substance softening the gum-like mucus. In the past, a soap solution was used, but this is not a good idea as it irritates the intestine and may poisons the body. According to the principle that the simplest solutions are the most efficient ones, most often the ordinary water is enough.

If you intend to make a dry fasting, first carefully cleanse the intestine. Start the cleansing at least a week before you stop drinking. First week fast on water only. Before you stop drinking, the large intestine must be clean inside. Thanks to this, it is much easier to fast without water, because the body needs it much less, compared with the time when the body is removing toxins (which entered the body from the intestine).

On the second or third day of fasting, you may want to cause diarrhoea. For this purpose, eat herbal or non-toxic chemical laxative. One glass of ~5% warm water solution of baking soda may be very efficient. Other is water solution of magnesium sulphate, that is Epsom salts, about 25 grams in one glass of warm water. Also 100% pear juice, about 1 litre bought in a store or produced by yourself, works well.

It is worth to remember that many people have abdominal pain after drinking large amount of pear juice. This can be quite painful, depends on how long man has been fasting before drinking the juice and what is remaining in the intestine. After drinking the juice, strong spasms and peristaltic movements occur in the intestine. If the intestine was not clogged too much, the diarrhoea may come within several minutes.

You can warm up about one litre of pear juice. Then drink it all within five minutes, but not too fast or you will cause vomiting.

Pear juice used in this way is effective for a few hours. This may be unpleasant. You may feel bad all the afternoon, because of abdominal pain, headache, etc, depending how sensitive you are. Pear juice works quite fast, therefore one to three days before using it, you would better rinse the intestine with water, so that it is not clogged so much. If it is, the pain and the spasms are stronger.

Of course, not everybody will experience pearl juice in the same way. There are people who, with full intestine, if they drink one litre of pear juice, feel not more than just a little rumble in the belly. There are also people who have nausea and feel strong pain after drinking only two glasses of the juice – this method may not be suitable for them.

I have described this method for those who would like to try it and experience how it works in their case. If you are not sure how it will work on you, you may start from just one glass of the juice and see what will happen. In the next try, you may increase the amount of the juice if one glass has too weak effect.

There are other methods for cleaning the intestine, not only the large one, but also the thin intestine. The entire digestive track and the gall bladder are cleaned. The most known and efficient method originated from yoga practise. It is described in the chapter "alimentary canal cleansing".

COFFEE ENEMA

Water is absorbed from the large intestine into the blood. Therefore all substances dissolved in water are also absorbed into the blood. Doctors have been using this function to efficiently apply medication or food to the patient. Body's absorption of the water soluble substances from the water poured into the large intestine, while doing enema, is several times more efficient than the absorption of these substances when they are eaten. This method of applying medications is much more efficient than swallowing.

When you pour a water and coffee solution into the large intestine, all substances that have been dissolved in the water, will enter the blood circulation. There are many poisonous compounds in the burned coffee powder that were produced as the result of roasting the coffee beans and further industrial processing. Therefore, drinking coffee is less harmful for the body than putting it into the large intestine.

A coffee enema is popular among those who do enemas. However, you may want to think twice about whether or not to do a coffee enema because this contaminates the entire body with harmful compounds. Simply cleansing the large intestine with water results in the same mechanical efficiency.

If you prefer to add something to increase the cleansing efficiency, simply add cabbage, lemon or grapefruit juice to the water. If you insist on an even stronger cleansing, you can prepare a solution by dissolving 1 tablespoon of baking soda and 1 tablespoon of table salt in 1 litre of warm water.

MOVING MUSCLES

Many people, who are fasting or adapting the body for living without food, complain about considerable weakness of the body, which may be accompanied by muscle pain. In case of some people the muscles begin to atrophy.

These people feel very weak, therefore doing any physical work tires them more than before,when they were eating. Performing such a simple act as moving a heavy object, becomes a big effort, causing short breath and legs trembling to these people.

Such weakness of the muscles requires exercising. When the muscles have too little movement, they atrophy. When man is fasting or forcible adapting the body for living without food, the atrophy is much faster, if man does not exercise the muscles regularly. The body, considering the muscles less needed, may eat them.

Therefore, if you want the muscle mass to remain, do exercisere gularly. It is more advantageous when the exercises do not tire the body too much, so do not use too much force. Let the muscle exercises to be moderate and regular in time. Instead of bending the knees a hundred times and pressing-up thirty times at once, stagger them to five sessions in one day. Little jogging and moderate swimming are also very beneficial for the muscles.

Energizing exercises mentioned earlier are very beneficial for the muscles and the entire body, especially for the energetic field. I have mentioned that the energizing exercises do not tire the body, they just make the muscles work gently, and this clearly makes them stronger.

It is worth to know some techniques and even try them out, but you do not have to become a student of yoga or any school. You can exercise alone or rely on your feeling of the body and the energy flow, which induce the muscles to move, as I described it earlier. In this case, the movement of the muscles is the most important, which will not allow them to atrophy, which will strengthen them and give the body more energy. To do the exercises aesthetically perfect is much less important in this case.

ALIMENTARY CANAL CLEANSING

I like to compare the alimentary canal to a pipe that is several meters long or to a rolled hose with enlargements. This is to be cleaned from remaining food remnants rotting inside.

Search for the expression *shankh prakshalan* on the Internet.
You will find much detailed information with photos and films, describing the procedure of this ancient effective method of cleansing the stomach, duodenum and intestines, all of which constitute the alimentary canal.

The descriptions state that the water and salt (NaCl) solution should be approximately 1%, which is about 1 table spoon of salt dissolved in 1 litre of water.

I successfully cleansed my alimentary canal using this composition:
1 litre of warm water + 1 tablespoon of table salt + 1 teaspoon of baking soda ($NaHCO_3$).

Adding baking soda increases the pH of the solution and causes diarrhoea. Increasing the pH is beneficial because it de-acidifies the blood, urine and also kills fungi. Fungi and many bacteria cannot live in alkaline environment (pH over 7).
On the other hand, diarrhoea is also advantageous because it helps clean out the intestine.

I believe that it is more beneficial for the body to use K_2CO_3 or $KHCO_3$ instead of $NaHCO_3$ or Na_2CO_3 because sodium (Na) is in almost every food product. Thus additional consumption of sodium may disturb the sodium-potassium balance. The body does not usually lack sodium but the insufficiency of potassium is not rare.

My important reminder is, make sure about the purity of these carbonates. They must all be food grade, never use the industrial grade ones.

I also cleansed my alimentary canal using this composition:

1 litre of warm water + 1 tablespoon of table salt + 1 tablespoon of Epsom salt (MgSO$_4$·7H$_2$O). This solution also cleanses the gall bladder and its ducts. However, I do not recommend this solution because not everyone can tolerate this intensive cleaning. The cleaning procedure is quite unpleasant. It may cause dizziness, vomiting and fainting. Never do that if your have a wound, ulcer or cancer anywhere inside the digestive tract. In case of any doubt, consult a wise doctor who knows about *shankh prakshalan*.

If you wish to have a strong cleansing and if you have your doctor's approval, you can prepare this solution:
1 litre of warm water + 1 tablespoon of table salt + 1 teaspoon of baking soda + 1 tablespoon of Epsom salt.

One litre of this solution is usually not enough, unless you have a small body. I, for example, with a body weight of 80 kg and a height of 186 cm, need to drink 2.5 litres of this solution. Later, I drink only clean water until my diarrhoea becomes like colourless water. Sometimes I shorten the procedure if it has made me tired.

Be aware that this cleaning is sometimes very unpleasant. Man ought to be healthy enough to apply this procedure. This is why you should seek advice from a doctor who has experience about *shankh prakshalan*.

To cleanse the alimentary track, you can use solutions made with herbs instead of the solutions mentioned above. This may be a better remedy for you. Find out which herbs clean intestines (cause diarrhoea) and are available in your area. Consult a competent herbalist.

RESUMING EATING

When the body shows any of the signs of emaciation, that is:
- it is weak most of the time;
- it is becoming thinner and thinner;
- it is losing weight (even if only 0.5 kg a week);
- your mood is getting worse or is bad most of the time;

this indicates that it is about the time to resume eating. To continue the starving (sometimes wrongly called inedia) can bring the body to a state in which it will not be usable for living any more, it will be starved to death.

Instead of keeping the state of starving, it is worth to see things and think differently, wiser, as if it was another valuable experience in this life. In such situations, I say: "Life never ends, so what you have not experienced till now, you can experience later. What you have not achieved till now, you can do in the future."

Therefore, it is not worth worrying, because if you do, you make your life difficult and suffer, therefore the amount of Love naturally manifested from you is limited. Next time, with yet bigger experience, with more expanded sphere of the Consciousness, it will go better. Maybe then the stage will be achieved in which eating will naturally, without any force, fall out of you.

On the other hand, it is not worth to fight with the body, because such action will not result in anything beneficial. Fighting causes wounds and suffering. If you fight with your body; who will be wounded and suffering? So when going back to eating is a wiser solution, it is worth to choose it. Your world will not stop, even if people will not consider you an enlightened master any more.

Resumption of eating again is quite a risky process, because if done improperly, it may make the health worse than before you gave up eating. The process of rebuilding the body after starving, can be compared to accelerated growth of a baby's body. First of all, this means that the body builds itself mainly on what it eats. So if man eats other substances than the body needs, their body material structure will be weaker than the ideal one. A body built in this way is weaker, gets ill easier, wears out and ages faster.

The most advantageous solution, when returning to eating after fasting, is to use the conscious eating method. Conscious eating gives the body the food, the amount and time all according the the real body needs. Thanks to this method, having starved or fasted, one can build a strong and resistant body. The resumption of eating again is even more important than the heal fasting itself.

If you do not have the patience for conscious eating, it is worth that you follow the principles of the proper eating, described later. Here are the three most important ones:

1. Limit the amount of eaten food, even if you have a limosis. The less time has passed from the end of your fasting, the less food should you eat. Increase the amount slowly and gradually. Limosis may occur very fast; if you support it, you may seriously hurt your body.
2. Use the conscious method from the first food. Long, long chewing is the most essential part or your eating.
3. The nearer to nature and the less processed is the food, the better mater-

ial is delivered to the body, from which it builds itself. So the less processing of what nature is giving man for eating, the more advantages for the body.

FAILURES

The experience and knowledge obtained about errors done during the process of realizing something give you potentially bigger possibilities. Thanks to this, next time you can enter the realization of a goal with more knowledge, trust and certainty. This is true also when applying to inedia or non-eating. The so-called 'unsuccessful try to adapt the body for inedia' makes a valuable part of the experience on this way.

Before beginning another try for life without food, it is worth to make sure that the body is healthy and nourished well and the instinct is sufficiently educated for this task. So it is worth to use some time to nourish the body well and to do some mental, spiritual exercises. Therefore, focus less on just non-eating but rather use more time and energy for expansion of the Consciousness sphere and programming of the instinct, because inedia is more the skill of the mind than of the body. The contemplation exercise and especially 'allowing your Inner Joy to emanate' described earlier, may bring you a lot of benefits.

Anyway, it is not worth, in such a situation, to acknowledge that you have failed. If, in addition, you feel guilty or you make the body guilty, you put yourself in a much worse situation. Such an approach does not help, it becomes another barrier created by you on the way of conscious self-development.

If the goal pursued has not been achieved, it does not necessarily mean that you have failed. If you think that you have not succeeded, you may be wrong because in fact it may be something else. Then, if you look for the true answer deep inside you, you may find that your true goal was not giving up food but the experience that you have gone through.

In case that you have not succeeded to live without food, the best thing that you can do is to regard the eating again as coming back home after a very interesting journey full of valuable experiences. It is worth mentioning the health benefits which the non-eating-try time gave your body.

During the try of adapting the body for living without food, and also later, feeling Love flowing from you is very important for the body. Love is there when Life is created. The body needs Life, thus it needs your Love especially in moments regarded as difficult.

PROPER BODY WEIGHT

Social suggestion has influenced people so much that they believe even non truths. The appearance and weight of the body is one example. In a society where the majority of people are overweight, a somewhat overweight man is regarded as looking well and healthy. Obesity results from the improper functioning of the body; this means that the body is ill, although there are exceptions.
In the same society, a man of proper body weight is regarded as thin.

Proper body weight is one of the characteristics of a perfectly healthy body.

> When the body is not subject to overeating or under-eating and when the body systems are functioning properly, the body is at the ideal weight, regardless of how it looks and how people judge it.

The judgement of man's appearance is often contrary to their proper body weight. It is important to be aware of this.

When your body is in total health, you feel perfect and this is a normal state for you that lasts for months and years, you have a body of ideal weight. Whether people judge you as fat or thin, it has no significance because that is only their opinion. If you start to modify your diet in order to lose weight or to gain weight, you would probably harm the body.

> Focus on your body's health, not its appearance or people's opinions.

Provide the body with all that it needs for proper functioning. The correct diet and proper physical activity for your body are necessary for good health. Focus on this, not on the judgement of people about your appearance. If you follow the direction of adjusting the appearance of your body to suit people's opinion, you may probably harm it.

ASK YOURSELF

I suggest that you think deeply over these questions, analyse them and answer them to yourself.

1. Why almost everything that human eats is later excreted as faeces, urine, mucus, sebum, gases etc.? Does it mean that this perfect organism is a machine for processing almost all eaten things to produce excretions?
2. Why there are no illnesses caused by non-eating or by fasting, but there are so many diseases caused by eating?
3. Why do so many diseases (often bothering man for years) completely disappear during long enough fasting?
4. Why do fasting statistics show the highest efficiency rate among physical healing methods available on Earth?
5. When treated for drug addiction (either alcohol or nicotine, narcotics, caffeine, sugar etc.), the body shows some unpleasant reaction (called clinical symptoms). When stopping eating, people show the same clinical symptoms. Why are the symptoms in both cases the same? When a recovered addict returns to their addiction, the reactions in their body are the same as appear in man who restarts eating after a long period of fasting. Again, why the reactions are the same in both cases?
6. Researches show that some people can live without food for months or years, but others die after just a dozen of days. Why?
7. Why do different individuals, having the same weight and height, eating food which differs very much by quantity and composition (every man eats something different) enjoy perfect health?
8. Why are some people eating very 'healthy food' often ill, but other people eating junk food very healthy?
9. When people and animals are ill, they have no appetite. In such cases animals fast until they become healthy. If an ill human fasts, they also become healthy much faster. Why does the body react like this?

Do you have any other question related to this subject?

REASONS OF EATING

Why does man eat? What is the reason that man decides to put inside their body a piece of matter defined as food? This question may seem strange because a simple answer can be given: 'Because man feels hunger'. Therefore let us ask: When and in which circumstances man feels hunger?

There are many reasons why man eats. They may be catalogued in different lists; here is one of them:

1. Real needs of the body (RNB).
2. Emotions.
3. Habit.
4. Addiction.
5. Belief and fear.
6. Boredom.
7. Decision to change.
8. Company.
9. Taste, smell, appearance.
10. Poverty, thrift.
11. Compelling.
12. Reward.
13. Grounding.

Other reasons, which make people eat something, most often are contained in one of the above points.

For man aspiring to inedia or non-eating, to know the reasons of eating is one of the most advantageous steps on the way. This makes man understand better their psyche and body.

RNB

Real **n**eeds of the **b**ody. Human body (with exceptions) sometimes needs specific substances from outside. There are thousands of these substances. Some of them are known, named and catalogued, for example: carbohydrates, fats, proteins, minerals, trace elements and enzymes. The body works best if it receives them exactly in the right moment and exactly in the right amount.

Let me ask a question. Who knows, what substance, in what amount and at what time the body needs? Every body is different and lives in different conditions; so how about the general dietetic recommendations? How misleading are they?

You simply will answer that you rather do not know any man, who would know what, how much and when the body needs. As for the second question, you also know the answer: there is no diet good for all people.

Let me add that the ideal diet is a matter which is changing constantly. What is the perfect diet for man today, may be a harmful diet tomorrow. Man is constantly changing. As the circumstances of man's life changes, so their needs undergo changes, including the diet.

RNB is the only circumstance, in which eating something gives advantages for the work of the body. Eating for any other reason harms the body, although this can give man advantages in other matter.
When RNB occurs, the best solution is to give the body what it asks for. If RNB is not gratified, the body is harmed and suffers.

Alenara suggested a method to determine whether feeling hungry is caused by RNB or by an emerging emotion. In order to determine this, man imagines that they will not eat the thing they feel hungry for. When imaging this, man pays attention to the emotional reaction of the body. If there is no reaction, it shows rather for RNB. If there was an emotional reaction, particularly one grounded on fear, it indicates another cause. Most often it is about fear or an emotion being released.

The conscious eating method (described earlier) develops the skill of telling the difference, whether it is about RNB or an emotion. Conscious eating makes it much easier, to establish and keep the most proper diet.

Emotions are the factor which most often makes man take food. In the instinct there are blocked emotional reactions, feelings, pictures and thoughts. They are being accumulated in there since the conception, some of them have the origin in previous lives. The intellect does not know about their existence. The instinct, which cannot cope with processing the data, tries to send them to the intellect for solution. The instinct's work is storing data and running programs (processes functioning without any attention from the intellect) – I have already written about it.

Therefore, when the instinct is trying to send data to the intellect, man first may feel hungry. If at this moment, man turns sufficient attention only to the feeling of hunger, and man asks themselves if they really feel hunger, then the answer most probably will be 'no', it is not a hunger. However, most people, when they feel hungry, do not stop on the thought, they immediately start inserting things into their body. As the result, the body suffers because it receives something harmful.

The conscious eating method, even if it is done only partially at the moment of feeling hungry, helps to learn how to distinguish the RNB from an emotional reaction.

What happens when man, instead of focusing on the appearing hunger, thinks about eating? The blocked emotions, feelings, pictures and thoughts are pushed back deeper inside the instinct. The problem remains unsolved because man has not thought about it and has not reached deeper. This unresolved problem is still gnawing man inside.

The emotions being released during fasting, if there are many of them, may make man feel quite unpleasant. Then this man, not fully understanding what is happening to them, becomes so sensitive, nervous and impatient. At that time man still associates such situation with the hunger and when man starts eating again, they feel relief. But if at that time, man (instead of eating) would focus on feeling what the heart communicates, the hunger would decrease or vanish and the psyche would have a chance to be cleared from the problem.

Clearing the psyche during fasting is more unpleasant and difficult to bear by overweight people. They are exactly those people who made themselves fat because when their psyche wanted to solve harmful programs, which was felt as hunger, they immediately start eating. As you can conjecture exactly they are the people who most need fasting and who go through fasting with biggest difficulties. In extreme cases, people die during fasting; not because the body does not receive food, but because of emotions being released, which they cannot cope with.

Here another role can be seen, which food plays for man on earth. Food is a drug which allows people not to think about unpleasant things. How many people overuse this drug, it is visible mainly by the fatness of the society.

Hunger can be caused also by microbes living in the body (e.g. mould in intestine). As an example, candida can influence the brain centres of feeling hunger or taste in a way that makes man hungry for the specific substances needed by candida. Many people addicted to sweets have the body full of candida, especially in their intestines.

HABIT

is the activity usually performed in specified circumstances. Habits in regard to eating are one of the main reasons why people eat when there is no RNB. As similarly to other habits, man does not think whether the body needs what in this moment they are consuming. Man just eats because they are used to doing this.

One of the most common habits is to sit at the eating table because of so-called mealtime. The division: breakfast, lunch, dinner, or any other division, makes man eat frequently.

Another habit is about the type of food. Examples. Tea without sugar but with a biscuit for the teatime. Instant coffee with milk and sugar in the morning after getting up. Dumpling with sauerkraut and sauce. Beer with fries when watching TV. Ice cream when walking in the city. These are a few examples of habits. You probably could mention here also yours. Man chooses, prefers one food and does not like others, depending on the circumstances. This depends on some factors of which the most important is the society suggestion.

A habit produces automatic reaction of the body, this is why in a specific circumstance (e.g. time, environment) man feels hunger for a specific food. This is a good example how the society suggestion is programming the instinct.

A habit can be removed much easier than an addiction. How to distinguish between a habit and an addiction? Look at the emotional reaction. In general, if giving up a specific action does not trigger emotional reaction, the action was a habit. If you try to give up an addiction, unpleasant emotional reactions occur (which may be accompanied by unpleasant body reactions), for example: irritability, anger, explosions of hatred. In other words, the less intensive emotional reaction, the weaker addiction. There is no sharp line between a habit and an addiction.

ADDICTION

to eating is one of the most often occurring addictions on Earth. Yes, one may become dependent on eating or drinking, addicted to eating generally or to eating something specific. An addiction looks like a habit but when you try to give it up, you feel that the body and the psyche are revolting.

Man most often becomes addicted to sugar, coffee, soft drinks, salt, dairy, rice, bread or meat. When an addict suddenly decides to give up the addicting product, they feel that the body craves for it. For example, a body addicted to meat and deprived of it, will crave for it with the taste, and even will influence the mood. Man will be feeling, for weeks, that they have unbearable craving for, let us say, a steak; they may even dream about eating it.

In case of an addiction, it is easy to mistakenly determine if craving for a specific food is caused by the addiction, RNB or parasites. That is why man who is not an expert in the method of conscious eating may not in every case faultlessly determine what, how much and when the body needs. However, exercising the method of conscious eating regularly leads to the skill to be able to distinguish quickly between RNB, addiction and other factors.

A strong craving for a particular food may be cause also by parasites. There are many more parasites, willing to live in the human body, than an ordinary man may expect. Many of them can strongly influence taste preferences of man. Practically, it can be said that some parasites can enslave man so much that the victimised man will eat mostly what supports the parasites to grow well. Fungus may be a good example. If their colony has grown enough in the intestine, man becomes an addicted glutton of sweets.

The more addicted to eating man is, the more difficult they find fasting to be and the fasting process alone is also more unpleasant. In case of man addicted to eating, the body symptoms are the same as those occurring in case of man addicted to alcohol, cigarettes or drugs. This is one of clinical proofs confirming that eating is a kind of man's addiction. Man lives in this addiction almost from their birth.

Eating as an addict (living with the addiction to food) is one of the main factors why the body of an ordinary human withstands less than a hundred years, often being ill and ageing during the whole life.

BELIEF OR FEAR

often are important factors considered by man creating their own. In this case, the belief is built on the fear that the body lacks some substance, so it has to be given by eating specific food. Apart from the fear, that the body lacks something, man can believe that eating something gives advantages to the body.

Here are some examples. I have chosen only the false ones.

- Drinking milk makes the bones and teeth harder because it contains a lot of calcium.
- Man needs to eat everything.
- Man has to eat a lot of fruits and vegetables.
- Meat is necessary for the body to grow properly and because it provides the body with vitamins B12.
- Man has to drink at least 2 litres of water daily.
- Man has to eat often but in small quantities.
- Man has to eat a lot to be able to work heavily.
- Eat a lot so that you will grow big and strong.

These and many other beliefs, passed on from generation to generation and often blindly followed, influence man's diet. People with such or other beliefs about eating, eat some food only because they believe about its specific influence on the body. This kind of beliefs are applied when a diet is created and promoted, e.g. to lose weight, to detoxify the body, to heal it.

As a matter of fact, the body is self-sufficient and it needs only a mind which operates it properly. The stronger man believes that the body needs something from outside, the more man makes the functioning of the body dependent on it.
Another fact is that every man is a different world, creates and adopts different needs and beliefs. This is why there is no such thing as a proper diet for everyone. An individually suited proper diet for one man is a diet which fully meets RNB of this man.

Especially often found belief is the conviction that man has to eat a lot in order to have enough energy and thus also strength. Man who believes that food is an essential fuel, which gives energy to the body (as gas does to an engine), will be more predisposed to overeating. Most people have the instinct programmed in this way. I have explained it already.

False beliefs make man eat food that the body does not need, that overloads it, that damages it. For example, the belief that "man should eat a lot of fruits", is misleading. The thing is that one should not increase the amount of eaten food by adding fruits. It may bring more advantages to the body, to increase the proportion of fruits in the diet.

As you can easily conjecture, fear and beliefs related to eating and food cause more harm than give advantages to man Especially defenceless children suffer more, when they are forced by their parents to eat.

I also heard of a belief that if man does not eat all of the received serving, they are tempting the destiny which in future may punish them by lack of food.

One more essential matter concerning beliefs. If a food contains high amount of a substance (vitamin, mineral, element) it does not mean that it has to be consumed in order to give the body the substance. Cow milk, containing a lot of calcium, can be a good example. People may believe that drinking lots of milk frequently prevents deficiency of calcium in the body. However, the result of such behaviour is the opposite. Drinking a lot of cow milk, especially the boiled one, causes deficiency of calcium in the body. Explaining why this happens would require penetrating in another topic concerning influence of specific foods on human body.

BOREDOM

and eating also are related in some ways. Did you ever start to eat just because it was a less boring activity at that moment or it let you forget about boredom? "Why do you eat?" – "Because there is nothing else for me to do." or "To kill the time." Do you know these or similar expressions?

The activities related with preparing food, eating it and afterwards cleaning, are attractive enough to make man to start performing them, when they find no other occupation.

When you are bored then, instead of eating, you can contemplate or do other so-called spiritual exercises. You probably already know that eating due to boredom creates unnecessary overload for the body, wastes time, money and energy.

Man who decides to eat because they are bored, often does this also because they like the taste. In this way, the relationship is created: boredom >> the will to get rid of it >> temporary upswing of the mood. This kind of relationship, as you can easily conjecture, is quite self-destructive for man. This most often manifests by obesity and related diseases of the body. It is easy to get addicted then.

DECISION TO CHANGE

which usually is based on beliefs, becomes a reason for changing the diet. Such a decision may concern the appearance of the body, the way it works, the mood or psyche.

One of the most frequently taken decisions is to slim down an obese body. Most people know that the excess of eaten food causes obesity. Some of them decide to change the diet in order to lose the excess body fat.

Having made the decision, man selects the food, amount, time and way of eating. When creating such a diet, the knowledge and beliefs of man have crucial influence.

The decisions concerning the diet can be often noticed among people interested in conscious self-development. These people decide to consume selected foods and give up the other. They also change the time of eating. If this develops in accordance with RNB, then their decisions advantageously influence them, if not, then probably they hurt the bodies.

When making any decision concerning the diet, it is worth to know that most advantageous is to follow RNB. If you aspire to non-eating and RNB indicates the need to take food, then the right way goes through working on changing RNB.

MEETING

with others may make man willing to eat. Social gathering usually include eating food – it is one of the customs harmful to health. During that time, most often food not needed by the body is eaten. Additional harm causes overeating because, for example, the hosts are encouraging the guests to try everything. Also the conditions are not favourable for consuming food because people are talking while eating.

Can you imagine a social meeting without any food? It is possible and it may be quite successful if all the participants are informed in advance, why without eating. At most, people who do not like the idea will not come. You can organize a party and ask the participants to bring their own food. Tell them that you do not know what their RNB is, so you are not going to prepare any food for them. Encourage them to take care of their own RNB and bring their own food.

TASTE, SMELL, APPEARANCE

may be so tempting that man decides to consume something although they do not feel any hunger or thirst. The so-called cooking art is a large branch of man's life on Earth. A fact is that what often looks tasteful, comes out not such at all after you try it.

One of the biggest harms that people have done to themselves is using condiments. Salt, sugar, spices, taste intensifiers, substances improving the smell and look belong to condiments. Why using them harms the body? Mainly because this cheats the senses and makes the natural body function, which is finding the nutritional substances with the sense of taste, work improperly.

"This is tasteless." "It tastes like sawdust." If man feels like that about a dish, this clearly indicates that the body does not need this food. It is better for the body if man does not eat the dish instead of flavouring it and in this way cheating the natural body function. The sense of taste, directly dependent on RNB, works perfectly. When the body needs something, the taste sense lets man eat it with pleasure, even if it does not contain any flavouring. It may even happen that adding a flavouring will spoil the taste of the dish.

Potatoes without salt taste great if the body needs them but they are tasteless when eating them harms the body. Strawberry, berry, raspberry, have amazing taste when the body needs them. But when eating them causes overloading the body, the senses inform man that they are too sour, not sweet enough, etc. This is why some people say that this fruit "tastes better with whipped cream and sugar".

Using substances which change the taste or appearance of food, cheats the body and makes man eat more for taste instead due to RNB. Having made the body used to the taste caused by the condiments, man more often crave for the taste than feels hunger for the food specified by RNB.

Condiments make man addicted. Sugar and salt are the most often used food drugs and substances cheating the taste sense, the natural body function which controls eating according to RNB.

Giving up the condiments, especially for the taste, is very advantageous for the human body. Then the taste sense informs more precisely what and how much the body needs. This body function works in this simple way – if something is tasteless without any condiments, this means, the body does not need it.

There are people who, utilising their knowledge about how condiments work, mainly the tasty ones, have built well profiting companies. Some companies selling fast food are a good example of this. Their big money profits, in addition to the big health damage caused to millions of people, is the sum of their operation and universal ignorance concerning the taste sense.

POVERTY, THRIFT

make some people feel that 'it's a waste' not to finish a dish and later throw it away. It seems that such behaviour of man is caused mainly by their thrift. It is a fact, throwing food away is a waste, whereas conserving it for later use saves money and time. However psychic analysis more often show that there is a fear in the basis of such behaviour of man.

Even if here we forget the RNB, eating food which was left earlier, especially if it was heated up, harms the body more. Many prepared meals go bad much faster than the raw material used for preparing them. Heating up produces more substances harming the body.

People, especially those who have experienced hunger caused by poverty, natural disaster or war, may have a strong conviction that food should not be wasted. If they consider the hunger wide spread among millions of people on Earth, they feel guilty or even as if they were sharing responsibility for this.

My grandfather (man of a great heart) was like that. He chose to eat boiled potatoes which were in the fridge for a few days, instead of throwing them away, even if he was not hungry. That is also why he was breeding a pig so that no food would be waisted.

On the other hand, there are people who buy food considering only the price. They are poor, so they cannot buy what they would need. In order to save money, they buy only the cheapest products.
There are also rich people, who still consider food prices and select the less expensive food instead of the ones that their bodies need.

COMPELLING

concerning eating is associated with one of the most serious harms that parents can do to their children – to force them to eat more than they want to or what they do not feel hunger for. Concerning food and its quantity, the children should be left free to choose. But it is better for their health to protect them (so that they will not get addicted) against toxins like chips, fries, pizza and also products made of milk or baked flour.

Some children are deceived in order to make them eat. They are told that all that is on the dish has to be eaten, because if not, something bad may happen; for example, the child will have freckles or someone/something will take them away. Also this kind of suggestions are kind of compelling. They harm the child's psyche, which may manifest with harm in the food sphere later in their life.

Compelling in eating is applied also to mealtime. Some people do not allow others or themselves to eat when they are hungry, but ask them to wait till a meal will be ready. "Don't eat now, wait, dinner will be ready soon!" Or even worse, they order others to eat because it is mealtime – "It is dinner time now, eat everything nicely!"

Compelling yourself or other people to eat at fixed times of the day introduces rhythm to the day order, makes man dependent and almost never accords with RNB.

To forbid something, also is a kind of forcing. If man forbids another man to eat something that RNB indicates for, they harm the body.

Compelling, forbidding to eat something may be temporarily used in order to protect yourself or other people, especially children, against eating toxic substances, such as candy, fried, backed or fumed food and products made from animal milk. However, in this case it pays better to give more attention and work to the psyche and education. Eating these foods is discordant with RNB, it is caused by an addiction. The addiction may be psychical, for the taste or caused by parasites.

REWARD

in the form of food as consolation for yourself or another man, may be a sufficient reason for eating. Did it happen to you to eat something in order to console yourself when feeling sad, discontent or to reward yourself for something?

Examples. "It was a day full of nervousness, so now I will at least eat something good." "I have not passed the exam, so why not buy an ice cream as consolation." "We shall be happy, so let's go to a restaurant for a good dinner."

In this case eating may be considered to be a kind of recoil or even refuge from a problem, difficulties, unpleasant situation. Man considers the act of eating and the food taste as something giving a pleasure. This program often originates from childhood. Many parents commit this mistake, they reward children with candy or ice cream for doing something 'good'. In this way, they build in the child's instinct a suggestion that eating something tasteful may be a reward or consolation.

Rewards are also all food products, most often sweets, which are given to, for example, winners of a contest, pupils at the graduation, children for good behaviour. Acting in this way, strongly suggests that eating specific food is a price which is worth to work for or even fight for.

Eating only for reward or consolation is discordant with RNB, so it harms the body. This also makes man more addicted to taste and does not let blocked psychical reactions manifest outside. It is worth to examine yourself to find out if you have this program, so that, if need be, you can consciously remove it. This liberates you from one of your addictions.

GROUNDING

is one of the special reasons of eating, which often concerns people trying to adapt the body to inedia or non-eating. This helps them to be 'grounded' in order not to be 'flying' too much in the clouds of spirituality. Also inediates need to be in balance between the matter and the spirit.

One of the functions of eating is to keep the connection between man and the physical matter, particularly Earth. It can be said, explaining in a graphical way, that eating food makes man heavy enough so that they will not lift off the ground like a balloon. On the other hand, too much food can weigh down man to Earth so much that they won't be able to 'rise in the spirit'.

In case of some non-eaters who still have not learned to keep the balance between the matter and the spirit, eating becomes a helping factor, thanks to which they can ground themselves. This is the reason why a non-eater sometimes may want to eat something heavy. The lower the vibrations of the food, the better and longer it grounds man. For example, a glass of carrot juice grounds man less and for a shorter time than an oily hamburger of the same weight.

A non-eater may interpret differently their wish for eating something. they may, for example, feel and say that it is the taste sense, trained for the whole life, demands sensations. Besides this, quite often the need for grounding parallels with RNB. Then eating is more advantageous.

Also other people, not only non-eaters, may feel the need to ground themselves. Usually these are people focused on the spiritual side of the life. In the respect of their subtle nature and the way I feel these people, I used to call them angels. They, in order not to 'fly' too high, sometimes need to eat something heavy, which makes them feel better and improves their health. When the contact with Earth (the matter) loosens too much, man may be losing so-called 'feeling of the reality'. One of the results of this loosening can be a body illness.

I know people who are in weak contact with Earth. They suffer because of this. For example, it is difficult for them to find a good job, they are in constant debt, they are chronically ill. In some cases, physical examination does not show any illness but they may feel pain. When their diet is changed for a heavier one, the mood may improve because the illness leaves or the symptoms significantly decrease, and man can see clearer solutions of their financial problem.

What is called death because of starving, is not always so although it was caused by not eating for too long. Many, among people left without food, died, but not because of the organic hunger, the reason was excess bond loosening between them and the matter. A being who is insufficiently bonded to the matter, is not able to live in human body on Earth and they may decide to go to another dimension, where the matter is not so dense.

INEDIATES and NON-EATERS

How many inediates or non-eaters do live on Earth? I do not know any statistic data of this type. I heard and read numbers given by others, ranging from a few to more than hundred thousand. According to my present feeling, there are hundreds of thousands of people who do not need food for living on Earth.

It is a fact that many non-eaters are people seen as highly developed spiritually. Most of them are not interested in being famous. They remain unpopular because the mass media do not talk about them.

The other (the largest) part of non-eaters are people who have never heard about the hypotheses, philosophy and movement concerning non-eating. They do not eat because they just do not feel like eating. Also, it often happens that the society in which they live thinks that they are ill, not normal or extraordinary. This makes them feel uneasy.

Particular case are people called anorectic. One fact is that anorexia is an illness caused by disturbances in the psyche. Another fact is that not all of these people are real anorectic. Some of them are people who do not know about their inborn or developed non-eating ability and they succumb to common beliefs. Strong suggestion that they experience from the society has the power to make them ill or even die.

Some non-eaters are not obviously recognizable as such because they let you invite them for a coffee, for a dinner or they even take part in a banquet. Then they eat just for social reasons because they do not want to become a subject of an interest for others. This is the only reason why they eat because they do not need food.

I listed below, in alphabetical order, only those very few who were made famous by the mass media or who are / were actively promoting this life style. These people were or are inediates / non-eaters but I do not guarantee this. I found this information but I have not investigated those people. Most of this info comes from the year 2001.

Alenara

From Sweden. When she was a teenager she discovered how bad food influences her body. Since then she was moving in direction of 'breatharian-

ism', especially when she did not feel to be compelled to eat. Alenara, although she does not call herself a breatharian, has a lot of knowledge about living without food. She can explain breatharianism from different view. Her web sites contains a lot of information:
www.ethereallights.com and www.angelfire.com/stars3/breathe_light.

Balayogini Sarasvati

Amma, India, for 3 years was consuming only water as reported by „Rosicrucian Digest" June 1959.

Barbara Moore

"A heroic figure is Barbara Moore, M.D. of London" - a news release by the London Sunday Chronicle dated 17 June 1951 reads:
A woman of 50, who looks like she was only 30, claimed yesterday that she hates food, has beaten old age, and expects to live at least 150 years. She has set out to do it by giving up food. Twenty years ago she ate three normal meals a day. Slowly for 12 years she reduced her eating until she was keeping fit on one meal a day of grass, chickweed, clover, dandelion and an occasional glass of fruit juice. Five years ago she switched entirely to juices and raw tomatoes, oranges, grasses and herbs. Now she drinks nothing but a glass of water flavoured with a few drops of lemon juice. She says, "There is much more in sunlight and air than can be seen by the naked eye or with scientific instruments. The secret is to find the way to absorb that extra - that cosmic radiation - and turn it into food".
Each year she goes to Switzerland for the better air and climbs mountains on a diet of water from the streams. "You see - she explains - my body cells and blood have changed considerably in composition. I'm impervious to heat or hunger or fatigue".
Barbara died in a car accident, during her travels across United States.

Christopher Schneider

He says about himself: "I have been non-eating since August 1998 [...] it gives me a lot of experiences and events. I eat some chocolate, sweets, cheese, sometimes every day, and sometimes once a week. I eat for fulfil my tastes, touching ground, not for necessity of eating. Nearly every day I drink Cappuccino, tthis is something like a ritual, or watered juices".
In Germany, since 1999, Chris run courses dedicated to the 21-day proced-

ure. People determined to accommodate to live on light; he helps in passing on this process. He is also a nature therapist, rebirthing therapist and a kinesiology, reiki and spiritual healler. He organizes courses and helps others by sharing this knowledge. As he says "all this work is dedicated to find power and connection with internal unity and Divine One Within". Christopher's web site is www.chi-production.de.

Evelyn Levy

Brazilian, lives with her husband Steve in Brazil. After coming back from personal journey to Peru, where she did not eat for five days, she got interested in immortality and living on light. During this time she began a natural process of accommodation to high vibrations, which resulted in lack of being hungry. Later, when in 1999 her husband decided to stop eating, she decided to do the same. Evelyn's web site is: vivendodaluz.com.

Giri Bala

Indian woman, born in 1868, has not taken food or drink since 1880. The entire life she was living in Bengal village of Biur. Her inedia has been rigorously investigated by the Maharaja of Burdwan. She used a certain yoga technique to recharge her body with cosmic energy from the ether, sun and air.
The story of Giri Bala was told to Yagananda when he met with her when she was 68. By that time, she had not eaten nor taken fluids for over 56 years. Still living the life of a humble and simple villager, she had in her early years, as rumour spread, been taken to the palace of the leader of her province. There she was kept under strict observation and eventually released with the sanction that yes she did exist purely on Light.
As a child she enjoyed a voracious appetite for which she was often chided and teased. At age nine she was betrothed and was soon ensconced in her husband's family abode. One day Giri suffered so greatly at her mother-in-law's tongue and teasing at her gluttony that she exclaimed "I shall soon prove to you that I shall never touch food again as long as I live".
She ran out of the village crying, and prayed for guru who could teach her how to live on God Light only. Then, the guru appeared and showed her Kirija Yoga technique, which made her body free from material feeding. Since that time, Giri practised yoga to power the body energy from the sun and the air, and she took neither food nor liquids.

Hira Ratan Manek

Born and living in India. Seven doctors started examining him a few days before he began a long fast. First he lived only on water for 211 days, and then for 411 days. HRM's official web site is www.solarhealing.com.

Jack Davis

He lives in Hawaii. After he attended a seminar conducted by Wiley Brooks he said "During those years I drastically reduced and altered the types of food consumed. [...] By 1982 I was ready for the lessons of Wiley Brooks." His story in details was on breatharian.info.

Jasmuheen

An Australian, who after completing the 21 day procedure in1993, did not eat for two years. Then she started, as she said, some experiments with small amount of delicacies, coffee and tea. She claims to be free from eating, but is lenient with her taste senses, that is why she drinks coffee, eats sweets and even potatoes during long flights in order to reduce her energy to be able to sleep. According to her statement, the average amount of daily food is less than 300 calories per day. Jasmuheen's web site contains a lot of interesting data www.jasmuheen.com.

Joachim M Werdin

You have probably read my story written in this book. More info can be found on my web sites: inedia.info and breatharian.info.

Kamilla

A Polish woman who lives in London, interested in secrets of life, esotericism from the philosophical point of view. She began the lifestyle without eating on August 1999, when being in a monastery, in complete seclusion, she obtained the initiation. Her decision resulted from participating in Jasmusheen's lecture a few weeks earlier. From the very first moment of that meeting, Kamila "knows immediately, that she passed through the process". Then she admitted: "This is like the operation without scalpel and you feel

it very deeply".
She also does not practise asceticism and as she said: "I take sometimes one or two teaspoonfuls of horseradish, mushroom in vinegar and eat it with pleasure". The spiritual change of Kamilla, which resulted in living without addiction to so-called food, was beneficial for her health. Previous examinations showed that she suffered from blood cancer, diabetes and paralyse of the right leg. All these things disappeared and Kamila bursts with health.

Kazimierz Karwot

A Polish. Before starting "living on Light", during the years 1999 and 2000, he was living in nature, where he was working on his spiritual growth. As in case of other non-eating people, his transformations resulted after more than a dozen of years on a spiritual path. Kazimierz did this in very modest conditions, living on the outskirts of a village. He did the initiation, the 21 day process, in seclusion, in February 2001. Now he says: "I am living on Light". His web site is http://karwot1.pl.

Martha Robin

A French, born in 1902 (Chateauneuf-de-Galaure), never left her home village. From March 1928 on, she was unable to eat any food, when she tried, the body vomited everything. She could neither swallow, nor digest, nor could she drink, not even pure water. She was also unable to sleep. Physicians were helpless. She lived solely on the Eucharist. She spent a lot of time praying and contemplating.

Prahlad Jani

An article published in "India Times" on 2003 11 21, "BBC News" and other mass media informed about man who claimed that he had been living 68 years without any food and drink. Medical tests made by many doctors in a hospital proved that after ten days of strict observation, without any food or water, he was in perfect health state and his body did not change the weight.

Steve Torrence

An American, Evelyn's husband. At the beginning of 1999, he was impressed by the book "Life and Teaching of Far East Masters". As he said, he came to a conclusion that "our bodies do not need physical food and have been accommodated to it because we forced them. Eating is not only unnecessary, but also harmful for our health and good temper".

Sunyogi Umasankar

Umasankar has discovered a method of absorbing energy directly from the sun, which is called sun-gazing, which can remove the need to eat, drink or sleep. In "India Monitor" he said: "From 17th August 1996 to 7th December 1996, I stopped having food altogether, but after continued requests by a relative, I resumed my normal intake."

Surya Jowel

Involved in The Suryayogi Fundation, more information can be found on his web site: www.suryayog.org.

Theresa Neumann

She was born in 1898 in Northern Bavaria. At the age of 20 she had an accident and became blind and paralysed. Then in 1923 she was miraculously healed. Since then Theresa had not consumed any foods or liquids except for one small consecrated wafer a day.
Stigmata, or sacred wounds of Christ, began to appear on her head, breast, hands and feet every Friday while she was experiencing the passion of Christ. Yogananda later said that in her past life she was Mary Magdalene. She is here to show (like Giri Bala) that it is possible to "live on God's Light".
Throughout the 36 years that Theresa bore the stigmata, thousands of tourists visited her small cottage to witness the miracle. Theresa died in 1962. Paola Giovetti's book "Theresa Neumann" presents her life.

Vasanta Ejma

For many years Vasanta was praying: "I ask you my Lord for being in You, only in your energies for 24 hours a day. I am asking for grace of serving You, please, be my employer." For 10 years Vasanta was often fasting, praying, meditating and visiting secluded places to find God in herself. "I did not know how God carries out my request, but on August 13th 2001 I felt that I began 21-day process of living on light. This is unbelievable grace of God, making the mind free from the third dimension. I have experienced passing on to divine freedom. Then I have understood what is the difference between getting know the way and passing it on, when during 21-day of transformation I experienced freedom states. It is impossible to describe this, the world of freedom, without rules and limitations, where everything is possible? I experience this, being in God's world." Vasanta's web site has more www.vasanta.prv.pl.

Vona Tansey

A quote from her web site: www.vonatansey.com – "Vona has lived on Universal Soul Light since September 2001. She no longer needs food to fuel or sustain her body yet sustains body weight and maintains optimal physical energy. As her body becomes more spiritual, it vibrates at a faster frequency of energy and comes into resonance with God-conscious soul frequency of unconditional love."

Wiley Brooks

An American, one of the longest known breatharians. As he claims, he has not eaten for over 30 years. He says that eating is an acquired habit. To know more, you can visit his web site www.breatharian.com.

Will van der Meer

A Dutch man living in Montana. When he was giving a seminar in Poland, November 2003, he claimed to be free of food since March 2001.

Xu Fan

A Chinese woman. The December 1996 issue of the Japanese magazine "Borderland", based on a report by Pung Chung, published an article (in Japanese) about her mysterious ability to stay healthy without food for nine years (at the time of publication). More info is in the book "Control for Life Extension" Valery Mamonov, www.longevitywatch.com.

Zinaida Baranova

A Russian woman, age 67, teacher, living without food and drink since March of 2000, as described by an article "Guest from Krasnodar Taught Rostov Citizens to Give Up Meals" in "Pravda" 20030718.

thousands of others

How many people all over the world live without eating and often also without drinking? People who belong to different categories, different life styles, various beliefs and behaviours. Every one of them has a unique story of why and how to free yourself from food. The majority of them never confess that they do not eat, to avoid possible negative reactions from the society.

You can find information about them on the Internet. There are many articles, photos and films, so I decided not to develop this chapter here.
I merely want to advice you that much information on the Internet is false. You do not have to believe what the self-claimed non-eaters are saying and what others write about them. You can consider it as a possibility, not as something for sure. Acting like this, you do not create new beliefs based on suggestions from other people but you remain free and have more information.

A LIST

On the Internet, you will find many people described as non-eaters, inediates, pranarians, breatharians, Light eaters, etc.
I listed here, in alphabetic order, the names of people which I found on the Internet:
AlwayLoveMe
Anne-Dominique Bindschedler
Anne Catherine Emmerich
Elizabeth the Good
Helen of Enselmini
Camila Castillos
Dirk Schröde
Edith Ubuntu
Elitom ben Yisrael
Erika Witthun
Genesis Sunfire

Henri Monfort
Isabelle Hercelin
Louise Lateau
Maria Domenica Lazzeri
Mary J. Fancher
Master Fu Hui
Master Guang Qin
Master Jue Tong
Master Liao Fong-Sheng
Mony Vital
Nun Shi Hongqing
Oberom C. Silva Kirby
Oleg Maslow
Olga Podorovskaya
Peter Sorcher
Peter Straubinger
Phan Tấn Lộc
Ray Maor
Reine-Claire Lussier
Ricardo Akahi
Veni – Zofia Buczma
Victor Truviano
ViSaBi

Are you one of them? Please, contact me, tell me your story, share with me your experience on forum.breatharian.info.

FASTING FOR HEALTH

From the statistical point of view, fasting is the most efficient physical method to restore health of man. It is the cheapest and fastest way to:
- get rid of the most serious illnesses, e.g. cancer, diabetes, coronary diseases, high blood pressure, eczema, asthma, and so on;
- permanently improve health;
- rejuvenate the body;
- slim the body;
- get rid of the accumulated toxins;
- raise body's life energy level;
- improve the psyche mood.

In case of most people suffering so-called civilization diseases, which are commonly considered incurable, heal fasting is a way to restore full health.

Depending on an individual, heal fasting can take from a single day untill several months. In case of an ordinary, not overweight man, an inhabitant of so-called western civilization, the maximum fasting time is about seven weeks. Most often fasting takes from seven to twenty eight days. Almost every mentally healthy man can fast if they are not afraid and not forced to do it. Do-called negative emotions awaken by fear during fasting can kill the body.

There are a few main methods of healing man via fasting:
1. Dry fasting – nothing is taken into the mouth, even not a drop of water.
2. Ordinary or water fasting – only water is consumed.
3. With herbs – the only consumed thing are liquid herb infusions.
4. With juices – in fact, this is not fasting, the proper name for this is 'juice diet' or 'liquidarian diet', because only juices are consumed.

DRY FASTING

According to the principle, 'the simplest solutions are the most efficient ones', dry fasting, when nothing is taken into the mouth even not a drop of water, produces the deepest cleansing and cure of the body. Actually, to make it most efficient, one does not even (literally) touch any water. The body should remain without any liquid during the whole fasting period.

It can be said that a week of dry fasting is as efficient as two to three weeks of fasting on just water. During the ideal dry fasting, man does not drink water and even do not touch water, which means no body wash. However, in many cases this is too extreme, so taking bath is recommended.

Fasting without any water can last from 1 to 14 days. It depends on some factors. The drier and the hotter the air, the shorter time man can stay without drinking. The more physical activity causing perspiring is involved, the shorter the body can stand without water. When the conditions like temperature, air humidity, physical activity of man are normal, an ordinary inhabitant of the mild climate region can dry fast for 7 days.

The body can slightly dehydrate during dry fasting. It is allowed to let the body dehydrate a little, but it is important, during the whole time of dry fasting, to regularly check the body. When the dehydration of the body crosses a critical level, this process cannot be normally reversed. Restoring the proper hydration of the body becomes impossible and then the body stops working (dies).
Ordinarily the first 3 days without drinking do not require any special care, but later the hydration level of the body should be monitored. Observe your skin flexibility closely. Is it flexible or becoming more similar to paper?

Another important factor, which determine the period of time the body can dry fast without any harm, is the amount of substances to be excreted from the body. For example, if man has eaten a lot of salty food, which resulted in more salt be accumulated in the body, it would not be wise to start dry fasting without first removing the excess salt. Before starting a dry fast, in this case it is worth to do water fasting for a few days prior to dry fasting.

A good procedure can be something like this. You start with water fasting. From the day eight do not take water any more. In this way, you start dry fasting when the body has got rid of the excess salt and other substances which need water in order to be removed.

Usually after only two to three days of fasting, the body's need for water becomes quite small, so giving up water after a week of fasting is not a real challenge.

WATER FASTING

During water fasting, water is the only substance allowed to be consumed. The water should be clean, energized by nature and properly structured. The best is rain or snow water collected far from polluted air or distilled water. If you use distilled water, first cool it till ice starts to appear. Then put it back in room temperature, now it is ready for drinking. Drink warm or room temperature water.

Nothing is added to the water, no sugar, not even a drop of lemon juice, no honey, no tea. Drinking water with added substances disturbs the digesting process and does not allow the body to switch on the internal nourishment. Fasting when the internal nourishing is not working, wears the body away faster. This manifests, among others, via faster weight losing and worse mood, and may cause accelerated depletion of minerals. This process is called starvation; if it is being extended, it brings death to the body.

Water fast can take from one day to a few (in extreme cases even more than a dozen) months. The length depends on, among others, the total weight of the accumulated excess matter, mainly fat, in the body and the physical activity of fasting man. In average, it can be assumed, to 'burn' 1 kg of body fat, 2 to 6 days are needed. For example, man having 20 kg of excess fat can fast for 40 to 120 days. Every fasting is beneficial for the body, but more advantageous is a fast lasting for at least 14 days.

If you have never fasted, it is worth to first practise it. The first fast can last for only 1 day. After a few days you can fast for 2 days and nights. Make a break for a week and then fast for 3 days. You can repeat such 3 days fasting for a few times, till you feel that short fasting is nothing extraordinary for you and you can easily fast longer.

Then do 4 or even 5 days fasting. Extend the next fasts, make them last for 7, 9, 10, 12 days and nights. Every fast is longer. You can do it in a different way, according to your own feeling, until you reach 14 days of fasting. Once you are able to fast for 2 weeks, you will most probably feel that you are able to fast for a few weeks.

Fasting for several weeks may cause 'miracles' in body heath. It may biologically rejuvenate the body; it is a fact many times proved clinically, visually and mentally. Sufficiently long removes almost all illnesses, smooths out wrinkled skin, restores the natural colour and strength to the hair and beautifies the body.

People who fasted for health talk with conviction about many advantageous, mental and psychical health changes that they have experienced.
"I never imagined that I could feel so good." "If you have not experienced this, you do not know, what the true good health is, even if you have been feeling very well." These and similar opinions may be heard.

There is one serious danger, which may make the body to stop working, that is to say die, it is fear. The society suggestion inculcated a belief (program) in the mind that man has to eat and that fasting harms the body. Well, if you believe this, do not start 40 days fasting right away, because if you do, the body may stop working earlier, just because of the belief. It is better to first exercise fasting in order to experience it for yourself that such beliefs result from insufficient basic knowledge about how human body works.

SYMPTOMS

During fasting the body cleans itself, removes toxins and parasites – this may cause unpleasant reactions. Every man feels this differently. One feels nothing extraordinary during the whole fasting time and has no unpleasant reactions, while another fasting man feels so bad that they may compare this to the state of dying.

Therefore, if during fasting you feel well, you may enjoy the coming benefits for the body and psyche, and you can continue your daily life as usual, except for the eating, of course. If you belong to those people whose body manifest the unpleasant reactions, know that they are beneficial symptoms of biological and mental self-cleaning and rejuvenation of the body. Therefore, you can calmly wait for them to pass. In very few cases, the symptoms may require you to stop the fasting.

Here are some of many unpleasant reactions which may appear during fasting. They all are temporary.

- headache, pain of any internal organ, pain of a bone, joint, eyes or anything else in the body;
- more hair falling out;
- body weakness;
- dehydration of the body;
- dizziness and fainting;
- weight loss;
- joint swelling;
- psychic instability;
- sudden or acute illness (strong activation of old or chronic disease);
- rash, allergy intensification;
- kidney, liver, gall bladder stone movements or elimination resulting in severe pain;
- fever;
- drop of blood pressure;

- heart palpitations;
- nausea, vomiting.

If some of the above symptoms appear, just wait till they pass after a few hours, days or weeks. These symptoms do not harm the body by themselves. However, it is worth to pay attention to them because things like dizziness and fainting may cause you to fall down and hurt the body.

If your blood pressure is low, pay even more attention, because it may go even lower, reaching a dangerous level for the proper work of the body. Better control and plan your activity in consideration of this matter.

If there are big stones in your kidneys, it may happen that a bigger piece will block the ureter causing extreme pain, which may need a doctor intervention. There would be no need to stop fasting but do unblock the ureter.

It can be said shortly that every of the unpleasant reactions appearing during fasting, indicates undergoing processes of removing the excesses accumulated for years like toxins, dead cells, fat. The proces of body self-reparation and self-regulation may also caue unpleasant symptoms. The body, a perfect electro-biological self-controlling machine, restores the state of the most efficient functions for itself, if it is allowed to do this, if given the time and if not overloaded with the digesting.

Fasting is a period of time when the body is not disturbed and is allowed to do all the necessary reparations, cleaning, renovations etc. Thanks to this, the body can work better and longer. Fasting regularly is one of the most important secrets of long life.

INTESTINE WASHING (enema)

It is really worth to wash the large intestine with water during fasting. Also during dry fasting, the intestine can be washed, although in some rare cases, this makes the fasting less efficient because water is delivered to the body.

Some people think with disgust about enema. If you belong to them, you do not have to clean the intestine. However, be aware of the simple fact that it contains putrefying matter. The poisoning toxins produced by the putrefying intestine content are entering the blood. Then they circulate throughout the whole body, causing unpleasant reactions and additionally loading the excreting system. This can go for a longtime.

The not excreted matter of the large intestine remains in it as fecalith, which may be the cause of diseases including intestine cancer. Anyway, it is up to you to decide what you prefer, to see the disgusting dirt flowing out of your body or to putrefy inside.

The large intestine is a tube 60 to 80 cm long, with many nooks, so it needs many deep washings in order to be well cleaned. It is enough to use clean water for washing the large intestine. On the internal side of the large intestine, something similar to gum-like mucus is being accumulated for years. It may be difficult to remove it completely. In some cases, fasting for a few weeks, with deep enemas, is needed. Then it gradually tears off and flows out.

Wash the intestine once a day during the first week of fasting. Then wash it every second day during the second week of fasting. Later, enema twice a week or fewer should be enough. When only clean water will be flowing from the intestine even though you wash it deeply, you can make only one enema a week.

If you are planning complete dry fasting, wash the intestine well before starting it. During complete dry fasting, no enema is done so that no water is given to the body. Therefore, in order not to suffer, it is worth to do water fasting for a week, doing deep enema every day, and then start the dry fasting.

The large intestine washing, even when you are not fasting, is an efficient cure, which in many cases removes the cause of illnesses. Most people have no idea what can be accumulated in the intestine. Remains of eaten food may stay in the intestine for years, in form of fecalith and gum-like mucus glued to the sides. These remains, plus candida, are main material causes forming intestine tumours.

PHYSICAL ACTIVITY

It is necessary to move the body also during fasting. Move it even more than usually if you lead so-called 'seating life style'. Strolling, little jogging, swimming and general gimnastics are recommended. The movement helps the body to remove toxins faster.

Being physically active is particularly recommended when you are not feeling very well. However, when the body is really (very) weak and it requires a rest, never force it, let it rest. Be reasonable in this matter.

Energizing exercising are worth of special attention during fasting. Among others *qì-gōng, tàj-jí,* hatha yoga and isometric gymnastic belong to them. You do not need to worry if you know none of these. The most important thing, when doing an energizing exercise, is to stay focussed on the feeling of the energy flow through the body and do not think about movements of the body. The body, when feeling the flowing energy, will start moving the muscles. I have already described it.

INEDIA / NON-EATING or FASTING

To remind you:
Inedia – state of the mind, which reflects through the body, making it energised so much that it never asks for food.
Fasting – a medical procedure or a religious practise, forcing the body to refrain from food for a period of time, for healing purpose.

Man's body can function without eating for a very long time. It depends on many factors, mainly: the Conscience sphere in which man lives, fat and muscle reserves, psyche state, environment conditions and physical activity. The longest fasts (not inedia) documented by research lasted over fifteen months. The fasting man drunk up to two glasses of water per day and felt very well during the entire time. Fasts lasting up to three months are nothing extraordinary and not really dangerous for the body of an overweight man.

Inedia differs from fasting mainly by:
- body weight changes;
- disposition;
- way of building the body.

BODY WEIGHT CHANGES

When man stops inserting food and drink into their body, the body first removes substances constituting the biggest obstacles in its functioning. Water, as a solvent, is needed by the body so that the body can remove redundant and toxic substances. This is why the body needs water during the initial few days to a few weeks of fasting. How much – you may ask? Usually not much, from one cup to one litre per day; this depends on the body constitution, climate, physical activity and other factors.
Having sufficiently cleansed itself, the body decreases its water requirement to the level of a few to a dozen spoons per day. Drinking may become unnecessary in favourable environmental conditions when the body needs no water.

Drinking impacts body weight. If a fasting man drinks only as much as their body demands for, their body weight goes down until the best level for this man is reached. The proper body weight for a given man may considerably differ from what is defined by so-called common sense and some data published in tables or calculated by formulas like BMI, etc.

> The proper body weight means that the body has no excess and no deficiency. That may differ from what appeals to majority of people.

Most people do not believe that a body of the proper weight looks almost like a skeleton covered with skin.

Man feels best when they have a body of the proper weight because then their body functions properly. Difference in body weight between two people of same height may be as much as 15%, even if each man has body of proper weight.

During fasting, the body of a non-emaciated man is going in the direction of the proper weight. The body will reach the proper weight after fasting for a period of time which depends on e.g. man's Consciousness sphere, the initial excess of fat, water and muscles, psychic and physical activity. In case of very fat man, achieving the proper weight may take a few months.

What happens to the body when it has reached the proper weight?

If man can live without food, that is, they can be an inediate, their body maintains the proper weight. However, if man cannot live without food, their body weight will continue to go down. This happens because the body is constantly using and removing cells and it does not receive any material to build them. This man is not a non-eater. If this process, called also emaciation or self-eating, continues, the body eventually stops functioning, it starves to death.

> Remember.
> In inedia or non-eating, the body weight is stable or fluctuating around the proper, perfect shape.
> During fasting, the body weight is constantly decreasing until the body enters emaciation and finally stops functioning.

DISPOSITION

During the initial two to three weeks of fasting your disposition can be quite changeable. There is no need to be worry (within limits of reason, of course) about your body weakness, pain, dizziness, nausea or other symptoms occurring during this time. These are signs of body cleansing or self-healing. However, later, when the body approaches its proper weight, which usually takes two to three weeks or much longer in case of obese man, your disposition becomes perfect. Then you understand what it means to feel well and to be in perfect health. You have so much energy, will to live, work and to be physically active. Also, much creativity manifests in your mind.

What follows with the flow of time?

If you are in inedia or non-eating, the good disposition and everything associated with it will remain. Good mood, happiness, self-satisfaction and optimistic lovely attitude towards others indicate good state of the body and psyche. "Healthy spirit dwells in healthy body." – a Polish saying.

However, if you are unable to live without food, you will be fasting or emaciating. Then you will feel weak, unwilling to do anything or even feel sad. The more your body will need food, the worse you may feel physically and psychically. This indicates that you should return to eating.

BUILDING THE BODY

The building material for inediate's body cells is created from qì/prana, the source of which is the mind. Therefore, an inediate needs nothing to insert into the digesting track.

The building material for the non-inediate is delivered from the outside in form of food, drink, air and radiation. If the amount of the building material is too little, the body will show deficiencies which manifests as defects and dysfunctions.
In fact, also in case of the non-inediate, the body cells are built from qì/prana, however this process is not enough to sustain the body.

Summary.
If you have not eaten for several weeks and you still feel very well and the body weight does not go below the proper value, this looks like you can live without food. However, if after several weeks your body's weight goes under the proper value and you feel bad, this should make you conclude that the body is being harmed. In this case, if you do not give food to the body, you may make it fail.

BEINGS and NON-EATING

Humans living on Earth consider food something necessary. In other words, an average human is a kind of a being for whom eating is an inherent and indispensable part of life. Eating is an essential experience of human life on Earth because it is relating the human body with the rest of the matter on this planet.

Among different reasons why many beings come to live on Earth there is one, to experience eating. Experiencing the entire myriad of things associated with food and eating is attractive enough to make a being live here. This is why, for most people on Earth, forcing non-eating means being deprived from going through the expected experience. This, of course, makes them to leaving the material body.

On other planets, the relation to what people call food or eating is much different. There is a big diversity, from beings who eat nothing on one end of the line, to beings who eat constantly and create a unity with food, on the opposite end of the line.

Beings living in this universe can be divided into three groups:
1. Immaterial beings.
2. Partly material beings.
3. Material beings.

IMMATERIAL BEINGS

Immaterial beings usually have the body invisible for human eyes and impalpable though more sensitive people can see or feel them. Their bodies do not have what we would call internal organs. These beings can take any shape depending on their will.

One can easily guess that the immaterial beings have nothing common with what people call material food. An average inhabitant of their world may even not know what material food is. What they consume is what we call 'energy'. That is why people emanating energy from emotions are a rich source of food for the immaterial beings.

Eating, like humans do on Earth, is an unattainable experience for the immaterial beings, so some of them dream about experiencing life in the hard matter in order to be able to eat. Then they come to live on planets like

Earth. Life here is hard for them, no wonder, they have suddenly changed their life circumstances. When they are in human body, they may experience problems with eating. Many anorectic or bulimic people or those frequently overeating or striving to inedia originate from immaterial beings.

Immaterial beings, having entered into human body, find themselves not completely adapted to living in this environment. This is caused mostly by difficulty with adaptation to matter. Eating constitutes a strong link between matter and the being. This is where the striving to freedom of eating originates from, which previously was their natural state. Self-grounding providing more stable relation with matter, helps them to dwell in the body more easily.

Many of these beings are unable to remain without eating in the human body because their link with the body may become too loose, which results in breaking it permanently. Eating is not only a necessity for them, it is also a part of intended experience with matter. Therefore, for them, giving up food may mean the lost of meaning of life.

I sometimes meet these people on Earth. The majority of them do not know what causes their issues with (non)eating. I explain to them about this so that they have information useful for understanding the background of the issues. With more useful information in this matter, they can more consciously choose to experience matter or to be an inediate.

If you meet somebody, most often they will be fat or thin, who emanates Love and warmth like a sun, has sensible angelic nature and problems with (non)eating, you can presume that they came from a less dense world where food was not known. Statistically, the bigger the issue with (non)eating they experience, the shorter experience with matter on Earth they have.

PARTLY MATERIAL BEINGS

The density of their bodies varies in the range between almost invisible and impalpable (similar to fog) to almost as dense as would be the human body without bones, like a jelly. Such a being can be a foggy ghost constantly changing the shape, similar to a jelly-like substance or something like plasticine. It is an interesting experience to insert your hand into or even throughout the body of this being, if they allow you to.

As you may easily guess, the food eaten by these beings also is of loose consistence. They eat jelly-like substances, liquids, gases, fire, radiation and emotion of other beings. There are many born non-eaters among these beings. Adapting the body to inedia or non-eating is relatively easy for them, compared to people.

Partly material beings choose rather other planets than Earth for living. Living here, even though possible, is not very favourable for them because here they quickly lose energy. It is more difficult for them to find large variety of food here.

If an ordinary human would decide to be fed as partly material beings, they might quickly become thin, weak and feel bad. To compare, this would be like in case of man, who normally eats heavy food, but suddenly switches to only drinking juices.

MATERIAL BEINGS

People can easily understand what it means to be bound by food to matter. Material beings are so fixed in dense matter that attempting to break this bond may cause death to them. It is really difficult for them to do without inserting food into the body. The deeper they are in matter, the more difficult the adaptation to living without food is for them.

This is important information because it means that striving to live without food causes transformation of a material being into a less material being. Like other changes, if this transformation is forced or too quick, it may fail.

On the other hand, there are planets with people like us here on Earth, where people do not eat at all. They look like the people on Earth, they have same digestive tract, but they do not eat. The act of eating is considered taking drugs, something similar like drinking alcohol here on Earth. Therefore, the act of eating over there is harmful for their bodies.

The digestive tract of those people living on other planets works as a sense for the nerve system. When you are in inedia on Earth, your digestive tract work exactly the same, as a sense for your nerve system.

PRINCIPLES OF PROPER NOURISHMENT

Although this book is about inedia, non-eating and fasting, it is highly advisable to start with healthy body. One of factors defining body health is diet. Use this information for your benefit and share with others.

1. CONSCIOUS EATING

> Every man is a different universe, that is why a true universal diet does not exist.
> When you follow a diet, you harm your body. When you follow the real needs of your body, you strengthen it.

I suggest that you reread the Conscious Eating method described in "Inedia, Non-Eating, Fasting" and apply it for your benefit. Conscious eating is the most important principle of proper nourishment. In fact, when you apply CE, you do not need to read the rest of this text.

2. CHEWING

From the moment when man puts something into their mouth, chewing becomes the most important thing in eating. Proper chewing of food is paramount, so that the body can process the food properly. Insufficiently chewed food coming into the stomach has no chance to be processed properly by the digestive system. Therefore it becomes a burden because this food will petrify and thus harm the digestive tract.

The stomach is the second centre of the body's digestive system. The stomach is to accept matter which is already properly prepared, that is, it is sufficiently broken down, mixed with saliva and initially digested. If only one of these processes is not performed, the stomach is unable to fulfil its work completely.
Then this improperly prepared matter goes from the stomach into the duodenum. This process continues to the point of excretion. Due to this incomplete digestion, the body excretes matter which is not fully processed. The body cannot assimilate what it might have from the eaten food, if it was not chewed properly and mixed with saliva. Petrification occurs. This is one of the causes of body diseases and ageing.

This simple act of chewing has a huge impact on the entire body. If you want to compare, you can easily do a test. For one day, swallow your food without chewing to the extent that is possible. After a few days break, so that the body can recover, eat your food chewing it properly. Now, when you compare your health, feeling, and the appearance of the body excretions, you will have no doubts.

What is proper chewing?
Before something is swallowed, it first has to be chewed in order to bring it to a the maximum liquid consistency possible, and it has to change the taste. For example, when you are eating bread, you need at least three minutes of continuous chewing before you swallow it, so that the bread bite changes into a liquid, that has a different taste from the initial bread bite.
If the taste becomes unpleasant, it is an indication that the body does not want it. Then, without hesitation, spit it out. The body already has taken everything that it needed from the chewed food. If you swallow it, you unnecessarily charge the body's self-cleansing system.

It is also beneficial to chew liquids, that is, mix them well with saliva by sloshing them around the teeth. Liquids need a shorter chewing time before they are swallowed.
It is important to mix cold drinks with saliva because the additional advantage is warming them before they are swallowed on the way to the stomach.

When following the principle of proper chewing, man soon notices that their body can be sufficiently nourished only by chewing food. The body seldom needs to swallow food that has been chewed for a long time.

In this way, it is easy to notice that the body rejects most of the processed foods by letting you know with its sense of taste. A good example is eating highly processed food, e.g. cake, pizza, chips, sausage and dairy. When these far-from-nature products are chewed for a long time, their taste change to disgusting. Few people would feel like swallowing it.

Fruits and some other not processed foods, after longer chewing change the taste to even nicer than the initial bite. Of course, in this case, one ought to swallow, not spite out the food.

As a result of long chewing, man can feel when and which foods are beneficial for the body. Also, man can feel when they have eaten the right amount.
In addition, the experience achieved from proper chewing helps you to cre-

ate essential knowledge on the path to non-eating.

Chewing, as described above, is a component of the Conscious Eating method.

3. WITHOUT DRINKING

Drinking while chewing makes it more difficult for the digestive system to process food properly. People usually sip a drink in between bites of food while eating in order to soften and break down solid food faster. As you can imagine, when solid food is turned into mash faster with drinking liquids, it makes one feel like swallowing sooner, before it is well mixed with saliva. Thus the stomach receives improperly processed matter.
Drinking while eating solid food also disturbs the digestion process, because it dilutes the saliva and digestive juices. Then the diluted digestive juices digest the food more slowly, which creates the conditions for premature rotting of matter in the intestines.

Abstain from drinking prior to eating so that the digestive juices are not diluted. Do not fill the stomach with a liquid just before eating food. If you feel thirsty before eating, drink enough to quench your thirst but wait a quarter of an hour before beginnings to eat.
Washing down your food immediately after eating is even worse then drinking beforehand. This practise deteriorates the process by diluting the digestive juices. It is better to drink after the digested food leaves the stomach.

If you feel that you do not have enough saliva when eating something, you can change what you are eating to something more moist, instead of drinking to assist your chewing. However, remember that longer chewing mashes any food changing it into a liquid form.

4. PROPER COMBINING OF FOOD

One of the most important principles of proper nourishment is to have only one type of food in one meal. For example, when you eat rice (carbohydrates), do not combine it with eggs or meat (protein) in the same meal. Eat only rice and eat the eggs later when the rice will have moved out of the stomach and into the intestines.

Every food needs specific digestive juices. The chemical composition of digestive juice for a given food can differ from the composition required for processing another food efficiently. These different compositions can cause adverse chemical reaction between both digestive juices, mainly enzymes. Thus, when two different types of foods are combined in one meal, the secreted digestive juices cannot process the mixture properly. This manifests itself by putrefying process in the intestine, flatulence, constipation and other digestive disorders.

The proper combining of foods is especially important in the case of unnatural processed foodstuff, that is everything that was prepared by cooking, frying, baking, smoking, etc. prior to eating. When man eats unprocessed food directly from nature, the body manages the processing much more easily in respect to combining different foods in one meal. The difference comes from the enzymes found in the food (more about that later).

- Here are examples of errors most often made in combining foods:
- Food containing much protein (e.g. meat, egg, soya, bean) eaten in the same meal with food containing much carbohydrates (e.g. potatoes, bread, rice, pasta).
- Fruits mixed with dairy (e.g. yoghurt with a fruit cocktail).
- Salads or juices made with a combination of fruits and vegetables (e.g. apple with carrot).
- Food containing much carbohydrates / sugars (e.g. rice, potatoes, bread) combined with oil (coconut oil, butter, lard).

I suggest that you look up more information on the combining of foods.

Usually eating only one type of food in a meal is the most beneficial for the human body. For example, you can make a breakfast consisting of mainly carbohydrates (e.g. rice and sweet potato), lunch consisting of only vegetables and dinner consisting of mainly proteins (e.g. bean and egg).
If you feel this way is too difficult to follow or your meals are too plain, you can do your own research on combining foods properly.

5. FOOD DIRECTLY FROM NATURE

Nature is an integral whole consisting of elements perfectly adjusted with each other. When observing nature, you see how everything functions perfectly. Sometimes it may seem to you that some programs of nature can be improved. However, when you learn about these programs, you can see that they are already perfect. The elements that constitute nature are already ideally harmonious and working in a way that any man's 'correction' can only harm this order.

Some of nature's elements are programs of transformation. In this transformation, some bodies change themselves by using bodies of others organisms. A typical example is eating. A plant eats (absorbs) water, air, minerals and sunlight. Man eats fruits of plants or entire plants. Earth and air eat (absorb) the products of man or the body of man.

The transformations taking place in each of these stages do not need any intervention as the materials, energy and the products of metabolism are found in nature in the proper form. For instance, if man intervenes in nature's functions, the products of nature are then modified and the transformations are disturbed. By disturbing nature man brings about results that are incompatible with the programs of nature, thereby causing harm to people.

A typical example of intervention in nature's transformation is food processing. Cooking, frying, backing, smoking, etc. produce something artificial that is not found in nature (with some exceptions).
The human body is a product of nature and it is subject to nature's mechanisms. Feeding man with artificial substances that are not found in nature, causes perturbation to the natural transformations in nature. Thus what follows is an intervention in the laws of nature. As the experience and observation of nature show, the interventions in its programs disturb the life of people, animals, plants, water, soil and air.

Except for man, which beings in nature, cook, bake, etc. their food? Except for man, which beings on Earth genetically modify their food? As a result of this kind of activity, the appearance, health and life expectancy of man's body is deteriorating.

Food prepared for man by nature is ready to eat. Every food prepared for man by nature has a perfect composition so that the body can digest it properly. Any processing of nature's food leads to the production of substances which are not known in nature, thus human body has difficulty accepting it.

The thermal processing of nature's food destroys the enzymes. The enzymes found in nature's food are necessary for proper digestion. Destroying the enzymes with temperature, renders the food indigestible, causing it to be poisonous for the body. This food forces the body to use its own supply of enzymes. This provision is normally non-renewable. When the enzymes are fully depleted, the body dies. There are enough enzymes in the body to last many years. This is why people eating raw food, among others, have healthier body and live longer.

Be aware that there is no natural food in the shops, unless it is brought from real nature. All other sold food is industrial products. It may be labelled 'ecological' or 'organic', but is is still industrial products. Even the most natural farm is an industry. Nature does not know farming.

The body of an Earth inhabitant is forced to eat processed food almost from birth. This is one of the reasons why the sudden change to eating only raw food can cause unpleasant reactions, much like the symptoms of drug rehabilitation. So it is important to transition gradually because the body does not like sudden changes, although it is very flexible in terms of adaptation.
By the way, think about the resulting savings for you, society and the environment when people eat only raw food. Another book can be written about just this topic.

A big part of humanity lives in regions which are not inhabitable for human all year round. People live there because they have learned to heat their houses and store their food for times when the soil does not yield crops (food), mainly in winter.
Earth has assigned the subtropical and tropical zones for man to live in year round, where food is always available and does not have to be preserved. If you live in a cold climate, it is difficult for you to eat raw food year round. For the season of winter, better go to a warmer region where you have fresh food at your disposal.

6. WITHOUT SEASONING & FLAVOURING

Have you heard comments similar to these? "Without salt, it is tasteless." "Without sugar, it is too bitter." "A meal without seasoning tastes bad." "Meals have to be well spiced."
When man's body does not need a specific food, man does not feel like eating it, in other words, they are not hungry for it. But if this food is seasoned with flavouring (sugar, salt, herbs, vinegar, oil, etc.), most people would eat the food with pleasure. This proves that people often eat food not because it is really needed by the body, but because of the taste.

When something not needed enters the body, poisoning occurs, therefore the body is forced to remove or store the excess matter. This is one of the reasons for accelerated ageing and premature death of the body.

Seasoning and flavourings are substances that deceive our senses of taste and smell, which serves as indications of real body needs in nature. Look at nature and tell me, which being, except for man, puts flavours in food?

When the body demands food, man knows what they feel like eating because they are hungry specifically for this thing. The taste of food indicates to man what their body need, then it tastes good even without any seasoning.

You can verify this theory yourself. When you are satiated, you do not feel like eating a meal without seasoning. Later, you will feel like eating it but only if it is sufficiently tasty, that is, with seasoning and looking appetizing. Eating the food raw will not appeal to you.
Do not eat it but wait longer. After a few hours or days, you will clearly feel like eating this food with pleasure because you are hungry even though it has no seasoning or may even be raw. This happens only when your body really needs this food.

Another example. Most people, who like to eat meat would never eat it raw. This is because they like to eat a product made from meat that is duly prepared and spiced. If their body would need meat, they would eat it raw with appetite. Some people, after having fasted a sufficiently long time, would feel like eating meat even raw.
Nature does not cook, so it provides only raw meat for eating. If you do not feel like eating raw meat, this means that your body does not really need it. If you force your body to eat meat, you harm the body.

You have probably heard that using herbs assists in digesting. This is a fact, herbs and other substances affect digesting, taste, and appetite. Another fact is that the human body does not need these things. What man needs is to eat the right substances in the proper quantity and at the right time. Being close to nature and observing the body taste indications encourage proper nourishment.

Addiction to regular and overconsumption of a specific food deceives the body senses. Focus attention on this body need and do not follow the sense of taste.
Be aware of this and do not follow the sense of taste.
Attraction to the taste of things like candy, chips, fries, doughnut, cake, wheat bun, chocolate bar, ice cream, hot-dog, pizza, cornflake, popcorn, soda and colourful yoghurt almost always means wrong indication due to addiction.

7. ONLY WHEN HUNGRY OR THIRSTY

This topic comes as a consequence of the preceding principles of proper nourishment, because it is about real body needs, which are manifested through hunger or thirst.
Let me emphasize here that the common practises of eating meals at fixed times and, associated with this, cooking the same meal for all, results in more harm than benefit.

On the one hand, the body of man eating meals at fixed times (breakfast, lunch, dinner), that have been cooked for the entire family, is forced to accept food when it does not ask for nourishment. On the other hand, the body is more often given substances which it does not need.

Using the CE method leads man to feel that fixed mealtimes do not serve the human body well. The body is served best by what it demands for, and it has to be consumed exactly when it is needed. Also the amount is defined best by the body.

Allow me to speak about forcing children to eat. Parents complain that their children do not want to eat at mealtimes, but they cry out for food at other times. This is natural behaviour, because the body of a child knows well when and what it needs. Parents who care about their children, are guided by the children's indication in this respect. They give the children the freedom to choose the time to eat and the type of food. At the same time, the parent protects the child against poisons like those mentioned above.

Forcing children to eat, or to finish the food that was prepared for them, causes trauma to be inflicted on the defenceless child during the development of their body and psyche. In this way, the seeds of future mental illnesses are sown, which may reflect on eating, e.g. anorexia or bulimia.

8. DRINKING AND WATER

Only things that nature provides for man to drink are suitable for them. The main drink that nature provides for man is water naturally flowing in a spring or river and lake water.

When you open a fruit (e.g. coconut), cut a plant (e.g. cactus, birch), a fluid comes out; sometimes you can drink it. Note that this liquid is not pasteurized, contains no preservatives and does not come in a plastic bottle. You will never find a plastic container in nature.

Man has already lost the ability to check the quality of water by smelling or tasting it, the way animals easily do. Let us perform a simple experiment. Take some water and divide it into two parts. For the duration of one night, store one part of the water in a glass bottle, and the other part in a typical plastic bottle made for holding water. Next, place two identical glasses or metal bowls, side by side, in the middle of a room. Pour the water from the glass bottle into the bowl on the left and then pour the water from the plastic bottle into the bowl on the right.

Call a dog, cat, rabbit, or other animal to the bowls of water. Let the animal to chose the bowl of water to drink from. What do you suppose, from which bowl the animal will drink? You probably guess that if the animal smells both waters, it will choose the one that was kept during the night in the glass bottle.

Now, you go and smell both waters. Can you smell the difference?
No?
Then drink both of them.
Do you also not feel the difference in taste?
Oh dear!
You see, this is the basic ability, checking the quality of water. How does it function in you?
Not many people living outside of nature are still able to perform that function.

Man's body is composed mostly of water. The quality of consumed water has a direct impact on human body, even if man does not feel it. For example, chlorine or fluorine added to water harms our nerve system, bones, teeth and eyes. Bathing in such water harms our skin and hair.

If you are living in a city, your tap water is probably poisoned. For the sake of your health, do whatever you can in order to purify the water before you drink it, or buy good water.

Water stored in a plastic bottle also is not drinking water. Water dissolves poisoning chemical components contained in the plastic, even if it has food grade certificate. When you buy / store water, chose only containers made of glass, wood, stainless steel, silver, porcelain or other material that does not poison water by leaching poisons.

How to treat water for drinking; it is a different large theme for a separate book, so I am not going to develop it here. However, there is an abundance of valuable information available about this topic, just look for it. It is worth. What is more important than health?

How much water to drink every day? Well, exactly as much as the body needs. More than that is harmful and less than that is also harmful. Advertised recommendations saying to drink something like two litres of water a day, may be not good for your body. Follow your body's real need.

9. NOT AFTER 4 PM

There is a general consensus that for most people, 4 pm is the optimal time to finish eating daily. Taking into consideration the functioning of our organs, the best time frame for finishing eating is between 2 pm and 6 pm. The most important aspect is to finish eating your last meal on a given day 4 to 8 hours (depending on food type) before going to bed. The later the last meal is eaten, the lighter it should be for digestion purposes.

Among other reasons, eating to late results in the incomplete digestion of the food consumed before sleeping. This means that the digesting organs are forced to work too much. As the result, the content of the alimentary canal is poorly processed. Food staying in the digestive track for too long, putrefies and poisons the body.

Forcing the organs to work during the time intended for rest, regeneration, and the removal of toxins from the body, contributes to the feeling of weakness the following morning. One does not feel like getting up and feels weak. In addition, the bones, head and stomach can ache.

Eating just before going to bed is not only a sign of addiction. It is akin to the action comparable to a slow suicide. The body of man behaving like this attracts illness and has little chance to be healthy.

10. IN SILENCE

There is a Polish expression: "One should not gab while eating, because things fit badly in the belly." („*Przy jedzeniu się nie gada, bo się w brzuchu źle układa.*") The actions of eating and talking are incompatible, that is, they badly influence each other. One who chokes can resonate with this.

When one talks while eating, the food is not chewed as well. Having a discussion during a meal can cause stress that may later manifest in a stomach ache or diarrhoea.

Parties are examples of people meeting to sit at tables to talk. Some people cannot imagine a social meeting without snacks. However, an unusual party, when people exercise eating in total silence, can be organized.
Eating in total silence allows one to focus only on eating. Thanks to this, the life energy is directed more consciously to the digestive system. Man, when eating in silence can better focus on the chewing, swallowing, and feeling the impact of the consumed food on the body.

Eating in silence is practised by people who occupy themselves with spiritual development. This is a well-known practice in yoga and followed in many monasteries. The main purpose of this practise is the recognition and enjoyment of what is being eaten and also the focusing on the presently performed action.
The method of Conscious Eating, previously described, can be properly performed in silence.

CO-OPERATION FOR DEVELOPMENT

One of growth characteristics of the human civilization on Earth is that man is discovering more and more of their abilities, which proves how big and largely unknown power they possess in themselves. This growth is caused by expansion of the Consciousness sphere that man lives in.

One of this abilities is to maintain the body in proper functioning without inserting into it substances commonly recognized as food. This ability, although still very little known on Earth, becomes a part of life style of more and more people.

One of the reasons why people choose worse solutions for themselves is insufficient amount of information they have. False beliefs, superstitions, falsehood and misunderstandings are caused by lack of true information. Nowadays an average man has almost no knowledge about the ability to live completely without food. This is why I feel that it is worth to give people more true and scientifically researched information so that they can decide with more certainty about making advantageous changes in their life.

I am open for cooperation especially with scientists, doctors, journalists, editors and institutions interested in serious research about inedia, non-eating and fasting. The goal of this cooperation is to create a comprehensive documentation, which can be beneficially used by people. Furthermore inedia is an interesting subject for master, doctorate or other dissertation.

Please, do not fear the establishment, have the spirit to explore this subject with an open mind. I will readily cooperate with you for the good of people, so do not hesitate to contact me.

F. A. Q.

These are the questions I am asked most often personally or on the breatharian forum. If you have other questions, that you think may be worth including here, please write them on
forum.breatharian.info.

What is the best diet for humans?

There is not such thing as the best diet for every body. Every body is a different world, therefore every human needs different substances at different times and in different amounts.

If you still think about the perfect nourishing of your body, use Conscious Eating. When you master CE, this natural ability of man, you give you body what it needs, at the right time and amount.

If you are not going to eat consciously and you are still looking for the perfect nourishment, observe humans in nature. You will see that the food of the humanoid life forms in nature is based, in statistical average, 98% on plant food and 2% of meat (including eggs, fish, sea food, worms, etc). The older is the body, the less meat it really needs.
There is no natural vegan in nature. Some fanatic vegans strongly belief that monkeys are vegans. In fact, they eat insects, worms, eggs and sometimes catch small animals. Especially the chimpanzees and gorillas, once in a dozen days they will chase a small animal and eat it alive.

Nature shows you that forcing only plant food may be harmful. There are many people who harmed their body by forcing pure plant based diet. Only when they introduced eggs, fish or other animal food, they recovered. Especially the nerve system of humans is sensitive to lack of natural nourishment.

Why do we have alimentary canal?

The answer is obvious – in order to process and excrete everything that is thrown into the body. The human body is an electro-biological machine controlled by instinct and is the subject of so-called 'laws of nature' (set of programs constituting the material world).

Man has 'free will', which is manifested by creativity of the intellect, so that they can experience life in a way that IAM decides. The human body is a tool through which man experiences matter.

Instinct, which creates and maintains the body, falls under the influence of social suggestion, therefore many products created by the mind of a given man are the same as those created by other people's minds. If a body is born in a society of people who eat, it has systems and organs properly adapted to digesting and excreting. The program set of a society that man is born in decides about their body.

The human body is very flexible in adapting itself to defined life conditions so that it can broadly experience matter. It is the most sophisticated, self-controlled machine known in nature. All its senses and organs are needed so that man can experience life. They all can broadly adapt themselves to specific requirements.

The digestive and excreting systems are tools which make it possible for you to experience the program set called material food. As long as man remains in experiencing matter in form of food (taste, consistency, temperature, illnesses caused by eating, alcoholic stupor and many other) these systems are indispensable for man. When this experience is finished, the alimentary canal becomes useless to the body and therefore it disappears (atrophies), as researches made on inediates show, or becomes transformed into something else.

In other words, as long as man stays in the field of experiencing matter by inserting it into the body (the tool to experience this), their body will possess, develop and transform systems which make this experience possible. When man finishes this experience, his body will be adapted to new circumstances and the alimentary canal will be transformed or replaced by other system.

Why do people die from starvation?

The hunger itself does not cause death from starvation, but the human body can die if it is given insufficient food. This is how programs in man's instinct work.

Potentially every man on Earth can live without food. But a potential does not automatically mean the associated skill. A potential only means that a given ability can be developed and realized. If the skill to maintain body in perfect working is insufficiently developed, the body will die if it does not receive food for too long.

Life completely without food is possible only for those people who have properly changed functions of those programs in the instinct which deal with food and eating. Only those people who are born in inediate's society can live without food from the moment of their birth. In their instinct, the programs responsible for the relation between food and the body, function differently compared to people eating normally.

The instinct does not think, it just functions exactly along the way its programs perform regardless of the results. If specific programs are not modified, then those programs are run which cause death to the body if it lacks food. So if man believes that they will die without food, this certainly will happen. The inediate knows that food is not needed by their body to function perfectly.

Why non-eaters do not go to places where people starve and do not teach them?

You can ask this question to every non-eater you meet. I suppose that everyone sees this differently. If you ask me – here is my answer.

The task I have undertaken is answering questions, so I am a source of information. I do not look for people seeking help and I do not offer it. I do help if I am asked, I can and I want to. This is why I go to places where people invite me. I do not have any invitation from places, where people are starving. If I had one, I would consider whether to go there or not.

Besides this, here is additional information.

There are people on Earth who have profitable interests in keeping people in starvation, "incurable" illnesses, illiteracy and having nature polluted and so on. These people, with very big money and power, are ready to do a lot in order to keep others in poverty, ignorance and feebleness, because such people are unconscious and easily manipulable slaves.

People teaching about inedia in places where people are starving, may easily endanger their life. It is easier to manipulate the behaviour of desperate people who are ready 'to do anything' in order to receive a slice of bread or 'a bowl of rice'.

Another method, which often is more efficient, is to educate people 'with a full stomach', because they may be an example for others. This happens because people living in so-called (industrially) 'undeveloped' countries follow solutions or taken examples from 'developed' countries.

By the way, we could ask: Why powerful and influential organizations which take care of feeding the starving are much less (or are not) interested in educating these people? Why simple solutions, which provide sufficient food productivity and which could have solved the global starvation problem long ago, are not allowed to be used in regions where people suffer starvation? You may find very interesting and shocking answers to these questions if you dig deep enough.

What to do in order to become a non-eater? Can I also live without food?

There is no such thing as a universal method for every body, because every man has their own way, every man is a different world. There are as many ways leading to inedia or non-eating as there are inediates or non-eaters.

If you know that inedia or non-eating is for you, you are already walking the right way. You probably have put on your way the activity aiming at expansion of Consciousness sphere in which you live.

If you ask someone whether you are able to live without food, the answer is ... no, you are not. As long as you do not know this, you are not able to do this, although you possess the potential. Information alone is not enough, but as soon as you start to feel the knowledge and power associated with it in you, you will stand at the gate giving choice of this life style. Then you will know what and how to do this.

If you already feel that inedia or non-eating is for you, you are already walking the way on which non-eating exists. There are many possibilities in front of you, so you can realize them according to your plan.

What to do? Do what you feel is the best for you. First of all, do not consider food bad for you (many people make this mistake), relax and take it easy. Life never ends and is not a race so you always have time. What you are unable to do now, you will be able to do later.

It is a nonsense that people can live without food. How are you going to prove it to me?

Hereby I declare that I do not feel any need to prove that living without food is possible or that me or any other man is a non-eater. I do not intend to prove this. However I am open to experiments the outcome of which may be considered proof to some people.

Man living on Earth walks their own unique way, experiencing and building their own knowledge. Man builds their own world. Every man is a different world. All these worlds are different although they contain similar or even common elements.

To prove something or not, you can only to yourself. Regarding other things or what others say, you can only believe it or not, because they will not prove anything to you. You can also define a belief level which will mean a proof for you. So if you believe that this is nonsense – yes, you are right, this is true for you.

People build their world by their own beliefs, experiences and knowledge. Therefore what is true to one man (in their world), may not exist or be false to another man (in their world). This means that the truth is relative to people's worlds.

When for one man the possibility of living without food is true, it does not mean automatically that this happens to every man. The possibility to live without food is true for some people – they may even practise it. However, at the same time, this is false and an impossible thing for other people. Therefore, when one man lives happily without any food, another man may die when trying this.

This is only one example of a thing which simultaneously can be possible and impossible, true and false. Of course, this does not make man unable to collect information, change beliefs, experience life and build their own knowledge.

Man characterized by natural tolerance, allows other people to experience whatever they choose to, because they know that this is a manifestation of man's free will.

Where do the non-eaters take energy for living from?

When man thinks about non-eating, they most often first think about delivering energy. Man anticipates that the energy needed for living (that is e.g. to build body cells, function its organs, think, emotions) comes from outside.

Scientists researching material and energetic functioning of the body are biased on this belief. How energy is drawn by the body for its functioning, and what is the influence of specific compounds, called carbohydrates, proteins, minerals etc., on bodily functions. Scientists first try to find out how it happens that the human body functions, then they formulate hypothesizes and create theories. Then other people accept these theories as the only truth.

Without going deep into the matter, it is a fact that man lives on what they believe that it give them energy. If man believes that bread, potatoes or apples give energy to their body, then this really does happen. If man believes that the sun is the source of energy for their bodily functions, then this indeed is the case. Similarly – when man believes that breath, prana or Light is the source of energy needed by their body to function – this happens.

Man lives on what they believe that powers them. This is also true in case of the non-eaters. One non-eater can live on energy drawn from the sun and another non-eater will power their body with prana or from the air breathed in.

However, when you know that yourself are the energy source of your body/mind's life, then this does happen. But if you believe only, it will not suffice. Your knowledge and clear feeling of it are indispensable. In this case you need nothing from outside. IAM, being the representative of the Consciousness, creates everything. This is the motto of this book: IAM is the Consciousness and everything else is Its creation. Thus I know that IAM is the source of my life.

This is it, more or less complicated, how much I am able to explain with the intellect. But the intellect does not feel, it is only able to think (analyse, solve, create), so it cannot comprehend the above explanation.

Until man knows this by deep experience, their intellect is not able to understand how man can live completely without eating, drinking and without breathing. Until this happens the intellect will not know and probably will deny it. It depends on how much the intellect of a given man already knows, how much experience man has gone through and how large is the Consciousness sphere that man lives in.

I suggest, if you are interested in the theme of energy of the body in relation to what man eats, read the book "Man's Higher Consciousness" by Hilton Hotema. You will find a lot of interesting material in his book.

Physicists are trying to discover the material world and explain it to the intellect. This makes them create more fantastic hypothesizes than science-fiction stories written just a few decades ago. If you are interested in present-day physics describing elementary particles, waves, energy, quantum and information, you probably will find intellectual explanation to this question. Why can a human live without eating, drinking, breathing and warm environment?

Why did you return to eating?

This results from my experience that non-eating and inedia are convenient factors in human life. Perfect health, fast, clear and creative thinking, much energy, extraordinary abilities help man to slowly transform themselves into a superman, that is to the man's natural state. In my past, I experienced that and even more. That is why I am now sharing this knowledge.

Presently, non-eating is not on my path because this impedes me in accomplishing the activities that I have undertaken on Earth. I am choosing the normal, primitive life of an ordinary man. This helps me to learn life on Earth more efficiently.

Approximately 90% of human life is related to food. As a scientist experimenting on his own body and mind, I still am to experience this 90% so that I can learn and understand more and do not become detached from the reality on Earth. This is the main reason why I have returned to so-called normal eating.
I am aiming for a better understanding of people living on Earth, aiming to know which information they need and are able to use on their way to achieving the natural state of man.
The more people return to their natural state, the more they will restore the natural life, that is, life in alignment with the laws of nature on Earth.

The full understanding of an enslaved man, who has lost their basic know-

ledge, is possible only when one lives as an ordinary man.
The same principle applies to a journalist who wants to write a good report about the homeless. Therefore, he lives among them for some time on the street, without money and the conveniences of a home. This is why I need to live in a normal fashion, as others do, and experience the life of an ordinary man, who is continually learning and evolving and developing themselves. This is also the reason why I now eat normally.

What do you eat now?

I eat at random, whatever is in reach of my hands. I pay little attention to it. I usually eat the leftovers after my family members have finished their meal. In short, my diet is not good; it is mostly harmful for the body. This is the diet of the ordinary man.

When I am a guest, I eat and drink whatever I am served. When they ask me what I wish to eat, I reply, whatever they plan to serve. In this way, I do not cause any problems to people who invited me.

I am not a fanatic of any -isms. I see that -isms often bring more problems than benefits. I already have mentioned this that man limits themselves with beliefs.

Once or twice a year I allow my body to rest, usually in early spring and autumn. I fast, consume only little water, for a period of a few days to a few weeks. Sometimes I follow a diet on herbal drinks or juices, depending on the needs of my body in respect to healing.

Can an inediate, a non-eater or man who fasts be sexually active?

Of course they can, according to their will and preferences, just like people who eat normally.

The body, which is an electro-biological machine, uses energy to function. Man's sexual activity results from a basic program, the goal of which is for two bodies to produce another body. This is one of the most important programs of the instinct.

Normally during the sexual intercourse, the man discharges energy through the semen and the woman receives this energy. Generally, this is in accord-

ance with the biology of nature, where the body of the male creates a dose of energy in order to place it in the body of the female, where new life can be created and developed.
Man can change this process but this is a separate topic.

The energy in the body follows thoughts and stimuli. Man, who is aware of the energy flow in his body, can control it, e.g. to direct, focus, take, give. Due to a disconnection with nature and environmental stimuli, the ordinary man usually controls the energy in his body poorly, accumulating his energy in the physical area associated with reproduction. The younger the man, usually the weaker his control over his emotions and energy.

In the case of the inediates, their energy usually accumulates in the upper region of the body; this is why their sexual activity decreases. They can still perform but feel less need sexually.

If an inediate, a non-eater or man who fasts can use techniques of energy control during arousal so that the semen is not released, then he can be much more sexually active. If he cannot do that, he loses his life energy with every ejaculation of his semen. How to control that and why, etc. is a large topic that is described in many books.

In the case of a woman who fasts, is an inediate or a non-eater, she does not lose any energy during the intercourse. She is usually also less willing, because her energy accumulates more in the upper body region.

Does a woman lose her period during non-eating or fasting?

When a woman lives without food long enough and she has a totally healthy body, then there is no bleeding during her periods. This means good health, that is, the body has returned to proper functioning.

As almost all women lose blood during their periods, this fact is considered normal. In fact, the uterus is a sensitive indicator of a woman's health. As a consequence, a woman's body loses blood during her period only when her body is insufficiently healthy, regardless of her nourishment. A perfectly healthy woman does not lose any blood during her period.

In the case of a healthy woman, the absence of blood during period, does not mean infertility. On the contrary, this indicates a full readiness to be impregnated. Fasting can help heal infertile women. Fasting is very effective cure for a women who are obese and suffer due to excessive bleeding. Experience is required in this case, therefore it is better to follow a doctor having sufficient knowledge in this field.

When a woman is not able to live naturally without food, that is, her body is starving, menstruation disorders can occur, resulting a lack of bleeding. In this case, a woman also can become infertile. Do not force your body to fast, when you are intending to become pregnant.

Who ought not to fast?

Those who do not want to.
Those who are afraid of fasting.
One must not be forced to fast.
In addition, read the list in the chapter "seven-week adaptation".

Can one take medicine and herbs during *bì-gǔ* ?

In respect to this question, please seek advice from a doctor who is experienced in healing with fasting. To make the complicated story simple, chemical components known as medicine are consumed in order to remove or avoid symptoms of illness. During fasting, the causes of illnesses are removed, then, why to continue consuming chemicals? The same thing happens with herbs because they also contain chemical compounds.
During fasting, the body is much more sensitive to substances inserted into it, that is why the medicine is stopped or the dose is significantly reduced.

Sometimes during fasting, the chemicals are introduced for a specific reason, e.g. to cause diarrhoea. This would depend on the specific or individual case, which is a good reason to consult a qualified doctor.

ABOUT THE AUTHOR

SHORT STORY

I came to this material world on June 2nd 1963. When I was a teenager I become more interested in the so-called paranormal phenomena. After starting with radiesthesia, the circle of my interests expanded to include yoga, bioenergotherapy, conscious self-development and related practices. As a consequence of this kind of activities, I became interested also in healthy dieting, (self)healing and healing by fasting.

When I was a teenager in Poland, it was difficult to find literature dedicated to esoteric topics. It was possible to find only some very expensive copied books. There were also organizations of radiesthesists, which often organized meetings about so-called paranormal matters. In order to learn and experience more, I participated in them whenever possible.

In 1984, before I was taken to the obligatory military service, I spent four months in a catholic seminary. It was another interesting experience for me and I was also able to learn more about the clergy life.

Since 1989 I was travelling for over three years in Asian countries as a teacher and promoter for the international, auxiliary language Esperanto. During that time I was able to find much more literature about esoteric topics. Whenever I had the opportunity, I read and practised what I learned. I also visited, whenever it happened to be on my way, some spiritual development centres. But despite reading valuable books, speaking with 'enlightened' people, visiting centres of spiritual practices, I had not found, as I can see now, what I was looking for.

Now I know that this thing is in me and I am the source of it. The deeper I went inside myself, the better I saw that all knowledge I needed, everything that I was looking for, and much more was there, in me; it had always been in me from the beginning. The only thing I needed to do was to allow myself to let it manifest itself in me. All the great renowned 'spiritual masters' are not capable of giving me what I have always had. They can only, themselves being a source of information, turn my attention to it.

CAREER

After my graduation in 1983, I worked as a chemist in "The Institute of Heavy Organic Synthesis" in *Kędzierzyn-Koźle* (south Poland) for a year. During my tenure at that institute, I often travelled through Europe to participate in Esperanto meetings. I left the institute in 1988 and went to Asian countries to teach Esperanto.

When travelling in over forty countries I had the opportunity to deeply experience and understand the meaning of the Polish saying: "Travelling educates". No other school had ever given me so much experience and knowledge.

In Taiwan, at the end of my last sojourn, I started a private business, a publishing company. I published a book and was issuing the magazine "MONO" (money) in Polish and Esperanto.

After coming back to Poland I founded a foreign language school, which functioned for the next two years. We were teaching English, German, Chinese and Esperanto.

In 1996 I closed the school and started a trading company ROSPEROS. The principal activity of ROSPEROS was importing computer parts called "CPU upgrades", mostly from Taiwan. CPU upgrades enable inexpensive, efficient and ecological upgrading of old computers. It is a good solution for those who need more powerful computers but have limited finances. I closed ROSPEROS in 2005, that was the end of my business activity.

Since 2006, I am conducting a research with the goal to build a device which gives free electricity, so that man will not have to be tied to the grid. Having a generator of free electricity, you do not have to buy fuel, pay for light, warmth and functioning of electrical devices. You do not have to work like a slave for something which always has been there for free.

EXPERIMENTATION

Since 1979, when I was 16, I have been taking steps and doing experiments on myself on my path toward a conscious self-development. My decision to start the living without food, from July 1st, 2001, was one of those steps and experiments.

On July 2001 my family left the house for a five week vacation. During that time I worked daily as usual in my office. Every day I contemplated more than usual in order to adapt the body for the changes in its functioning.

I planned to adapt the body to the changes in its functioning within three to five weeks, but it took me longer than that. Most of the occurring change was not something new for me, because I had been fasting at least once a year to clean and heal the body since I was 16.

Having decided to experience life without food, I just put food aside. However, I later realized that for the majority of people, according to their beliefs, it is practically impossible to just put aside the food. That is the reason why I decided to first research and then describe methods of adapting the human body to living without food. This is why I started this book.

Having considered the matter, I came to the conclusion that the experimental path would provide me with the best data and experiences. As a natural progression of this idea, my next step was to revert to the 'normal' material body feeding and to make the body dependent on food again. So now I can say that by dint of the knowledge I have built up about the subject I can provide more information to people who are interested in it.

At the time when the first edition of this book was out, I had not yet decided when to begin the next experiment. I was putting off my final decision, trying to get some co-operation from qualified professionals like scientists, doctors, biotherapists or clairvoyants, who might be interested in the subject. There were some interested individuals but they either expressed formal interest or they were stopped by the establishment.

For me, the life style without food was the most convenient one. It gave me many benefits. That was the main reason for not giving it up for over six months despite feeling increased pressure from the outside. However, I was feeling that there are things more important, according to the tasks undertaken by me for this life, but the non-eating would prevent me from accomplishing some of them. Finally I decided to stop the non-eating phase in March 2003.

MORE ABOUT THE NON-EATING EXPERIMENT

Many people, having read "Life Style Without Food" published in 2005, asked me to write more about my experiment with non-eating, which I performed between the years of 2001 and 2003. I have not written about this,

because I believe that:
- Every man is a different universe, therefore information about my experience with inedia and non-eating should not be an indication for other people.
- Every man, as a unique unique world, has their own way and ought to rely on their own Inner Power, not on suggestion from another man.
- I do not like to talk about myself, especially about things which are in my immaterial sphere.

However, many people persuaded me, saying that all of this is important information and that I should share it with them. I am fulfilling their wish.

I had decided to give up food in order to experience freedom from this strongest material addiction on Earth. On June 30, I had dinner which was my last meal before the non-eating began. We had pizza which I ate until I got stomach ache. From July 1, I did not take anything into my mouth.

At that time, I was managing a company, working 14 hours a day in the office and the storeroom. I made no changes in the type of work I did and my place. I continued to do everything in the same way as I had been doing before starting the non-eating.

The first few weeks were not different with anything special, compared to longer fasts which I had done before in my life. Typical symptoms of body self-cleaning were occurring, e.g. headache and dizziness when I got up too fast, passing aches in different parts of my body, and heart pain. The dizziness continued for approximately five weeks before that finally ceased. The longest lasting symptom was pain in the area of the diaphragm. For about three weeks, the pain was increasing with each passing day. Later, it gradually subsided and ceased completely after approximately two months. My diaphragm, the muscles of my back and chest had some hard work to do in adapting to the changing dimensions of my organs.

At the end of the fourth month, I suddenly felt an extraordinary strong pain in the area of my kidneys. An X-ray photo revealed that my ureter was blocked by a jelly-like substance, this was confirmed by the doctor. Fortunately, after receiving an anti-spasm and analgesic injection, the ureter cleaned itself and the pain disappeared completely.

During these first four months, I was also feeling changes in my psyche. The sensitivity of my psyche was increasing; that is why in the beginning, I often felt irritated for insignificant reasons, which manifested itself in the form of nervousness and impatience. Later, I stabilized my psyche by performing mind exercises.

Noticeable changes were occurring in my psyche for about half a year and then I stabilized everything. Then calmness prevailed. I could feel that my mind served me better than before the period of non-eating. I could evoke the state of intellect passiveness more easily and sustain it longer. This led to noticeable development of my telepathy. I could perceive more often what people were thinking and feeling.

My intellect was functioning much more efficiently. From morning until late night, I could be occupied with tasks that required an active intellect, e. g. office work. At the end of my work time, at night, I felt that my intellect was as efficient as it had been in the morning. In addition, I could think faster and focus better on one task without distraction.

I also observed changes in my instinct. For example, the boundary between my night dreams and daily reality become less sharp. The transition from night dream to daytime awareness became smoother. The dream contents were more related to my daily activities, as if one was continuation of the other.

I allocated five to eight hours for sleeping. Although six hours of sleep was sufficient for my body, I stayed in bed longer to do some mind exercising while lying down.

There was one trait of my mind state accompanying me in those days, which was not so pleasant. I saw the illusion of Life much more clearly, deeply and with more details. I saw how my mind was creating all of this, the entire matter and beings acting in it.
The bodies of people, animals, plants, and minerals are only programs which function in accordance to other programs. In true reality nothing exists.
There is only IAM and nothing else. My body and even my mind are only pictures / programs / thoughts. An effort must be made in order to create all of this. I saw that all of this was just a meaningless game. Life and its purpose have to be created by creating the illusion of things like: existence, perfection, changes, opposites, development, spirituality and matter, so that the game can go on. Then, having started this mechanism of constant creation, everything has to be forgotten about IAM and about the creating power of IAM so that the game can go on in this senseless illusion.
Then, I also saw what food is; it is just a drug, an addiction formed during our very early time as babies, out of which man can lose themselves in this matter more deeply and play better.

I saw that and more. I still see it and I would like to forget so that I could play again as primitive man does.

One of the things that I liked most during my non-eating period was my physical stamina. I could work longer physically and yet remain much less tired compared to my days of normal eating.
On a hot day, my colleague and I carried 300 monitors, each one weighing 10 kg, for a distance of 50 m. It took us approximately 1.5 hours. I did not rest even for a moment because I did not feel any fatigue. After I completed caring the monitors, I went back to doing office work without feeling any tiredness. I sweated so little that I did not need to take a shower.

During the almost two years of non-eating, I drank mainly water in small quantities and sometimes juices, tea, coffee or herbal drinks. Sometimes it was not more than half a glass a day. For one week, I did not drink anything.
One evening, I performed an experiment. I drank 0.7 litres of red dry wine. I was surprised that I felt no effect; it was as if I had drank water.

During those two years, I sometimes ate something, for example, when I was a guest of my acquaintances abroad (I did not want to look like a crank); during family ceremony (I did not wish to sadden the family members and create feeling of isolation). I also tested the effect of some food on the body of a non-eater.
Usually, having eaten something, my body threw it out in the form of diarrhoea within several dozens of minutes after eating. My body reacted in the same manner after drinking more than a half a glass of a denser juice.

During this period of nearly two years, there were some days when my body was feeling weak, as if it was without any energy and hunger returned. At that time, I performed energizing exercises, that is, absorbing energy from nature, especially when bathing in sunshine, clad in no clothes. However, what was more important was doing the contemplation of passiveness regularly. The benefit of this exercise was that I could better feel the Inner Power manifested by IAM. As a result, any hunger disappeared, it turned out to be an illusion as my energy and power returned.

When I began the non-eating experiment, my body weight was 78 kg. My body weight decreased and remained between 68 and 71 kg. When I was very active emotionally and mentally, for example when conducting a seminar, my body weight dropped an additional 2 kg. Later, when I relaxed through mind exercising, my weight went back to the stabilized range.

To summarize my experiment with non-eating, I know that I do not need to eat to keep my body in a healthy state. It is possible for me to give up food without any preparation. However, a gradual transition which includes preparation is more beneficial for the body and psyche. I know that the body is just an image in the mind and this image is a subject of the mind.

FAT AND SICK

I practised non-eating from July 2001 to March 2003. That experience gave me enough knowledge required by my needs. It is through the gained knowledge that I can inform individuals about details regarding life without food. Continuing non-eating beyond March 2003, although convenient for me, would not have allowed me to fulfil my tasks. So at that time, I felt like man going down a road and having other people along the way telling me: "You can go this way but you would be able to do much more, if you were walking down that one because that would be more in accordance with your original intentions."

Since September 2002 I was trying to stop the non-eating phase in order to start my tasks. However, living without food was so beneficial to me that I kept delaying that end. Finally, in March 2003, I came back on track, I stopped the non-eating phase and proceeded with my tasks.

At that time, March 2003, this is what I planned to do within one year:
- to fatten the body to the maximum of 130 kg (286 lb). I had never experienced such a big overweight, that is why I was not able to fully understand all related physical and psychological processes.
- to get sick with diseases believed to be incurable, like cancer, diabetes, hypertension, heart diseases and others. Then to heal myself completely.

In March 2004 I decided to end the above experiment. I had learned enough and I did not want to force myself to suffer more. I was feeling worse than I could have imagined before starting the experiment (worsening health, low energy level and bad mood). Also I felt that it was the right time to continue farther with my plan.

On the 1st of March 2004 I started the next experiment with non-eating. On that day, I moved food away from me once again. As I was 30 kg (66 lb) overweight, I could feel significant differences between the two beginnings of the non-eating life style (the first in July 2001 and the current one in March 2004).

From my experiment with fattening up, although I reached only 100 kg, I learned many things about how an obese man feels. It concerns not only the every day activities (e.g. limits in movements, addictive appetite, feeling of hypertension) but also how fasting works in the case of such man.

Now I can understand why for obese people, those who most need it (as much as fish needs water), it is so difficult to go through fasting. Having my own fat body, upon experiencing on myself, I was able to recognize how difficult it is for an obese man to fast.

An obese man is more addicted to food. It is useful for such man to have a stronger will power in order to successfully pass a treatment, which is similar to the treatment of a drug addict, because man is suffering more.
I discovered and experienced many more aspects regarding obesity. It all gave me more knowledge about man. To describe them all, I would need to write another book. I know that it is worth for me to experiment in this way.

By the way, please remember, that this is my experience. I mean, what I was feeling does not have to be the same as what others feel. I am doing all these experiments in order to know more, for the very sake of playing and to be able to give information to people, should they ask me.

THE TASK

I know that my present main task is to pass valuable information on. For this purpose, I recall, collect, elaborate on and pass on information which is related to:
- Consciousness, Light, Love, Life;
- function of man's mind and body;
- adaptation abilities of human body;
- usage of energy in the way that does not harm life on Earth;
- individual abilities of man for conscious self-developing.

For example, this book is contained within the second point.

FORUM

If you have questions or want to share your experience, advices, etc.
I invite you to take part in the following Internet forums:
http://forum.niejedzenie.info (in Polish)
http://forum.breatharian.info (in English).

After opening http://inedia.info , you can find forums in other languages. Click on the language of your choice.

DONATION

By the way, if your would like to donate money, I accept donations. Please, use the link on the bottom left side of http://breatharian.info .
If you prefer other ways, please, contact the author.

TABLE OF CONTENT

WHY THIS BOOK?..4
THIS IS ONLY INFORMATION...6
DEFINITIONS..9
BEFORE WE START WITH THE TOPIC..................................14
   VOGUE..14
   WARNING..15
   BE A CO-AUTHOR OF THIS BOOK...................................16
INTRODUCTION..17
THE CONSCIOUSNESS...18
   SPHERES OF THE CONSCIOUSNESS................................22
   IAM..26
      CONTEMPLATION OF IAM..28
      THE MOST POWERFUL SAYING.................................29
THE MIND..31
   THE INSTINCT...31
      A SECRET..33
   THE INTELLECT...34
   THE INTUITION...36
      THE FUNCTIONS OF THE MIND..................................38
   MIND and BRAIN...38
WHAT IS LIFE?..39
A FABLE ABOUT A FISH..41
WHAT IS MAN ?..44
THE LIGHT...48
SUGGESTION BY THE SOCIETY..51
   REPROGRAMMING..53
POWERING THE BODY..56
   DIGESTIVE TRACT...57
   BREATHING..60
      QÌ or PRANA DRAWING EXERCISE..............................61
   SKIN...63
   MOVEMENT..65
   THE WILL OF LIFE..66
BODY CLEANSING, PURIFYING...67
NON-EATING or STARVING..71
HOW IS THIS POSSIBLE ?...74
   FOR THE OPEN-MINDED..75
   FOR THE ESOTERIC...75
   FOR THE SCIENTIFICALLY MINDED.................................76
   FOR THE BELIEVERS...77

  WITHOUT PHILOSOPHIZING..78
WHY INEDIA...81
  MAN IN NATURAL STATE..81
  PERFECT HEALTH..82
  FREEDOM..83
  ECONOMY...84
  ECOLOGY..85
  LIFE ENERGY...87
  CREATIVITY...88
  SPIRITUAL GROWTH..89
  REJUVENATION..90
  CURIOSITY...91
PREPARATION FOR A CHANGE IN YOUR LIFE STYLE....................92
  PERSONAL SURVEY..94
  Why? So What? ANALYSIS..95
  FAMILY MEMBERS..97
  COLLEAGUES...98
  FRIENDS...98
  ADDICTIONS...99
  HABITS...99
  DIET...100
  VISUALIZATION..101
  CONTEMPLATION OF PASSIVENESS..108
  CONTEMPLATION OF INNER JOY..114
  FOCUSSING ON YOUR INNER SUN..116
  CONTEMPLATION or VISUALIZATION..117
  ENERGIZING EXERCISES..117
    ENERGIZING BY SOUND VIBRATION....................................120
    ALTERNATE SHOWER..121
METHODS..123
  NATURAL...123
  SPIRITUAL...127
  SUDDEN..128
  FORCEFUL...130
  8 DAY PROCESS BY RICARDO AKAHI..131
  10 DAY PROCESS BY RAY MAOR...131
  11 DAY PROCESS BY VICTOR TRUVIANO......................................131
  THE 21 DAY PROCESS..132
  HYPNOTIC...133
  ALTERNATE..134
  TRYING...135
  PHILOSOPHICAL-INTELLECTUAL..136
  SUN-GAZING...137
  ALCHEMICAL...139
  CONSCIOUS EATING..140
    FOLLOWING A DIET..143
  YOUR OWN..143

ADAPTATION IN SEVEN WEEKS..144
SEVEN-WEEK ADAPTATION..147
PREPARATION..148
- 1. PROPER NOURISHMENT..149
- 2. ENERGIZING EXERCISES..149
- 3. MIND EXERCISES..149
- LOOSENING EXERCISES..150
- 4. SLEEP REGULATION..152
- 5. PROTECTION AGAINST HARMFUL RADIATION..153
- 6. GETTING CLOSE TO NATURE..156
- 7. CHANGE OF DIET..157

THE ADAPTATION..160
- MENTOR..161
- PLACE..162
- THE FIRST DAY..163
- THE SECOND DAY..165
- THE THIRD DAY..165
- THE SEVENTH AND EIGHTH DAYS..165
- THE DAYS THAT FOLLOW..165
- DURING ALL THE DAYS OF THE ADAPTATION..167
- THE LAST DAY..168

THE RETURN TO NORMAL LIFE..168

SYMPTOMS..170
- FEAR..171
- WEAKNESS..172
- DEHYDRATION..174
- DIZZINESS AND FAINTING..175
- NAUSEA AND VOMITING..176
- WEIGHT LOSS..177
- EMACIATION..178
- PAIN..179
- PSYCHICAL INSTABILITY..180
- DIFFERENT REALITY..182
- CHANGES ON SKIN..184
- FEELING COLD..185
- FEVER..186
- LOOSE TEETH..186
- HAIR FALLING OUT..187
- SWELLING JOINTS..187
- OTHER..188

WHAT TO PAY MOST ATTENTION TO..189
- FIRST OF ALL, COMMON SENSE..189
- SECLUSION..190
- WITHOUT FORCING..190
- LIMITED BELIEF IN INFORMATION..192
- ALONE OR WITH A MENTOR..193
- HALLUCINATIONS OR VISIONS..194
- GOOD HEALTH..195
- BODY TEMPERATURE..195

DRINKING WHEN NOT EATING..196
CLEANSING THE LARGE INTESTINE.......................................197
    COFFEE ENEMA..201
MOVING MUSCLES...202
ALIMENTARY CANAL CLEANSING...203
RESUMING EATING..204
FAILURES..206
PROPER BODY WEIGHT..207

ASK YOURSELF..208

REASONS OF EATING...209
RNB..209
HABIT...212
ADDICTION..212
BELIEF OR FEAR..213
BOREDOM...215
DECISION TO CHANGE..216
MEETING...216
TASTE, SMELL, APPEARANCE...217
POVERTY, THRIFT...218
COMPELLING..219
REWARD..219
GROUNDING...220

INEDIATES and NON-EATERS..222
    Alenara...222
    Balayogini Sarasvati..223
    Barbara Moore...223
    Christopher Schneider...223
    Evelyn Levy..224
    Giri Bala..224
    Hira Ratan Manek..225
    Jack Davis..225
    Jasmuheen...225
    Joachim M Werdin...225
    Kamilla..225
    Kazimierz Karwot...226
    Martha Robin...226
    Prahlad Jani...226
    Steve Torrence..226
    Sunyogi Umasankar...227
    Surya Jowel...227
    Theresa Neumann...227
    Vasanta Ejma..227
    Vona Tansey..228
    Wiley Brooks..228
    Will van der Meer...228
    Xu Fan..228
    Zinaida Baranova...229
    thousands of others...229
    A LIST...229

FASTING FOR HEALTH..231
   DRY FASTING...231
   WATER FASTING...232
   SYMPTOMS..234
   INTESTINE WASHING (enema)...235
   PHYSICAL ACTIVITY..236
INEDIA / NON-EATING or FASTING...238
   BODY WEIGHT CHANGES..238
   DISPOSITION..239
   BUILDING THE BODY...240
BEINGS and NON-EATING...241
   IMMATERIAL BEINGS..241
   PARTLY MATERIAL BEINGS...242
   MATERIAL BEINGS..243
PRINCIPLES OF PROPER NOURISHMENT..................................244
   1. CONSCIOUS EATING..244
   2. CHEWING..244
   3. WITHOUT DRINKING..246
   4. PROPER COMBINING OF FOOD......................................246
   5. FOOD DIRECTLY FROM NATURE..................................247
   6. WITHOUT SEASONING & FLAVOURING....................249
   7. ONLY WHEN HUNGRY OR THIRSTY...........................251
   8. DRINKING AND WATER...251
   9. NOT AFTER 4 PM..253
   10. IN SILENCE..253
CO-OPERATION FOR DEVELOPMENT...255
F. A. Q..256
      What is the best diet for humans?..256
      Why do we have alimentary canal?...256
      Why do people die from starvation?...257
      Why non-eaters do not go to places where people starve and do not teach them?...258
      What to do in order to become a non-eater? Can I also live without food?..............259
      It is a nonsense that people can live without food. How are you going to prove it to me?..260
      Where do the non-eaters take energy for living from?............................261
      Why did you return to eating?...262
      What do you eat now?...263
      Can an inediate, a non-eater or man who fasts be sexually active?..........................263
      Does a woman lose her period during non-eating or fasting?....................264
      Who ought not to fast?..265
      Can one take medicine and herbs during *bì-gǔ* ?..................265
ABOUT THE AUTHOR..266
   SHORT STORY..266
   CAREER..267
   EXPERIMENTATION...267
      MORE ABOUT THE NON-EATING EXPERIMENT............268
   FAT AND SICK..272

THE TASK	273
FORUM	274
DONATION	275

If you see any errors or mistakes or false information in this book, please, contact the author, so that he can correct them.

Thank you.

Printed in Great Britain
by Amazon